THE BLACK POWER REVOLT

THE

BLACK POWER

REVOLT

A Collection of Essays

Editor

Floyd B. Barbour

EXTENDING HORIZONS BOOKS

Porter Sargent Publisher 11 Beacon Street, Boston, Mass.

EXTENDING HORIZONS BOOKS

W. H. TRUITT, CO-EDITOR

DEPT. OF PHILOSOPHY, SUFFOLK UNIVERSITY

PREFACE

EXTENDING HORIZONS BOOKS is a collection of writings on social science and critical social philosophy. As a series it seeks to overcome the dichotomy between theory and practice which is characteristic of American social science, and which is revealed in society by the incompatibility between values and behavior.

Earlier titles in this series revive classic pioneering studies such as Kropotkin's MUTUAL AID and Sorokin's SOCIAL AND CULTURAL DYNAMICS. Tracing the forward movement of social theory, we have presented, for example, works on Toynbee and Georges Gurvitch.

To bring this spirit of rational criticism as an instrument for democratic social progress into the present moment, we present this collection of essays written by people concerned publicly and privately with Black Power.

W. H. T.
Boston, 1968

PUBLISHER'S NOTE

The Black Power Revolt is a report of the Editor's findings in a year of enquiry. The forces of flux and convergence are realistically examined. It is hoped that this work will aid understanding and inspire continuing study by those within and without Black Power.

If it furthers the social dialogue and helps to clear the way for freedom of action appropriate to a democracy, the publisher's aims will have been fulfilled.

F.P.S.
Boston, 1968

ACKNOWLEDGMENTS

For permission to reprint copyrighted material the following acknowledgments are gratefully made to:

Yale University Press, publishers, for the poem "Since 1619" which appeared in *For My People* by Margaret Walker. (Copyright © 1942 by Yale University Press.)

Dr. Herbert Aptheker, author of *A Documentary History of the Negro People in the United States,* published by Citadel Press, for selections appearing on pp. 23-5, 28, 93-7, 119-125, 226-233, 402-5, 451-4, 655, 656-7 and 753 of that book, here included in Section I: Black Power Through History. (Copyright © 1951 by Herbert Aptheker.)

Student Nonviolent Coordinating Committee, and A. Whitney Ellsworth, publisher of the *New York Review of Books,* for "Power and Racism" by Stokely Carmichael, from *New York Review of Books,* September 22, 1966. (Copyright © 1966 by Student Nonviolent Coordinating Committee.)

Scientific American, Inc., publishers of *Scientific American,* for "The Social Power of the Negro" by James P. Comer, April 1967. (Copyright© 1967 by Scientific American, Inc.)

The Christian Century Foundation, publishers of *The Christian Century,* and Mr. Kyle Haselden, Editor of that journal, for "Black Power and the American Christ", by Vincent Harding, *The Christian Century,* January 4, 1967. (Copyright © 1942 by The Christian Century Foundation.)

The National Medical Association, Inc., publishers of the *Journal of the National Medical Association,* and W. Montague Cobb, Editor of that journal, for "The Negro American: His

Self-Image and Integration", by Dr. Alvin Poussaint, in the *Journal of the National Medical Association,* vol. 58, pp. 419-423, 1966.

LeRoi Jones, author, and The Sterling Lord Agency, his agents, for "The Need for A Cultural Base to Civil Rites and Bpower Mooments." (Copyright © 1967 by LeRoi Jones.)

Marzani and Munsell, Inc., Publishers, for "Self-Defense: An American Tradition" from *Negroes with Guns* by Robert F. Williams, Chapter 7. (Copyright © 1962 by Marzani and Munsell.)

US Organization, Los Angeles, California, and Clyde Halisi and James Mtume, Editors, for quotations from *The Quotable Karenga* by Maulana Ron Karenga, pp. 1-7 and 9-14. (Copyright © 1967 by *US* Organization.)

McCall Corporation, publishers of *Redbook* magazine, and Mr. Sey Chassler, Editor of that magazine, for "I Learned to Feel Black" by Mrs. Jean Smith, *Redbook* magazine, August, 1967.

Merit Publishers, Inc., and Mrs. Betty Shabazz, widow of Malcolm X, for letters from *Malcolm X Speaks,* pp. 58-63. (Copyright © 1965 by Merit Publishers, Inc.)

Grateful acknowledgment is also made to the following, whose essays appear here in print for the first time:

Mrs. Gwenna Cummings: "Black Women—Often Discussed but Never Understood."

Dr. Charles V. Hamilton: "Riots, Revolts and Relevant Response."

Dr. Nathan Hare: "Black Power vs. the White Backlash."

Dr. Adelaide Cromwell Hill: "What Is Africa to Us?"

Julius W. Hobson: "Black Power: Right or Left?"

John E. Johnson: "Super Black Man."

Floyd B. McKissick: "Programs for Black Power."

Lawrence P. Neal: "International Implications of Black Power."

Byron Rushing: "I Was Born."
Chuck Stone: "The National Conference on Black Power."
Barbara Ann Teer: "Needed: A New Image."

and to:

Gaston Neal, for the poem "Today."
Prof. Richard Newman, compiler of the periodical readings on
Black Power.

INTRODUCTION

Repetition. *The Black Power Revolt* opens with Margaret Walker's "Since 1619" and concludes with Gaston Neal's "Today." In between is repetition and counterpoint. If repetition has a meaning, the meaning is force, and force is what brings down barricades!

Repetition, like the individual frames of a strip of film, is the same but always changing. The question remains: will there be a change even with all the repeating?

My research began with David Walker's *Appeal* and *The Autobiography of Malcolm X.* (I imply I began this book, let me amend that by saying the book began itself out of its own need to be. I have acted as vehicle.) As I see it, the *Autobiography* is almost Dantesque, falling as it does into sections comparable to the Inferno, the Purgatorio, and the Paradiso. The Inferno can be judged the time of least self-awareness: taught to honor the white world, I came to maturity with little or no appreciation for the cultural history of my own people. That is the Inferno. (The season when burning our past was the important thing; Fanon's time of colonization.) For Malcolm it was a period of wandering through the streets of cities without goal and with little hope of a goal.

In prison, Malcolm reached his own purgatorio where he burned with the urgency to know. He left prison with the knowledge that being black was the most important single factor in his life. And he preached who the enemy was. He praised his blackness the way Marcus Garvey had praised his. Perhaps I as a person and we as a people are currently passing through a needed stage of purgatory. We burn in our awakening to our blackness and in our ability to rejoice in ourselves for being ourselves. We are even capable of burning down what does not contribute to a fruitful awareness of our humanity. In thoughts and dreams we return to Africa; Fanon's time of decolonization.

One day we shall have a work which embraces something of the Paradiso, a work which does not separate but unifies. But, Malcolm had to travel to Mecca in order to realize that it is not inherent in blacks to hate whites, that it is not a color we must vent our fury upon, but a system. Before the Paradiso, however, comes the day of tribal togetherness. First, comes the Purgatorio.

I believe the term Black Power is more than a slogan and this collection more than a platform for that slogan. Black Power is the attempt of a people, my people, to find definition and liberation. There was no true way of dividing *The Black Power Revolt* since many of the pieces interlock, overlap. I have chosen, however, to divide this book into four sections, with the understanding that each section does interlock, overlap. The historical documents show that we have been shouting Black Power for a long time. The contemporary statements speak for themselves.

Different voices, different times, different approaches—a prism, its light held, refracting. And each voice an answer to what it is to be Black and think Black.

.   .   .   .

Acknowledgment must be made to the authors, who took time away from busy schedules to contribute not only their insight but their suggestions and enthusiasm; and to my friends, acquaintances, and co-workers for their continued encouragement. I wish especially to thank Willis Truitt whose idea it was to have such a collection, and Porter Sargent who made publication possible; Dr. Herbert Aptheker, whose studies in the history of black people proved invaluable; Dr. Howard Zinn for his help in the planning stages; Dr. Adelaide C. Hill and Dr. Nathan Wright for the extra attention they extended to me; Roberta Davies and Esther Doughty for their editorial assistance; and LeRoi Jones who demanded a "big black fist of a book." Thank you.

Floyd B. Barbour
Boston, 1968

CONTENTS

Since 1619

How many years since 1619 have I been singing Spirituals?
How long have I been praising God and shouting hallelujahs?
How long have I been hated and hating?
How long have I been living in hell for heaven?

When will I see my brother's face wearing another color?
When will I be ready to die in an honest fight?
When will I be conscious of the struggle—now to do or die?
When will these scales fall away from my eyes?

What will I say when days of wrath descend:
When the money-gods take all my life away;
When the death knell sounds
And peace is a flag of far-flung blood and filth?

When will I understand the cheated and the cheaters;
Their paltry pittances and cold concessions to my pride?
When will I burst from my kennel an angry mongrel,
Lean and hungry and tired of my dry bones and years?

—Margaret Walker

I

BLACK POWER THROUGH HISTORY

BENJAMIN BANNEKER

We open with an early letter from a black man to a white man. The year is 1791; the writer, Benjamin Banneker (1731-1806). One of a team of three who determined the boundaries for the present city of Washington, Banneker published annually after 1792 a widely used almanac devised by himself, and at the age of 50 began the study of mathematics for astronomical purposes.

LETTER TO THOMAS JEFFERSON, 1791

I am fully sensible of that freedom, which I take with you in the present occasion; a liberty which seemed to me scarcely allowable, when I reflected on that distinguished and dignified station in which you stand, and the almost general prejudice and prepossession, which is so prevalent in the world against those of my complexion.

I suppose it is a truth too well attested to you, to need a proof here, that we are a race of beings, who have long labored under the abuse and censure of the world; that we have long been looked upon with an eye of contempt; and that we have long been considered rather as brutish than human, and scarcely capable of mental endowments.

Sir, I hope I may safely admit, in consequence of that report which hath reached me, that you are a man less inflexible in sentiments of this nature, than many others; that you are measurably friendly, and well disposed towards us; and that you are willing and ready to lend your aid and assistance to our relief, from those many distresses, and numerous calamities, to which we are reduced.

Now Sir, if this is founded in truth, I apprehend you will embrace every opportunity, to eradicate that train of absurd and false ideas and opinions, which so generally prevails with respect to us; and that your sentiments are concurrent with mine, which are, that one universal Father hath given being to us all; and that he hath not only made us all of one flesh, but that he hath also, without partiality, afforded us all the same sensations and endowed us all with the same faculties; and that however variable we may be in society or religion, however diversified in situation or color, we are all in the same family and stand in the same relation to him.

Sir, if these are sentiments of which you are fully persuaded, I hope you cannot but acknowledge, that it is the indispensable duty of those, who maintain for themselves the rights of human nature, and who possess the obligations of Christianity, to extend their power and influence to the relief of every part of the human race, from whatever burden or oppression they may unjustly labor under; and this, I apprehend, a full conviction of the truth and obligation of these principles should lead all to.

Sir, I have long been convinced, that if your love for yourselves, and for those inestimable laws, which preserved to you the rights of human nature, was founded on sincerity, you could not but be solicitous, that every individual, of whatever rank or distinction, might with you equally enjoy the blessings thereof; neither could you rest satisfied short of the most active effusion of your exertions, in order for the promotion from any state of degradation, to which the unjustifiable cruelty and barbarism of men may have reduced them.

Sir, I freely and cheerfully acknowledge, that I am of the African race, and in that color which is natural to them of the deepest dye; and it is under a sense of the most profound gratitude to the Supreme Ruler of the Universe, that I now confess to you, that I am not under that state of tyrannical thraldom, and inhuman captivity, to which too many of my brethren are doomed, but that I have abundantly tasted of the fruition of those blessings, which proceed from that free and unequalled liberty with which you are favored; and which, I hope, you will willingly allow you have mercifully received, from the immediate hand of that Being, from whom proceedeth every good and perfect Gift.

Sir, suffer me to recall to your mind that time, in which the arms and tyranny of the British crown were exerted, with every powerful effort, in order to reduce you to a state of servitude; look back, I entreat you, on the variety of dangers to which you were exposed; reflect on that time, in which every human aid appeared unavailable, and in which even hope and fortitude wore the aspect of inability to the conflict, and you cannot but be led to a serious and grateful sense of your miraculous and providential preservation; you cannot but acknowledge, that the present freedom and tranquility which you enjoy you have mercifully received, and that it is the peculiar blessing of Heaven.

This, Sir, was a time when you clearly saw into the injustice of a state of slavery, and in which you had just apprehensions of the horror of its condition. It was now that your abhorrence thereof was so excited, that you publicly held forth this true and invaluable doctrine, which is worthy to be recorded and remembered in all succeeding ages: 'We hold these truths to be self-evident, that all men are created equal; that they are endowed by their Creator with certain unalienable rights, and that among these are, life, liberty, and the pursuit of happiness.'

Here was a time, in which your tender feelings for yourselves had engaged you thus to declare, you were then impressed with proper ideas of the great violation of liberty, and the free possession of those blessings, to which you were entitled by nature; but, Sir, how pitiable is it to reflect, that although you were so fully convinced of the benevolence of the Father of Mankind, and of his equal and impartial distribution of these rights and privileges, which he hath conferred upon them, that you should at the same time counteract his mercies, in detaining by fraud and violence so numerous a part of my brethren, under groaning captivity, and cruel oppression, that you should at the same time be found guilty of that most criminal act, which you professedly detested in others, with respect to yourselves.

I suppose that your knowledge of the situation of my brethren, is too extensive to need a recital here; neither shall I presume to prescribe methods by which they may be relieved, otherwise than by recommending to you and all others, to wean yourselves from those narrow prejudices which you have imbibed with respect to them, and as Job proposed to his friends, 'put your soul in their souls' stead'; thus shall your hearts be enlarged with kindness and benevolence towards them; and thus shall you need neither the direction of myself or others, in what manner to proceed herein.

And now, Sir, although my sympathy and affection for my brethren hath caused my enlargement thus far, I ardently hope, that your candor and generosity will plead with you in my behalf, when I make known to you, that it was not originally my design; but having taken up my pen in order to direct to you, as a present, a copy of my Almanac. . .

A Letter From and to Slave Rebels, 1793

In contrast to Banneker's appeal as a free man are the following words from a black man to a black man. It is unusual to have such documents reach us since the mails were not open to slaves and the law made teaching them how to read or write illegal. This letter was found in August, 1793, on a street in Yorktown, Virginia.

Dear Friend—The great secret that has been so long in being with our own color has come nearly to a head tho some in our Town has told of it but in such a slight manner it is not believed, we have got about five hundred Guns aplenty of lead but not much powder, I hope you have made a good collection of powder and ball and will hold yourself in readiness to strike whenever called for and never be out of the way it will not be long before it will take place, and I am fully satisfied we shall be in full possession of the whole country in a few weeks, since I wrote you last I got a letter from our friend in Charleston he tells me he has listed near six thousand men, there is a gentleman that says he will give us as much powder as we want, and when we begin he will help us all he can, the damn'd brutes patroles is going all night in Richmond but will soon cill [kill—ed.] them all, there an't many, we will appoint a night to begin with fire clubs and shot, we will kill all before us, it will begin in every town in one nite Keep ready to receive orders, when I hear from Charleston again I shall no and will rite to you, he that give you this is a good friend and don't let any body see it, rite me by the same hand he will give it to me out his hand he will be up next week don't be feared have a good heart fight brave and we will get free, I had like to get each [one word is illegible here—ed.] but God was for me, and I got away, no more now but remain your friend—Secret Keeper Richmond to secret keeper Norfolk.

DAVID WALKER

A great statement on Black Power is to be found in Walker's Appeal to the Colored Citizens of the World. David Walker was born of a free mother in Wilmington, North Carolina on September 28, 1785. He left the South when he was about thirty or thirty-five years old to settle in Boston where he made his living by dealing in old clothes. Always active in anti-slavery work, he published his Appeal in 1829, and from then until his strange disappearance sometime in 1830, supervised the distribution and reprinting of his booklet, which during the last year of his life went into its third edition, from which the extracts here are taken.

The Appeal created great controversy throughout the country, especially in the slave South.

From Walker's *Appeal,* 1829

I am fully aware, in making this appeal to my much afflicted and suffering brethren, that I shall not only be assailed by those whose greatest earthly desires are, to keep us in abject ignorance and wretchedness, and who are of the firm conviction that Heaven has designed us and our children to be slaves and *beasts of burden* to them and their children. I say, I do not only expect to be held up to the public as an ignorant, impudent and restless disturber of the public peace, by such avaricious creatures, as well as a mover of insubordination—and perhaps put in prison or to death, for giving a superficial exposition of our miseries, and exposing tyrants. But I am persuaded, that many of my brethren, particularly those who are ignorantly in league with slave-holders or tyrants, who acquire their daily bread by the blood and sweat of their more ignorant brethren—and not a few of those too, who are too ignorant to see an inch beyond their noses, will rise up and call me cursed—Yea, the jealous ones among us will perhaps use more abject subtlety, by affirming that this work is not worth perusing, that we are well situated, and there is no use in trying to better our condition, for we cannot. I will ask one question here.—Can our condition be any worse?—Can it be more mean and abject? If there are any changes, will they not be for the better, though they may appear for the worst at first? Can they get us any lower? Where can they get us? They are afraid to treat us worse, for they know well, the day they do it they are gone. But against all accusations which may or can be preferred against me, I appeal to Heaven for my motive in writing—who knows that my object is, if possible, to awaken in the breasts of my afflicted, degraded and slumbering brethren, a spirit of inquiry and investigation respecting our miseries and wretchedness in this *Republican Land of Liberty! ! ! ! !* . . . .

Our Wretchedness In Consequence of Slavery

My beloved brethren: The Indians of North and of South America —the Greeks—the Irish, subjected under the king of Great Britain—the Jews, that ancient people of the Lord—the inhabitants of the islands of the sea—in fine, all the inhabitants of the earth, (except however, the sons of Africa) are called *men,* and of course are, and ought to be free. But we, (coloured people) and our children are *brutes! !* and of course are, and *ought to be* SLAVES to the American people and their children forever! ! to dig their mines and work their farms; and thus go on enriching them, from one generation to another with our *blood* and our *tears! ! !* . . . .

O! that the coloured people were long since of Moses' excellent disposition, instead of courting favour with, and telling news and lies to our *natural enemies,* against each other—aiding them to keep their hellish chains of slavery upon us. Would we not long before this time, have been respectable men, instead of such wretched victims of oppression as we are? Would they be able to drag our mothers, our fathers, our wives, our children and ourselves, around the world in chains and hand-cuffs as they do, to dig up gold and silver for them and theirs? This question, my brethren, I leave for you to digest; and may God Almighty force it home to your hearts. Remember that unless you are united, keeping your tongues within your teeth, you will be afraid to trust your secrets to each other, and thus perpetuate our miseries under the *Christians! ! ! !* . . . .

Never make an attempt to gain our freedom or *natural right,* from under our cruel oppressors and murderers, until you see your way clear—(*It is not to be understood here, that I mean for us to wait until God shall take us by the hair of our heads and drag us out of abject wretchedness and slavery, nor do I mean to convey the idea for us to wait until our enemies shall make preparations, and call us to seize those preparations, take it away from them, and put every thing before us to death, in order to gain our freedom which God has given us. For you must remember that we are men as well as they. God has been pleased to give us two eyes, two hands, two feet, and some sense in our heads as well as they. They have no more right to hold us in slavery than we have to hold them, we have just as much right, in the sight of God, to hold them and their children in slavery and wretchedness, as they have to hold us, and no more. . . . [Note in original.])*— when that hour arrives and you move, be not afraid or dismayed; for be you assured that Jesus Christ the King of heaven and of earth who is the God of justice and of armies, will surely go before you. And those enemies who have for hundreds of years stolen our *rights,* and kept us ignorant of Him and His divine worship, he will remove. Millions of whom, are this day, so ignorant and avaricious, that they cannot conceive how God can have an attribute of justice, and show mercy to us because it pleased Him to make us black—which colour, Mr. Jefferson calls unfortunate!!!!!! As though we are not as thankful to our God, for having made us as it pleased himself, as they, (the whites,) are for having made them white. They think because they hold us in their infernal chains of slavery, that we wish to be white, or of their color—but they are dreadfully deceived—we wish to be just as it pleased our Creator to have made us, and no avaricious and unmerciful wretches, have any business to make slaves of, or hold us in slavery. How would they like for us to make slaves of, and hold them in cruel slavery, and murder them as they do us?—

Fear not the number and education of our *enemies,* against whom we shall have to contend for our lawful right; guaranteed to us by our Makers; for why should we be afraid, when God is, and will continue; (if we continue humble) to be on our side?

The man who would not fight under our Lord and Master Jesus Christ, in the glorious and heavenly cause of freedom and of God—to be delivered from the most wretched, abject and servile slavery, that ever a people was afflicted with since the foundation of the world, to the present day—ought to be kept with all of his children or family, in slavery, or in chains, to be butchered by his *cruel enemies. . . .*

Our Wretchedness In Consequence Of Ignorance

. . . . if you commence, make sure work—do not trifle, for they will not trifle with you—they want us for their slaves, and think nothing of murdering us in order to subject us to that wretched condition—therefore, if there is an *attempt* made by us, kill or be killed. Now, I ask you, had you not rather be killed than to be a slave to a tyrant, who takes the life of your mother, wife, and dear little children? Look upon your mother, wife, and children, and answer God Almighty; and believe this, that it is no more harm for you to kill a man, who is trying to kill you, than it is for you to take a drink of water when thirsty; in fact, the man who will stand still and let another murder him, is worse than an infidel, and, if he has common sense, ought not to be pitied. . . .

I pray that the Lord may undeceive my ignorant brethren, and permit them to throw away pretensions, and seek after the substance of learning. I would crawl on my hands and knees through mud and mire, to the feet of a learned man, where I would sit and humbly supplicate him to instil into me, that which neither devils nor tyrants could remove, only with my life—for colored people to acquire learning in this country, makes tyrants quake and tremble on their sandy foundation. Why, what is the matter? Why, they know that their infernal deeds of cruelty will be made known to the world. Do you suppose one man of good sense and learning would submit himself, his father, mother, wife and children, to be slaves to a wretched man like himself, who, instead of compensating him for his labours, chains, hand-cuffs and beats him and family almost to death, leaving life enough in them, however, to work for, and call him master? No! no! he would cut his devilish throat from ear to ear, and well do slave-holders know it. The bare name of educating the coloured people, scares our cruel oppressors almost to death. But if they do not have enough to be frightened for yet, it will be, because they can always keep us ignorant, and because God approbates their cruelties, with which they have been for centuries murdering us. The whites shall have enough of the blacks, yet, as true as God sits on his throne in Heaven. . . .

Our Wretchedness In Consequence Of The Colonizing Plan

. . . Let no man of us budge one step, and let slave-holders come to beat us from our country. America is more our country, than it is the whites—we have enriched it with our *blood and tears*. The greatest riches in all America have arisen from our blood and tears:—and will they drive us from our property and homes, which we have earned with our *blood*? They must look sharp or this very thing will bring swift destruction upon them. The

Americans have got so fat on our blood and groans, that they have almost forgotten the God of armies. But let them go on. . . .

Remember Americans, that we must and shall be free and enlightened as you are, will you wait until we shall, under God, obtain our liberty by the crushing arm of power? Will it not be dreadful for you? I speak Americans for your good. We must and shall be free I say, in spite of you. You may do your best to keep us in wretchedness and misery, to enrich you and your children, but God will deliver us from under you. And wo, wo, will be to you if we have to obtain our freedom by fighting. Throw away your fears and prejudices then, and enlighten us and treat us like men, and we will like you more than we do now hate you, and tell us no more about colonization, for America is as much our country, as it is yours.—Treat us like men, and there is no danger but we will all live in peace and happiness together. For we are not like you, hard hearted, unmerciful, and unforgiving. What a happy country this will be, if the whites will listen. What nation under heaven, will be able to do any thing with us, unless God gives us up into its hand? But Americans, I declare to you, while you keep us and our children in bondage, and treat us like brutes, to make us support you and your families, we cannot be your friends. You do not look for it, do you? Treat us then like men, and we will be your friends. And there is not a doubt in my mind, but that the whole of the past will be sunk into oblivion, and we yet, under God, will become a united and happy people. The whites may say it is impossible, but remember that nothing is impossible with God.

The Americans may say or do as they please, but they have to raise us from the condition of brutes to that of respectable men, and to make a national acknowledgement to us for the wrongs they have inflicted on us. As unexpected, strange, and wild as these propositions may to some appear, it is no less a fact, that unless they are complied with, the Americans of the United States, though they may for a little while escape, God will yet weigh them in a balance, and if they are not superior to other men, as they have represented themselves to be, he will give them wretchedness to their very heart's content. . . .

If any are anxious to ascertain who I am, know the world, that I am one of the oppressed, degraded and wretched sons of Africa, rendered so by the avaricious and unmerciful, among the whites. If any wish to plunge me into the wretched incapacity of a slave, or murder me for the truth, know ye, that I am in the hand of God, and at your disposal. I count my life not dear unto me, but I am ready to be offered at any moment. For what is the use of living, when in fact I am dead. But remember, Americans, that as miserable, wretched, degraded and abject as you have made us in preceding, and in this generation, to support you and your families, that some of you, (whites) on the continent of America, will yet curse the day that you ever were born. You want slaves, and want us for your slaves! ! ! My colour will yet, root some of you out of the very face of the earth! ! ! ! !

. . . Now, Americans! I ask you candidly, was your sufferings under Great Britain, one hundredth part as cruel and tyrannical as you have rendered ours under you? Some of you, no doubt, believe that we will never throw off your murderous government and "provide new guards for our future security." If Satan has made you believe it, will he not deceive you? (*The Lord has not taught the Americans that we will not some day or other throw off their chains and hand-cuffs, from our hands and feet, and their devilish lashes (which some of them shall have enough of yet) from off our backs.* [Note in original.]) Do the whites say, I being a black man, ought to be humble, which I readily admit? I ask them, ought they not to be as humble as I? or do they think that they can measure arms with Jehovah? Will not the Lord yet humble them? or will not these very coloured people whom they now treat worse than brutes, yet under God, humble them low down enough? Some of the whites are ignorant enough to tell us, that we ought to be submissive to them, that they may keep their feet on our throats. And if we do not submit to be beaten to death by them, we are bad creatures and of course must be damned, &c. If any man wishes to hear this doctrine openly preached to us by the American preachers, let him go into the Southern and Western sections of this country—I do not speak from hear say—what I have written, is what I have seen and heard myself. No man may think that my book is made up of conjecture—I have travelled and observed nearly the whole of those things myself, and what little I did not get by my own observation, I received from those among the whites and blacks, in whom the greatest confidence may be placed.

The Americans may be as vigilant as they please, but they cannot be vigilant enough for the Lord, neither can they hide themselves, where he will not find and bring them out.

NAT TURNER

Several authors in our collection repeat how unrest among blacks dates back to the earliest slave times. No slave revolt however is more famous than that led by Nat Turner on August 21, 1831 in Southampton County, Virginia. Sixty whites were killed in the uprising and at least one hundred blacks died in the course of its suppression. Thirteen slaves and three blacks were arrested immediately, tried and hanged. Nat Turner was not captured until October 30, and was executed—going to his death calmly, according to newspaper reports—on November 11, 1831.

An autobiographical statement made by Nat Turner follows:

From Turner's *Confessions,* 1831

. . . I was thirty-one years of age the second of October last, and born the property of Benjamin Turner, of this county. In my childhood a circumstance occurred which made an indelible impression on my mind, and laid the groundwork of that enthusiasm which has terminated so fatally to many, both white and black, and for which I am about to atone at the gallows. It is here necessary to relate this circumstance. Trifling as it may seem, it was the commencement of that belief which has grown with time; and even now, sir, in his dungeon, helpless and forsaken as I am, I cannot divest myself of. Being at play with other children, when three or four years old, I was telling them something, which my mother, overhearing, said it had happened before I was born. I stuck to my story, however, and related some things which went, in her opinion, to confirm it. Others being called on, were greatly astonished, knowing that these things had happened, and caused them to say, in my hearing, I surely would be a prophet, as the Lord had shown me things that had happened before my birth. And my mother and grandmother strengthened me in this my first impression, saying, in my presence, I was intended for some great purpose, which they had always thought from certain marks on my head and breast. . . .

My grandmother, who was very religious, and to whom I was much attached—my master, who belonged to the church, and other religious persons who visited the house, and whom I often saw at prayers, noticing the singularity of my manners, I suppose, and my uncommon intelligence for a child, remarked I had too much sense to be raised, and, if I was, I would never be of any service to any one as a slave. To a mind like mine, restless, inquisitive, and observant of everything that was passing, it is easy to suppose that religion was the subject to which it would be directed; and, although this subject principally occupied my thoughts, there was nothing that I saw or heard of to which my attention was not directed. The manner in which I learned to read and write, not only had great influence on my own mind, as I acquired it with the most perfect ease,—so much so, that I have no recollection whatever of learning the alphabet; but, to the astonishment of the family, one day, when a book was shown me, to keep me from crying, I began spelling the names of different objects. This was a source of wonder to all in the neighborhood, particularly the blacks—and this learning was constantly improved at all opportunities. When I got large enough to go to work, while employed I was reflecting on many things that would present themselves to my imagination; and whenever an opportunity occurred of looking at a book, when the school-children were getting their lessons, I would find many things that the fertility of my own imagination had depicted to me before. All my time, not devoted to my master's service, was spent either in prayer, or in making experiments in casting different things in moulds made of earth, in attempting to make paper, gunpowder, and many other experiments, that, although I could not perfect, yet convinced me of its practicability if I had the means. *(When questioned as to the manner of manufacturing those different articles, he was found well informed. [Footnote in original.])*

I was not addicted to stealing in my youth, nor have ever been; yet such was the confidence of the Negroes in the neighborhood, even at this early period of my life, in my superior judgment, that they would often carry me with them when they were going on any roguery, to plan for them. Growing up among them with this confidence in my superior judgment, and when this, in their opinions, was perfected by Divine inspiration, from the circumstances already alluded to in my infancy, and which belief was ever afterwards zealously inculcated by the austerity of my life and manners, which became the subject of remark by white and black; having soon discovered to be great, I must appear so, and therefore studiously avoided mixing in society, and wrapped myself in mystery, devoting my time to fasting and prayer.

By this time, having arrived to man's estate, and hearing the Scriptures commented on at meetings, I was struck with that particular passage which says, "Seek ye the kingdom of heaven, and all things shall be added unto you." I reflected much on this passage, and prayed daily for light on this subject. As I was praying one day at my plough, the Spirit spoke to me, saying, "Seek ye the kingdom of heaven, and all things shall be added unto you," *Question.* "What do you mean by the Spirit?" *Answer.* "The Spirit that spoke to the prophets in former days,"— and I was greatly astonished, and for two years prayed continually, whenever my duty would permit; and then again I had the same revelation, which fully confirmed me in the impression that I was ordained for some great purpose in the hands of the Almighty. Several years rolled round, in which many events occurred to strengthen me in this my belief. At this time I reverted in my mind to the remarks made of me in my childhood, and the things that had been shown me; and as it had been said of me in my childhood, by those by whom I had been taught to pray, both white and black, and in whom I had the greatest confidence, that I had too much sense to be raised, and if I was I would never be of any use to any one as a slave; now, finding I had arrived to man's estate, and was a slave, and these revelations being made known to me, I began to direct my attention to this great object, to fulfil the purpose for which, by this time, I felt assured I was intended. Knowing the influence I had obtained over the minds of my fellow-servants—(not by the means of conjuring and such-like tricks—for to them I always spoke of such things with contempt), but by the communion of the Spirit, whose revelations I often communicated to them, and they believed and said my wisdom came from God,—I now began to prepare them for my purpose, by telling them something was about to happen that would terminate in fulfilling the great promise that had been made to me.

About this time I was placed under an overseer, from whom I ran away, and after remaining in the woods thirty days, I returned, to the astonishment of the Negroes on the plantation, who thought I had made my escape to some other part of the country, as my father had done before. But the reason of my return was, that the Spirit appeared to me and said I had my wishes directed to the things of this world, and not to the kingdom of heaven, and that I should return to the service of my earthly master—"For he who knoweth his Master's will, and doeth it not, shall be beaten with many stripes, and thus have I chastened you." And the

Negroes found fault, and murmured against me, saying that if they had my sense they would not serve any master in the world. And about this time I had a vision—and I saw white spirits and black spirits engaged in battle, and the sun was darkened—the thunder rolled in the heavens, and blood flowed in streams—and I heard a voice saying, "Such is your luck, such you are called to see; and let it come rough or smooth, you must surely bear it."

I now withdrew myself as much as my situation would permit from the intercourse of my fellow-servants, for the avowed purpose of serving the Spirit more fully; and it appeared to me, and reminded me of the things it had already shown me, and that it would then reveal to me the knowledge of the elements, the revolution of the planets, the operation of tides, and changes of the seasons. After this revelation in the year 1825, and the knowledge of the elements being made known to me, I sought more than ever to obtain true holiness before the great day of judgment should appear, and then I began to receive the true knowledge of faith. And from the first steps of righteousness until the last, was I made perfect; and the Holy Ghost was with me, and said, "Behold me as I stand in the heavens." And I looked and saw the forms of men in different attitudes; and there were lights in the sky, to which the children of darkness gave other names than what they really were; for they were the lights of the Saviour's hands, stretched forth from east to west, even as they were extended on the cross on Calvary for the redemption of sinners. And I wondered greatly at these miracles, and prayed to be informed of a certainty of the meaning thereof; and shortly afterwards, while laboring in the field, I discovered drops of blood on the corn, as though it were dew from heaven; and I communicated it to many, both white and black, in the neighborhood—and I then found on the leaves in the woods hieroglyphic characters and numbers, with the forms of men in different attitudes, portrayed in blood, and representing the figures I had seen before in the heavens. And now the Holy Ghost had revealed itself to me, and made plain the miracles it had shown me; for as the blood of Christ had been shed on this earth, and had ascended to heaven for the salvation of sinners, and was now returning to earth again in the form of dew,—and as the leaves on the trees bore the impression of the figures I had seen in the heavens,—it was plain to me that the Saviour was about to lay down the yoke he had borne for the sins of men, and the great day of judgment was at hand.

About this time I told these things to a white man (Etheldred T. Brantley), on whom it had a wonderful effect; and he ceased from his wickedness, and was attacked immediately with a cutaneous eruption, and blood oozed from the pores of his skin, and after praying and fasting nine days he was healed. And the Spirit appeared to me again, and said, as the Saviour had been baptized, so should we be also; and when the white people would not let us be baptized by the church, we went down into the water together, in the sight of many who reviled us, and were baptized by the Spirit. After this I rejoiced greatly, and gave thanks to God. And on the 12th of May, 1828, I heard a loud noise in the heavens, and the Spirit instantly appeared to me and said the Serpent was loosened, and Christ had laid down the yoke he had borne for the sins of men, and that I should take it on and fight against the Serpent, for the time was fast approaching when the first should be last and the last should be first. *Ques.* "Do you not find yourself mistaken now?"—*Ans.* "Was not Christ crucified?" And by signs in the heavens that it would make known to me when I should commence the great work, and until the first sign appeared I should conceal it from the knowledge of men; and on the appearance of the sign (the eclipse of the sun, last February), I should arise and prepare myself, and slay my enemies with their own weapons. And immediately on the sign appearing in the heavens, the seal was removed from my lips, and I communicated the great work laid out for me to do, to four in whom I had the greatest confidence (Henry, Hark, Nelson, and Sam). It was intended by us to have begun the work of death on the 4th of July last. Many were the plans formed and rejected by us, and it affected my mind to such a degree that I fell sick, and the time passed without our coming to any determination how to commence—still forming new schemes and rejecting them, when the sign appeared again, which determined me not to wait longer.

Since the commencement of 1830 I had been living with Mr. Joseph Travis, who was to me a kind master, and placed the greatest confidence in me; in fact, I had no cause to complain of his treatment to me. On Saturday evening, the 20th of August, it was agreed between Henry, Hark, and myself, to prepare a dinner the next day for the men we expected, and then to concert a plan, as we had not yet determined on any. Hark, on the following morning, brought a pig, and Henry brandy; and being joined by Sam, Nelson, Will, and Jack, they prepared in the woods a dinner, where, about three o'clock, I joined them.

Q. Why were you so backward in joining them?

A. The same reason that had caused me not to mix with them years before.

I saluted them on coming up, and asked Will how came he there. He answered, his life was worth no more than others, and his liberty as dear to him. I asked him if he thought to obtain it. He said he would, or lose his life. This was enough to put him in full confidence. Jack, I knew, was only a tool in the hands of Hark. It was quickly agreed we should commence at home (Mr. J. Travis') on that night; and until we had armed and equipped ourselves, and gathered sufficient force, neither age nor sex was to be spared—which was invariably adhered to. We remained at the feast until about two hours in the night, when we went to the house and found Austin. . . .

I took my station in the rear, and, as it was my object to carry terror and devastation wherever we went, I placed fifteen or twenty of the best armed and most to be relied on in front, who generally approached the houses as fast as their horses could run. This was for two purposes—to prevent their escape, and strike terror to the inhabitants; on this account I never got to the houses, after leaving Mrs. Whitehead's, until the murders were committed, except in one case. I sometimes got in sight in time to see the work of death completed; viewed the mangled bodies as they lay, in silent satisfaction, and immediately started in quest of other victims. Having murdered Mrs. Waller and ten children, we started for Mr. Wm. Williams',—having killed him and two little boys that were there; while engaged in this, Mrs. Williams fled and got some distance from the house, but she was pursued, overtaken, and compelled to get up behind one of the company, who brought her back, and, after showing her the mangled body of her lifeless husband, she was told to get down and lay by his side, where she was shot dead.

The white men pursued and fired on us several times. Hark had his horse shot under him, and I caught another for him as it was running by me; five or six of my men were wounded, but none left on the field. Finding myself defeated here, I instantly determined to go through a private way, and cross the Nottoway River at the Cypress Bridge, three miles below Jerusalem, and attack

that place in the rear, as I expected they would look for me on the other road, and I had a great desire to get there to procure arms and ammunition. After going a short distance in this private way, accompanied by about twenty men, I overtook two or three, who told me the others were dispersed in every direction.

On this, I gave up all hope for the present; and on Thursday night, after having supplied myself with provisions from Mr. Travis', I scratched a hole under a pile of fence-rails in a field, where I concealed myself for six weeks, never leaving my hiding-place but for a few minutes in the dead of the night to get water, which was very near. Thinking by this time I could venture out, I began to go about in the night, and eavesdrop the houses in the neighborhood; pursuing this course for about a fortnight, and gathering little or no intelligence, afraid of speaking to any human being, and returning every morning to my cave before the dawn of day. I know not how long I might have led this life, if accident had not betrayed me. A dog in the neighborhood passing by my hiding-place one night while I was out, was attracted by some meat I had in my cave, and crawled in and stole it, and was coming out just as I returned. A few nights after, two Negroes having started to go hunting with the same dog, and passed that way, the dog came again to the place, and having just gone out to walk about, discovered me and barked; on which, thinking myself discovered, I spoke to them to beg concealment. On making myself known, they fled from me. Knowing then they would betray me, I immediately left my hiding-place, and was pursued almost incessantly, until I was taken, a fortnight afterwards, by Mr. Benjamin Phipps, in a little hole I had dug out with my sword, for the purpose of concealment, under the top of a fallen tree.

During the time I was pursued, I had many hair-breadth escapes, which your time will not permit you to relate. I am here loaded with chains, and willing to suffer the fate that awaits me.

HENRY GARNET

Twelve years after the death of Turner and a century before Carmichael, a twenty-seven year old man received nation-wide attention because of a speech he delivered before a National Negro Convention in Buffalo, New York. Henry Highland Garnet was the pastor of a Presbyterian Church in Troy, New York. His fiery words, reprinted below, failed by one vote of being adopted that August, 1843, as the resolution of the convention.

Call to Rebellion, 1843

Brethren and Fellow Citizens:—Your brethren of the North, East, and West have been accustomed to meet together in National Conventions, to sympathize with each other, and to weep over your unhappy condition. In these meetings we have addressed all classes of the free, but we have never, until this time, sent a word of consolation and advice to you. We have been contented in sitting still and mourning over your sorrows, earnestly hoping that before this day your sacred liberty would have been restored. But, we have hoped in vain. Years have rolled on, and tens of thousands have been borne on streams of blood and tears, to the shores of eternity. While you have been oppressed, we have also been partakers with you; nor can we be free while you are enslaved. We, therefore, write to you as being bound with you.

Many of you are bound to us, not only by the ties of a common humanity, but we are connected by the more tender relations of parents, wives, husbands, children, brothers, and sisters, and friends. As such we most affectionately address you.

Slavery has fixed a deep gulf between you and us, and while it shuts out from you the relief and consolation which your friends would willingly render, it affects and persecutes you with a fierceness which we might not expect to see in the fiends of hell. But still the Almighty Father of mercies has left to us a glimmering ray of hope, which shines out like a lone star in a cloudy sky. Mankind are becoming wiser, and better—the oppressor's power is fading, and you, every day, are becoming better informed, and more numerous. Your grievances, brethren, are many. We shall not attempt, in this short address, to present to the world all the dark catalogue of this nation's sins, which have been committed upon an innocent people. Nor is it indeed necessary, for you feel them from day to day, and all the civilized world look upon them

with amazement.

Two hundred and twenty-seven years ago, the first of our injured race were brought to the shores of America. They came not with glad spirits to select their homes in the New World. They came not with their own consent, to find an unmolested enjoyment of the blessings of this fruitful soil. The first dealings they had with men calling themselves Christians, exhibited to them the worst features of corrupt and sordid hearts; and convinced them that no cruelty is too great, no villainy and no robbery too abhorrent for even enlightened men to perform, when influenced by avarice and lust. Neither did they come flying upon the wings of Liberty, to a land of freedom. But they came with broken hearts, from their beloved native land, and were doomed to unrequited toil and deep degradation. Nor did the evil of their bondage end at their emancipation by death. Succeeding generations inherited their chains, and millions have come from eternity into time, and have returned again to the world of spirits, cursed and ruined by American slavery.

The propagators of the system, or their immediate ancestors, very soon discovered its growing evil, and its tremendous wickedness, and secret promises were made to destroy it. The gross inconsistency of a people holding slaves, who had themselves "ferried o'er the wave" for freedom's sake, was too apparent to be entirely overlooked. The voice of Freedom cried, "Emancipate yourselves." Humanity supplicated with tears for the deliverance of the children of Africa. Wisdom urged her solemn plea. The bleeding captive plead his innocence, and pointed to Christianity who stood weeping at the cross. Jehovah frowned upon the nefarious institution, and thunderbolts, red with vengeance, struggled to leap forth to blast the guilty wretches who maintained it. But all was in vain. Slavery had stretched its dark wings of death over the land, the Church stood silently by—the priests prophesied falsely, and the people loved to have it so. Its throne is established, and now it reigns triumphant.

Nearly three millions of your fellow-citizens are prohibited by law and public opinion, (which in this country is stronger than law,) from reading the Book of Life. Your intellect has been destroyed as much as possible, and every ray of light they have attempted to shut out from your minds. The oppressors themselves have become involved in the ruin. They have become weak, sensual, and rapacious—they have cursed you—they have cursed themselves—they have cursed the earth which they have trod.

The colonists threw the blame upon England. They said that the mother country entailed the evil upon them, and that they would rid themselves of it if they could. The world thought they were sincere, and the philanthropic pitied them. But time soon tested their sincerity.

In a few years the colonists grew strong, and severed themselves from the British Government. Their independence was declared, and they took their station among the sovereign powers of the earth. The declaration was a glorious document. Sages admired it, and the patriotic of every nation reverenced the God-like sentiments which it contained. When the power of Government returned to their hands, did they emancipate the slaves? No; they rather added new links to our chains. Were they ignorant of the principles of Liberty? Certainly they were not. The sentiments of their revolutionary orators fell in burning eloquence upon their hearts, and with one voice they cried, Liberty or Death. Oh what a sentence was that! It ran from soul to soul like electric fire, and nerved the arm of thousands to fight in the holy cause of Freedom. Among the diversity of opinions that are entertained in regard to physical resistance, there are but a few found to gainsay that stern declaration. We are among those who do not. Slavery! How much misery is comprehended in that single word. What mind is there that does not shrink from its direful effects? Unless the image of God be obliterated from the soul, all men cherish the love of Liberty. The nice discerning political economist does not regard the sacred right more than the un-tutored African who roams in the wilds of Congo. Nor has the one more right to the full enjoyment of his freedom than the other. In every man's mind the good seeds of liberty are planted, and he who brings his fellow down so low, as to make him contented with a condition of slavery, commits the highest crime against God and man. Brethren, your oppressors aim to do this. They endeavor to make you as much like brutes as possible. When they have blinded the eyes of your mind—when they have embittered the sweet waters of life—then, and not till then, has American slavery done its perfect work.

TO SUCH DEGRADATION IT IS SINFUL IN THE EXTREME FOR YOU TO MAKE VOLUNTARY SUBMISSION. The divine commandments you are in duty bound to reverence and obey. If you do not obey them, you will surely meet with the displeasure of the Almighty. He requires you to love him supremely, and your neighbor as yourself—to keep the Sabbath day holy—to search the Scriptures —and bring up your children with respect for his laws, and to worship no other God but him. But slavery sets all these at nought, and hurls defiance in the face of Jehovah. The forlorn condition in which you are placed, does not destroy your moral obligation to God. You are not certain of heaven, because you suffer yourselves to remain in a state of slavery, where you cannot obey the commandments of the Sovereign of the universe. If the ignorance of slavery is a passport to heaven, then it is a blessing, and no curse, and you should rather desire its perpetuity than its abolition. God will not receive slavery, nor ignorance, nor any other state of mind, for love and obedience to him. Your condition does not absolve you from your moral obligation. The diabolical injustice by which your liberties are cloven down, NEITHER GOD, NOR ANGELS, OR JUST MEN, COMMAND YOU TO SUFFER FOR A SINGLE MOMENT. THEREFORE IT IS YOUR SOLEMN AND IMPERATIVE DUTY TO USE EVERY MEANS, BOTH MORAL, INTELLECTUAL, AND PHYSICAL THAT PROMISES SUCCESS. If a band of heathen men should attempt to enslave a race of Christians, and to place their children under the influence of some false religion, surely Heaven would frown upon the men who would not resist such aggression, even to death. If, on the other hand, a band of Christians should attempt to enslave a race of heathen men, and to entail slavery upon them, and to keep them in heathenism in the midst of Christianity, the God of heaven would smile upon every effort which the injured might make to disenthral themselves.

Brethren, it is as wrong for your lordly oppressors to keep you in slavery, as it was for the man thief to steal our ancestors from the coast of Africa. You should therefore now use the same manner of resistance, as would have been just in our ancestors when the bloody foot-prints of the first remorseless soul-thief was placed upon the shores of our fatherland. The humblest peasant is as free in the sight of God as the proudest monarch that ever swayed a sceptre. Liberty is a spirit sent out from God, and like its great Author, is no respecter of persons.

Brethren, the time has come when you must act for yourselves. It is an old and true saying that, "if hereditary bondmen would be free, they must themselves strike the blow." You can plead your own cause, and do the work of emancipation better than any others. The nations of the world are moving in the great cause of universal freedom, and some of them at least will, ere long, do you justice. The combined powers of Europe have placed their broad seal of disapprobation upon the African slave-trade. But in the slave-holding parts of the United States, the trade is as brisk as ever. They buy and sell you as though you were brute beasts. The North has done much—her opinion of slavery in the abstract is known. But in regard to the South, we adopt the opinion of the *New York Evangelist*—We have advanced so far, that the cause apparently waits for a more effectual door to be thrown open than has been yet. We are about to point out that more effectual door. Look around you, and behold the bosoms of your loving wives heaving with untold agonies! Hear the cries of your poor children! Remember the stripes your fathers bore. Think of the torture and disgrace of your noble mothers. Think of your wretched sisters, loving virtue and purity, as they are driven into concubinage and are exposed to the unbridled lusts of incarnate devils. Think of the undying glory that hangs around the ancient name of Africa—and forget not that you are native born American citizens, and as such, you are justly entitled to all the rights that are granted to the freest. Think how many tears you have poured out upon the soil which you have cultivated with unrequited toil and enriched with your blood; and then go to your lordly enslavers and tell them plainly, that you *are determined to be free*. Appeal to their sense of justice, and tell them that they have no more right to oppress you, than you have to enslave them. Entreat them to remove the grievous burdens which they have imposed upon you, and to remunerate you for your labor. Promise them renewed diligence in the cultivation of the soil, if they will render to you an equivalent for your services. Point them to the increase of happiness and prosperity in the British West Indies since the Act of Emancipation.

Tell them in language which they cannot misunderstand, of the exceeding sinfulness of slavery, and of a future judgment, and of the righteous retributions of an indignant God. Inform them that all you desire is FREEDOM, and that nothing else will suffice. Do this, and for ever after cease to toil for the heartless tyrants, who give you no other reward but stripes and abuse. If they then commence the work of death, they, and not you, will be responsible for the consequences. You had better all die—*die immediately,* than live slaves and entail your wretchedness upon your posterity. If you would be free in this generation, here is your only hope. However much you and all of us may desire it, there is not much hope of redemption without the shedding of blood. If you must bleed, let it all come at once—rather *die freemen, than live to be slaves.* It is impossible like the children of Israel, to make a grand exodus from the land of bondage. The Pharaohs are on both sides of the blood-red waters! You cannot move *en masse,* to the dominions of the British Queen—nor can you pass through Florida and overrun Texas, and at last find peace in Mexico. The propagators of American slavery are spending their blood and treasure, that they may plant the black flag in the heart of Mexico and riot in the halls of the Montezeumas. In the language of the Rev. Robert Hall, when addressing the volunteers of Bristol, who were rushing forth to repel the invasion of Napoleon, who threatened to lay waste the fair homes of England, "Religion is too much interested in your behalf, not to shed over you her most gracious influences."

You will not be compelled to spend much time in order to become inured to hardships. From the first moment that you breathed the air of heaven, you have been accustomed to nothing else but hardships. The heroes of the American Revolution were never put upon harder fare than a peck of corn and a few herrings per week. You have not become enervated by the luxuries of life. Your sternest energies have been beaten out upon the anvil of severe trial. Slavery has done this, to make you subservient, to its own purposes; but it has done more than this, it has prepared you for any emergency. If you receive good treatment, it is what you could hardly expect; if you meet with pain, sorrow, and even death, these are the common lot of slaves.

Fellow men! Patient sufferers! behold your dearest rights crushed to the earth! See your sons murdered, and your wives, mothers and sisters doomed to prostitution. In the name of the merciful God, and by all that life is worth, let it no longer be a debatable question whether it is better to choose *Liberty or death.*

In 1822, Denmark Veazie [Vesey], of South Carolina, formed a plan for the liberation of his fellow men. In the whole history of human efforts to overthrow slavery, a more complicated and tremendous plan was never formed. He was betrayed by the treachery of his own people, and died a martyr to freedom. Many a brave hero fell, but history, faithful to her high trust, will transcribe his name on the same monument with Moses, Hampden, Tell, Bruce and Wallace, Toussaint L'Ouverture, Lafayette and Washington. That tremendous movement shook the whole empire of slavery. The guilty soul-thieves were overwhelmed with fear. It is a matter of fact, that at that time, and in consequence of the threatened revolution, the slave States talked strongly of emancipation. But they blew but one blast of the trumpet of freedom and then laid it aside. As these men became quiet, the slaveholders ceased to talk about emancipation; and now behold your condition today! Angels sigh over it, and humanity has long since exhausted her tears in weeping on your account!

The patriotic Nathaniel Turner followed Denmark Veazie [Vesey]. He was goaded to desperation by wrong and injustice. By despotism, his name has been recorded on the list of infamy, and future generations will remember him among the noble and brave.

Next arose the immortal Joseph Cinque, the hero of the *Amistad.* He was a native African, and by the help of God he emancipated a whole ship-load of his fellow men on the high seas. And he now sings of liberty on the sunny hills of Africa and beneath his native palm-trees, where he hears the lion roar and feels himself as free as that king of the forest.

Next arose Madison Washington that bright star of freedom, and took his station in the constellation of true heroism. He was a slave on board the brig *Creole,* of Richmond, bound to New Orleans, that great slave mart, with a hundred and four [sic] others. Nineteen struck for liberty or death. But one life was taken, and the whole were emancipated, and the vessel was carried into Nassau, New Providence.

Noble men! Those who have fallen in freedom's conflict, their memories will be cherished by the true-hearted and the God-fearing in all future generations; those who are living, their names are surrounded by a halo of glory.

Brethren, arise, arise! Strike for your lives and liberties. Now is the day and the hour. Let every slave throughout the land do this, and the days of slavery are numbered. You cannot be more oppressed than you have been—you cannot suffer greater cruelties than you have already. *Rather die free-men than live to be slaves.* Remember that you are FOUR MILLIONS!

It is in your power so to torment the God-cursed slaveholders that they will be glad to let you go free. If the scale was turned, and black men were the masters and white men the slaves, every destructive agent and element would be employed to lay the oppressor low. Danger and death would hang over their heads day and night. Yes, the tyrants would meet with plagues more terrible than those of Pharaoh. But you are a patient people. You act as though, you were made for the special use of these devils. You act as though your daughters were born to pamper the lusts of your masters and overseers. And worse than all, you tamely submit while your lords tear your wives from your embraces and defile them before your eyes. In the name of God, we ask, are you men? Where is the blood of your fathers? Has it all run out of your veins? Awake, awake; millions of voices are calling you! Your dead fathers speak to you from their graves. Heaven, as with a voice of thunder, calls on you to arise from the dust.

Let your motto be resistance! *resistance!* RESISTANCE! No oppressed people have ever secured their liberty without resistance. What kind of resistance you had better make, you must decide by the circumstances that surround you, and according to the suggestion of expediency. Brethren, adieu! Trust in the living God. Labor for the peace of the human race, and remember that you are FOUR MILLIONS.

FREDERICK DOUGLASS

One of those to hear Garnet at the above-mentioned National Convention was the remarkable Frederick Douglass (1817-1895). Born into slavery, Douglass was purchased in 1832 by a Baltimore shipbuilder, but made his escape in 1838. Having taught himself to read and write, he worked as a day laborer in the North until he was employed by the Anti-Slavery Society as one of its lecturers. His Autobiography was published in 1845, and afterward he made a successful lecturing tour in England. Upon his return in 1847, he and Martin R. Delaney founded The North Star, for sixteen years one of the great anti-slavery papers in the North.

Reprinted below is a letter he wrote to Gerrit Smith, the abolitionist.

No Progress Without Struggle!, 1849

Let me give you a word of the philosophy of reforms. The whole history of the progress of human liberty shows that all concessions, yet made to her august claims, have been born of earnest struggle. The conflict has been exciting, agitating, all-absorbing, and for the time being putting all other tumults to silence. It must do this or it does nothing. If there is no struggle, there is no progress. Those who profess to favor freedom, and yet depreciate agitation, are men who want crops without plowing up the ground. They want rain without thunder and lightning. They want the ocean without the awful roar of its many waters. This struggle may be a moral one; or it may be a physical one; or it may be both moral and physical; but it must be a struggle. Power concedes nothing without a demand. It never did, and it never will. Find out just what people will submit to, and you have found out the exact amount of injustice and wrong which will be imposed upon them; and these will continue till they are resisted with either words or blows, or with both. The limits of tyrants are prescribed by the endurance of those whom they oppress. In the light of these ideas, Negroes will be hunted at the North, and held and flogged at the South, so long as they submit to those devilish outrages, and make no resistance, either moral or physical. Men may not get all they pay for in this world; but they must certainly pay for all they get. If we ever get free from all the oppressions and wrongs heaped upon us, we must pay for their removal. We must do this by labor, by suffering, by sacrifice, and, if needs be, by our lives, and the lives of others.

JOHN S. ROCK

Dr. Rock, a distinguished Boston physician and lawyer, was the first black attorney admitted to the bar of the United States Supreme Court. The following speech, which could be subtitled Black is beautiful, was delivered in Boston at a meeting commemorating the Boston Massacre.

Comparing White and Black Americans, 1858

White Americans have taken great pains to try to prove that we are cowards. We are often insulted with the assertion, that if we had had the courage of the Indians or the white man, we would never have submitted to be slaves. I ask if Indians and white men have never been slaves? The white man tested the Indian's courage here when he had his organized armies, his battle-grounds, his places of retreat, with everything to hope for and everything to lose. The position of the African slave has been very different. Seized a prisoner of war, unarmed, bound hand and foot, and conveyed to a distant country among what to him were worse than cannibals; brutally beaten, half-starved, closely watched by armed men, with no means of knowing their own strength or the strength of their enemies, with no weapons, and without a probability of success. But if the white man will take the trouble to fight the black man in Africa or in Hayti, and fight him as fair as the black man will fight him there—if the black man does not come off victor, I am deceived in his prowess. But, take a man, armed or unarmed, from his home, his country, or his friends, and place him among savages, and who is he that would not make good his retreat? "Discretion is the better part of valor," but for a man to resist where he knows it will destroy him, shows more foolhardiness than courage. There have been many Anglo-Saxons and Anglo-Americans enslaved in Africa, but I have never heard that they successfully resisted any government. They always resort to running indispensables.

The courage of the Anglo-Saxon is best illustrated in his treatment of the Negro. A score or two of them can pounce upon a poor Negro, tie and beat him, and then call him a coward because he submits. Many of their most brilliant victories have been achieved in the same manner. But the greatest battles which they have fought have been upon paper. We can easily account for this; their trumpeter is dead. He died when they used to be exposed for sale in the Roman market, about the time that Cicero cautioned his friend Atticus not to buy them, on account of their stupidity. A little more than half a century ago, this race, in connection with their Celtic neighbors, who have long been considered (by themselves, of course,) the bravest soldiers in the world, so far forgot themselves, as to attack a few cowardly, stupid Negro slaves, who, according to their accounts, had not sense enough to go to bed. And what was the result? Why, sir, the Negroes drove them out from the island like so many sheep, and they have never dared to show their faces, except with hat in hand.

Our true and tried friend, Rev. Theodore Parker, said, in his speech at the State House, a few weeks since, that "the stroke of the axe would have settled the question long ago, but the black man would not strike." Mr. Parker makes a very low estimate of the courage of his race, if he means that one, two or three millions of these ignorant and cowardly black slaves could, without means, have brought to their knees five, ten, or twenty millions of intelligent, brave white men, backed up by a rich oligarchy. But I know of no one who is more familiar with the true character of the Anglo-Saxon race than Mr. Parker. I will not dispute this point with him, but I will thank him or any one else to tell us how it could have been done. His remark calls to my mind the day which is to come, when one shall chase a thousand, and two put ten thousand to flight. But when he says that "the black man *would not strike*," I am prepared to say that he does us great injustice. The black man is not a coward. The history of the bloody struggles for freedom in Hayti, in which the blacks whipped the French and the English, and gained their independence, in spite of the perfidy of that villainous First Consul, will be a lasting refutation of the malicious aspersions of our enemies. The history of the struggles for the liberty of the United States ought to silence every American calumniator. . . .

The white man contradicts himself who says, that if he were in our situation, he would throw off the yoke. Thirty millions of white men of this proud Caucasian race are at this moment held as slaves, and bought and sold with horses and cattle. The iron heel of oppression grinds the masses of all the European races to the dust. They suffer every kind of oppression, and no one dares to open his mouth to protest against it. Even in the Southern portion of this boasted land of liberty, no white man dares advocate so much of the Declaration of Independence as declares that "all men are created free and equal, and have an inalienable right to life, liberty," &c.

White men have no room to taunt us with tamely submitting. If they were black men, they would work wonders; but, as white men, they can do nothing. "O, Consistency, thou art a jewel!"

Now, it would not be surprising if the brutal treatment which we have received for 'the past two centuries should have crushed our spirits. But this is not the case. Nothing but a superior force keeps us down. And when I see the slaves rising up by hundreds annually, in the majesty of human nature, bidding defiance to every slave code and its penalties, making the issue Canada or death, and that too while they are closely watched by paid men armed with pistols, clubs and bowie-knives, with the army and navy of this great Model Republic arrayed against them, I am disposed to ask if the charge of cowardice does not come with ill-grace . . .

I do not envy the white American the little liberty which he enjoys. It is his right, and he ought to have it. I wish him success, though I do not think he deserves it. But I would have all men free. We have had much sad experience in this country, and it would be strange indeed if we do not profit by some of the lessons which we have so dearly paid for. Sooner or later, the clashing of arms will be heard in this country, and the black man's services will be needed: 150,000 freemen capable of bearing arms, and not all cowards and fools, and three quarter of a million slaves, wild with the enthusiasm caused by the dawn of the glorious opportunity of being able to strike a genuine blow for freedom, will be a power which white men will be "bound to respect." Will the blacks fight? Of course they will. The black man will never be neutral. He could not if he would and would not if he could. Will he fight for this country, right or wrong? This the common sense of every one answers; and when the time comes, and come it will, the black man will give an intelligent answer. Judge Taney may outlaw us; Caleb Cushing *(Attorney-General of the United States from 1853 to 1857.)* may show the depravity of his heart by abusing us; and this wicked government may oppress us; but the black man will live when Judge Taney, Caleb Cushing and this wicked government are no more. White man may despise, ridicule, slander and abuse us; they may seek as they always have done to divide us, and make us feel degraded; but no man shall cause me to turn my back upon my race. With it I will sink or swim.

The prejudice which some white men have, or affected to have, against my color gives me no pain. If any man does not fancy my color, that is his business, and I shall not meddle with it. I shall give myself no trouble because he lacks good taste. If he judges my intellectual capacity by my color, he certainly cannot expect much profundity, for it is only skin deep, and is really of no very great importance to any one but myself. I will not deny that I admire the talents and noble characters of many white men. But I cannot say that I am particularly pleased with their physical appearance. If old mother nature had held out as well as she commenced, we should, probably, have had fewer varieties in the races. When I contrast the fine tough muscular system, the beautiful, rich color, the full broad features, and the gracefully frizzled hair of the Negro, with the delicate physical organization, wan color, sharp features and lank hair of the Caucasian, I am inclined to believe that when the white man was created, nature was pretty well exhausted—but determined to keep up appearances, she pinched up his features, and did the best she could under the circumstances. (Great laughter.)

I would have you understand, that I not only love my race, but am pleased with my color; and while many colored persons may feel degraded by being called Negroes, and wish to be classed among other races more favored, I shall feel it my duty, my pleasure and my pride, to concentrate my feeble efforts in elevating to a fair position a race to which I am especially identified by feelings and by blood. . . .

In this country, where money is the great sympathetic nerve which ramifies society, and has a ganglia in every man's pocket, a man is respected in proportion to his success in business. When the avenues to wealth are opened to us, we will then become educated and wealthy, and then the roughest looking colored man that you ever saw, or ever will see, will be pleasanter than the harmonies of Orpheus, and black will be a very pretty color. It will make our jargon, wit—our words, oracles; flattery will then take the place of slander, and you will find no prejudice in the Yankee whatever. We do not expect to occupy a much better position than we now do, until we shall have our educated and wealthy men, who can wield a power that cannot be misunderstood. Then, and not till then, will the tongue of slander be silenced, and the lip of prejudice sealed. Then, and not till then, will we be able to enjoy true equality, which can exist only among peers.

ROBERT PURVIS

When the American Anti-Slavery Society met to cele-brate its 27th anniversary, Robert Purvis of Philadelphia delivered the following indictment of the American gov-ernment for its subjugation of black people. About half is printed below:

ON AMERICAN DEMOCRACY, 1860

What is the attitude of your boasting, braggart republic toward the 600,000 free people of color who swell its population and add to its wealth? I have already alluded to the dictum of Judge Taney in the notorious Dred Scott decision. That dictum reveals the animus of the whole government; it is a fair example of the cowardly and malignant spirit that pervades the entire policy of the country. The end of that policy is, undoubtedly, to destroy the colored man, as a man, to prevent him from having any existence in the land except as a "chattel personal to all intents, constructions and purposes whatsoever." With this view, it says a colored man shall not sue and recover his lawful property; he shall not bear arms and train in the militia; he shall not be a com-mander of a vessel, not even of the meanest craft that creeps along the creeks and bays of your Southern coast; he shall not carry a mailbag, or serve as a porter in a post-office; and he shall not even put his face in a United States court-room for any purpose, except by the sufferance of the white man.

I had occasion, a few days since, to go to the United States court-room in the city of Philadelphia. My errand was a proper one; it was to go bail for one of the noble band of colored men who had so bravely risked their lives for the rescue of a brother man on his way to eternal bondage. As I was about entering the door, I was stopped, and ordered back. I demanded the reason. "I have my orders," was the reply. What orders? "To keep out all colored people." Now, sir, who was the man that offered me this indignity? It was Deputy-Marshal Jenkins, the notorious slave-catcher. And why did he do it? Because he had his orders from pious, praying, Christian Democrats, who hold and teach the damnable doctrine that the "black man has no rights that the white man is bound to respect." It is true that Marshall Yost, to whom I indignantly appealed, reversed this man's orders, and apologized to me, assuring me that I could go in and out at my pleasure. But, sir, the apology made the matter worse; for, mark you, it was not me personally that was objected to, *but the race* with which I stand identified. Great God! who can think of such outrages, such meanness, such dastardly, cowardly cruelty, without burning with indignation, and choking for want of words with which to denounce it? And in the case of the noble little band referred to, the men who generously, heroically risked their lives to rescue the man who was about being carried back to slavery; look at their conduct; you know the circumstances. We recently had a slave trial in Philadelphia—no new thing in the city of *"Brotherly Love."* A victim of Virginia tyranny, a fugitive from Southern injustice, had made good his escape from the land of whips and chains to Pennsylvania, and had taken up his abode near the capital of the State. The place of his retreat was discovered; the bloodhounds of the law scented him out, and caught him; they put him in chains and brought him before Judge Cadwallader—a man whose pro-slavery antecedents made him a fitting instrument for the execution of the accursed Fugitive Slave Law.

The sequel can easily be imagined. Brewster, a leading Democrat—the man, who, like your O'Conor of this city, has the unblushing hardihood to defend the enslavement of the black man upon principle—advocated his return. The man was sent into life-long bondage. While the trial was going on, slaveholders, Southern students and pro-slavery Market-street salesmen were freely admitted; but the colored people, the class most interested, were carefully excluded. Prohibited from entering, they thronged around the door of the court-house. At last the prisoner was brought out, handcuffed and guarded by his captors; he was put into a carriage which started off in the direction of the South. Some ten or twelve brave black men made a rush for the carriage, in hopes of effecting a rescue; they were overpowered; beaten, put under arrest and carried to prison, there to await their trial, before this same Judge Cadwallader, for violating the Fugitive Slave law! Mark you, they may go into the court-room as *prisoners,* but not as *spectators!* They may not have an opportunity of hearing the law expounded, but they may be punished if they make themselves chargeable with violating it!

Sir, people talk of the bloody code of Draco, but I venture to assert, without fear of intelligent contradiction, that, all things considered, that code was mild, that code was a law of love, compared with the hellish laws and precedents that disgrace the statute-books of this modern Democratic, Christian Republic! I said that a man of color might not be a commander of the humblest craft that sails in your American waters. There was a man in Philadelphia, the other day, who stated that he owned and sailed a schooner between that city and different ports in the State of Maryland—that his vessel had been seized in the town of Easton, (I believe it was,) or some other town on the Eastern Shore, on the allegation that, contrary to law, there was no white man on board. The vessel constituted his entire property and sole means of supporting his family. He was advised to sue for its recovery, which he did, and, after a long and expensive litigation, the case was decided in his favor. But by this time the vessel had rotted and gone to wreck, and the man found himself reduced to beggary. His business in Philadelphia was to raise $50 with which to take himself and family out of this cursed land, to a country where liberty is not a mockery, and freedom a mere idle name! . . .

But, sir, narrow and proscriptive as, in my opinion, is the spirit of what is called Native Americanism, there is another thing I regard as tenfold more base and contemptible, and that is your American Democracy—your piebald and rotten Democracy, that talks loudly about equal rights, and at the same time tramples one-sixth of the population of the country in the dust, and declares that they have "no rights which a white man is bound to respect." And, sir, while I repudiate your Native Americanism and your bogus Democracy, allow me to add, at the same time, that I am not a Republican. I could not be a member of the Republican party if I were so disposed; I am disfranchised; I have no vote; I am put out of the pale of political society. The time was in Pennsylvania, under the old Constitution, when I could go to the polls as other men do, but your modern Democracy have taken away from me that right. Your Reform Convention, your Pierce

Butlers—the man who, a year ago, put up nearly four hundred human beings on the block in Georgia, and sold them to the highest bidder—your Pierce Butlers disfranchised me, and I am without any political rights whatever. I am taxed to support a government which takes my money and tramples on me. But, sir, I would not be a member of the Republican party if it were in my power. How could I, a colored man, join a party that styles itself emphatically the "white man's party!?" How could I, an Abolitionist, belong to a party that is and must of necessity be a pro-slavery party? The Republicans may be, and doubtless are, opposed to the extension of slavery, but they are sworn to support, and they *will* support, slavery where it already exists.

EDITORIAL

Resounding with the ring of contemporary events is the following statement reprinted from the Chicago Conservator, a black newspaper:

BLOOD, BRAND, OR LIBERTY; 1880

Clarksville, Tennessee, was visited last week by a terrible fire. The business portion of the town was burned, leaving a mere shell of suburban residence in place of the great tobacco mart of Tennessee. It is supposed to be the work of incendiaries and the colored people bear the blame. When the city was burning, they gathered in little knots and crowds; discussed the situation, witnessed with a good deal of manifest satisfaction the strenuous efforts to suppress the fire, but would not lend a helping hand, for love or money. We are loath to advocate lawlessness. We deplore the necessity of resorting to arson and rapine but if such things must come, let them come. If the colored people of Clarksville did fire the town, we regret the necessity but not the act. If they had been denied the rights and privileges of men; if, by studied persecution, their hearts have been hardened; if goaded by oppression to desperation they have lost all their interest in and love for their homes; we are proud to see them have the manhood to be the willing witnesses of its destruction.

The colored people of Clarksville were incensed over a multitude of wrongs. Not long ago, a colored man was lynched upon the charge of an attempt at outrage. An attempt, mind you. This is a comprehensive term in the South. It embraces a wink by a colored man at a white girl a half mile off. Such a crime is worthy of lynching, but a beastly attack upon a colored girl by a white man is only a wayward indiscretion. The colored people have stood such discriminations long enough.

The people of Clarksville have broken the ice, God grant it may extend from Virginia to Texas. Still later, a colored man was brutally killed by a policeman, and ever since, the people have given forth mutterings, not loud, but deep. . . . [President] Hayes has plainly told the colored people they must make peace at any price. We repeat it, but with a different signification—they must make peace at any price. It may cost treasure, it may cost blood, it may cost lives, but make it, be the cost what it may. . . . The trying scenes of a presidential contest will soon be upon us. We claim no prophetic vision, but we warn the southern whites that they need not expect such one-sided scenes of butchery in future. They will have to make a choice between Blood, the Brand, and Political Liberty.

JOHN E. BRUCE

In October of the year cited below, John E. Bruce, a journalist, gave a speech in consideration of violence. He called for "force under wise and discreet leaders."

Speech, 1889

I fully realize the delicacy of the position I occupy in this discussion and know too well that those who are to follow me will largely benefit by what I shall have to say in respect to the application of force as one of the means to the solution of the problem known as the Negro problem. I am not unmindful of the fact that there are those living who have faith in the efficacy of submission, who are still impregnated with the slavish fear which had its origin in oppression and the peculiar environments of the slave period. Those who are thus minded will advise a pacific policy in order as they believe to affect a settlement of this question, with which the statesmanship of a century has grappled without any particularly gratifying results. Agitation is a good thing, organization is a better thing. The million Negro voters of Georgia, and the undiscovered millions in other southern states—undiscovered so far as our knowledge of their number exists—could with proper organization and intelligent leadership meet force with force with most beneficial results. The issue upon us cannot be misunderstood by those who are watching current events . . . The man who will not fight for the protection of his wife and children is a *coward* and deserves to be ill treated. The man who takes his life in his hand and stands up for what he knows to be right will always command the respect of his enemy.

Submission to the *dicta* of southern bulldozers is the basest cowardice, and there is no just reason why manly men of any race should allow themselves to be continually outraged and oppressed by their equals before the law. . . .

Under the present condition of affairs the only hope, the only salvation for the Negro is to be found in a resort to force under wise and discreet leaders. He must sooner or later come to this in order to set at rest for all time to come the charge that he is a moral coward. . . .

The Negro must not be rash and indiscreet either in action or in words but he must be very determined and terribly in earnest, and of one mind to bring order out of chaos and to convince southern rowdies and cutthroats that more than two can play at the game with which they have amused their fellow conspirators in crime for nearly a quarter of a century. Under the Mosaic dispensation it was the custom to require an eye for an eye and a tooth for a tooth under a no less barbarous civilization than that which existed at that period of the world's history; let the Negro require at the hands of every white murderer in the south or else-where a life for a life. If they burn our houses, burn theirs, if they kill our wives and children kill theirs, pursue them relent-lessly, meet force with force everywhere it is offered. If they demand blood exchange it with them, until they are satiated. By a vigorous adherence to this course the shedding of human blood by white men will soon become a thing of the past. Wherever and whenever the Negro shows himself to be a man he can always command the respect even of a cutthroat. Organized resistance to organized resistance is the best remedy for the solution of the vexed problem of the century which to me seems practicable and feasible and I submit this view of the question, ladies and gentle-men, for your careful consideration.

W. E. B. DU BOIS

*Long before William Edward Burghardt Du Bois became
the intellectual father of Pan-Africanism and wrote in
1900 that "the problem of the Twentieth Century is the
problem of the color line"; before he became editor in
1910 of Crisis, the magazine of the National Association for the Advancement of Colored People, and published his great books The Souls of Black Folk and
Black Reconstruction, Dr. Du Bois penned the following
statement of his ideals and intentions as a student in
Berlin:*

PERSONAL NOTES, 1893

Program for the celebration of my twenty-fifth birthday. . . . I
awoke at eight and took coffee and oranges, read letters, thought
of my parents, sang, cried &c (O yes—the night before I heard
Shubert's beautiful unfinished symphony. . . .). Then I wandered
up to the reading room, then to the art gallery, then to a fine
dinner. . . . Then went to Potsdam for coffee & saw a pretty girl.
Then came back to the seminar, took a wander, supped on cocoa,
wine, oranges and cake, wrote my year book & letters—and now
I go to bed after one of the happiest days of my happy life.

Night—grand and wonderful. I am glad I am living. I rejoice
as a strong man to run a race. And I am strong—is it egotism or
is it assurance? . . . I know that I am either a genius or a fool.
O I wonder what I am—I wonder what the world is—I wonder
if life is worth the striving. I do not know—perhaps I never shall
know; but this I do know: be the Truth what it may I shall seek
it on the pure assumption that it is worth seeking—and Heaven
nor Hell, God nor Devil shall turn me from my purpose till I
die. . . .

I am striving to make my life all that life may be—and I am
limiting that strife only in so far as that strife is incompatible
with others of my brothers and sisters making their lives similar.
The crucial question now is where that limit comes . . . God
knows I am sorely puzzled. I am firmly convinced that my own
best development is not one and the same with the best development of the world and here I am willing to sacrifice. . . . The
general proposition of working for the world's good becomes too
soon sickly sentimentality. I therefore take the world that the
Unknown lay in my hands & work for the rise of the Negro
people, taking for granted that their best development means the

best development of the world. . . .

These are my plans: to make a name in science, to make a name in literature and thus to raise my race. . . .

I wonder what will be the outcome? Who knows?

I will go unto the King—which is not according to the law & if I perish—*I Perish.*

MARCUS GARVEY

"We have reached the time when every minute, every second must count for something done, something achieved in the cause of Africa. We need the freedom of Africa now. At this moment methinks I see the angel of God taking up the standard of the Red, the Black, and the Green, and saying: 'Men of the Negro race, Men of Ethiopia, follow me!'" These words were spoken in August, 1921, by Marcus Garvey, a figure with whom we conclude this section and who opens the door to the next.

Garvey (1887-1940) came to New York from Jamaica in 1917. He gained great support and popularity among blacks with his Black Star Line and Back-to-Africa movement. He established the Negro World, a weekly newspaper, and the Universal Negro Improvement Association to teach self-help and self-reliance. His was the vision of black power as racial enterprise and solidarity:

FROM *Philosophy and Opinions,* 1923

It comes to the individual, the race, the nation, once in a life time to decide upon the course to be pursued as a career. The hour has now struck for the individual Negro as well as the entire race to decide the course that will be pursued in the interest of our own liberty.

We who make up the Universal Negro Improvement Association have decided that we shall go forward, upward and onward toward the great goal of human liberty. We have determined among ourselves that all barriers placed in the way of our progress must be removed, must be cleared away for we desire to see the light of a brighter day.

The Negro is Ready

The Universal Negro Improvement Association for five years has been proclaiming to the world the readiness of the Negro to carve out a pathway for himself in the course of life. Men of other races and nations have become alarmed at this attitude of the Negro in his desire to do things for himself and by himself. This alarm has become so universal that organizations have been brought into being here, there and everywhere for the purpose of deterring and obstructing this forward move of our race. Propaganda has been waged here, there and everywhere for the purpose of misinterpreting the intention of this organization; some have said that this organization seeks to create discord and discontent among the races; some say we are organized for the purpose of hating other people. Every sensible, sane and honest-minded person knows that the Universal Negro Improvement Association has no such intention. We are organized for the absolute purpose of bettering our condition, industrially, commercially, socially, religiously and politically. We are organized not to hate other men, but to lift ourselves, and to demand respect of all humanity. We have a program that we believe to be righteous; we believe it to be just, and we have made up our minds to lay down ourselves on the altar of sacrifice for the realization of this great hope of ours, based upon the foundation of righteousness. We declare to the world that Africa must be free, that the entire Negro race must be emancipated from industrial bondage, peonage and serfdom; we make no compromise, we make no apology in this our declaration. We do not desire to create offense on the part of other races, but we are determined that we shall be heard, that we shall be given the rights to which we are entitled.

The Propaganda Of Our Enemies

For the purpose of creating doubts about the work of the Universal Negro Improvement Association, many attempts have been made to cast shadow and gloom over our work. They have even written the most uncharitable things about our organization; they have spoken so unkindly of our effort, but what do we care? They spoke unkindly and uncharitably about all the reform movements that have helped in the betterment of humanity. They maligned the great movement of the Christian religion; they maligned the great liberation movements of America, of France, of England, of Russia; can we expect, then, to escape being maligned in this, our desire for the liberation of Africa and the freedom of four hundred million Negroes of the world?

We have unscrupulous men and organizations working in opposition to us. Some trying to capitalize the new spirit that has come to the Negro to make profit out of it to their own selfish benefit; some are trying to set back the Negro from seeing the hope of his own liberty, and thereby poisoning our people's mind against the motives of our organization; but every sensible far-seeing Negro in this enlightened age knows what propaganda means. It is the medium of discrediting that which you are opposed to, so that the propaganda of our enemies will be of little avail as soon as we are rendered able to carry to our peoples scattered throughout the world the true message of our great organization.

"Crocodiles" As Friends

Men of the Negro race, let me say to you that a greater future is in store for us; we have no cause to lose hope, to become faint-hearted. We must realize that upon ourselves depend our destiny, our future; we must carve out that future, that destiny, and we who make up the Universal Negro Improvement Association have pledged ourselves that nothing in the world shall stand in our way, nothing in the world shall discourage us, but opposition shall make us work harder, shall bring us closer together so that as one man the millions of us will march on toward that goal that we have set for ourselves. The new Negro shall not be deceived. The new Negro refuses to take advice from anyone who has not felt with him, and suffered with him. We have suffered for three hundred years, therefore we feel that the time has come when only those who have suffered with us can interpret our feelings and our spirit. It takes the slave to interpret the feelings of the slave; it takes the unfortunate man to interpret the spirit of his unfortunate brother; and so it takes the suffering Negro to interpret the spirit of his comrade. It is strange that so many people are interested in the Negro now, willing to advise him how to act, and what organizations he should join, yet nobody was interested in the Negro to the extent of not making him a slave for two hundred and fifty years, reducing him to industrial peonage and serfdom after he was freed; it is strange that the same people can be so interested in the Negro now, as to tell him what organization he should follow and what leader he should support.

Whilst we are bordering on a future of brighter things, we are also at our danger period, when we must either accept the right philosophy, or go down by following deceptive propaganda which has hemmed us in for many centuries.

Deceiving The People

There is many a leader of our race who tells us that everything is well, and that all things will work out themselves and that a better day is coming. Yes, all of us know that a better day is coming; we all know that one day we will go home to Paradise, but whilst we are hoping by our Christian virtues to have an entry into Paradise we also realize that we are living on earth, and that the things that are practised in Paradise are not practiced here. You have to treat this world as the world treats you; we are living in a temporal, material age, an age of activity, an age of racial, national selfishness. What else can you expect but to give back to the world what the world gives to you, and we are calling upon the four hundred million Negroes of the world to take a decided stand, a determined stand, that we shall occupy a firm position; that position shall be an emancipated race and a free nation of our own. We are determined that we shall have a free country; we are determined that we shall have a flag; we are determined that we shall have a government second to none in the world.

An Eye For An Eye

Men may spurn the idea, they may scoff at it; the metropolitan press of this country may deride us; yes, white men may laugh at the idea of Negroes talking about government; but let me tell you there is going to be a government, and let me say to you also that whatsoever you give, in like measure it shall be returned to you. The world is sinful, and therefore man believes in the doctrine of an eye for an eye, a tooth for a tooth. Everybody believes that revenge is God's, but at the same time we are men, and revenge sometimes springs up, even in the most Christian heart.

Why should man write down a history that will react against him? Why should man perpetrate deeds of wickedness upon his brother which will return to him in like measure? Yes, the Germans maltreated the French in the Franco-Prussian war of 1870, but the French got even with the Germans in 1918. It is history, and history will repeat itself. Beat the Negro, brutalize the Negro, kill the Negro, burn the Negro, imprison the Negro, scoff at the Negro, deride the Negro, it may come back to you one of these fine days, because the supreme destiny of man is in the hands of God. God is no respecter of persons, whether that person be white, yellow or black. Today the one race is up, tomorrow it has fallen; today the Negro seems to be the footstool of the other races and nations of the world; tomorrow the Negro may occupy the highest rung of the great human ladder.

But, when we come to consider the history of man, was not the Negro a power, was he not great once? Yes, honest students of history can recall the day when Egypt, Ethiopia and Timbuctoo towered in their civilizations, towered above Europe, towered above Asia. When Europe was inhabited by a race of cannibals, a race of savages, naked men, heathens and pagans, Africa was peopled with a race of cultured black men, who were masters in art, science and literature; men who were cultured and refined; men who, it was said, were like the gods. Even the great poets of old sang in beautiful sonnets of the delight it afforded the gods to be in companionship with the Ethiopians. Why, then, should we lose hope? Black men, you were once great; you shall be great again. Lose not courage, lose not faith, go forward. The thing to do is to get organized; keep separated and you will be exploited, you will be robbed, you will be killed. Get organized, and you will compel the world to respect you. If the world fails to give you consideration, because you are black men, because you are Negroes, four hundred millions of you shall, through organization, shake the pillars of the universe and bring down creation, even as Sampson brought down the temple upon his head and upon the heads of the Philistines.

II

BLACK
POWER:
THE
CONCEPT

STOKELY CARMICHAEL

Power & Racism

One of the tragedies of the struggle against racism is that up to now there has been no national organization which could speak to the growing militancy of young black people in the urban ghetto. There has been only a civil rights movement, whose tone of voice was adapted to an audience of liberal whites. It served as a sort of buffer zone between them and angry young blacks. None of its so-called leaders could go into a rioting community and be listened to. In a sense, I blame ourselves—together with the mass media—for what has happened in Watts, Harlem, Chicago, Cleveland, Omaha. Each time the people in those cities saw Martin Luther King get slapped, they became angry; when they saw four little black girls bombed to death, they were angrier; and when nothing happened, they were steaming. We had nothing to offer that they could see, except to go out and be beaten again. We helped to build their frustration.

For too many years, black Americans marched and had their heads broken and got shot. They were saying to the country, "Look, you guys are supposed to be nice guys and we are only going to do what we are supposed to do—why do you beat us up, why don't you give us what we ask, why don't you straighten yourselves out?" After years of this, we are at almost the same point —because we demonstrated from a position of weakness. We cannot be expected any longer to march and have our heads broken in order to say to whites: come on, you're nice guys. For you are not nice guys. We have found you out.

An organization which claims to speak for the needs of a community—as does the Student Nonviolent Coordinating Committee—must speak in the tone of that community, not as somebody else's buffer zone. This is the significance of black power as a slogan. For once, black people are going to use the words they want to use—not just the words whites want to hear. And they will do this no matter how often the press tries to stop the use of the slogan by equating it with racism or separatism.

An organization which claims to be working for the needs of a community—as SNCC does—must work to provide that community with a position of strength from which to make its voice heard. This is the significance of black power beyond the slogan.

Black power can be clearly defined for those who do not attach the fears of white America to their questions about it. We should begin with the basic fact that black Americans have two problems: they are poor and they are black. All other problems arise from this two-sided reality: lack of education, the so-called apathy of black men. Any program to end racism must address itself to that double reality.

Almost from its beginning, SNCC sought to address itself to both conditions with a program aimed at winning political power for impoverished Southern blacks. We had to begin with politics because black Americans are a propertyless people in a country where property is valued above all. We had to work for power, because this country does not function by morality, love, and non-violence, but by power. Thus we determined to win political power, with the idea of moving on from there into activity that would have economic effects. With power, the masses could *make or participate in making* the decisions which govern their destinies, and thus create basic change in their day-to-day lives.

But if political power seemed to be the key to self-determination, it was also obvious that the key had been thrown down a deep well many years earlier. Disenfranchisement, maintained by racist terror, made it impossible to talk about organizing for political power in 1960. The right to vote had to be won, and SNCC workers devoted their energies to this from 1961 to 1965. They set up voter registration drives in the Deep South. They created pressure for the vote by holding mock elections in Mississippi in 1963 and by helping to establish the Mississippi Freedom Democratic Party (MFDP) in 1964. That struggle was eased, though not won, with the passage of the 1965 Voting Rights Act. SNCC workers could then address themselves to the question: "Who can we vote for, to have our needs met—how do we make our vote meaningful?"

SNCC had already gone to Atlantic City for recognition of the

Mississippi Freedom Democratic Party by the Democratic convention and been rejected; it had gone with the MFDP to Washington for recognition by Congress and been rejected. In Arkansas, SNCC helped thirty Negroes to run for School Board elections; all but one were defeated, and there was evidence of fraud and intimidation sufficient to cause their defeat. In Atlanta, Julian Bond ran for the state legislature and was elected—twice—and unseated—twice. In several states, black farmers ran in elections for agricultural committees which make crucial decisions concerning land use, loans, etc. Although they won places on a number of committees, they never gained the majorities needed to control them.

All of the efforts were attempts to win black power. Then, in Alabama, the opportunity came to see how blacks could be organized on an independent party basis. An unusual Alabama law provides that any group of citizens can nominate candidates for county office and, if they win 20 per cent of the vote, may be recognized as a county political party. The same then applies on a state level. SNCC went to organize in several counties such as Lowndes, where black people—who form 80 per cent of the population and have an average annual income of $943—felt they could accomplish nothing within the framework of the Alabama Democratic Party because of its racism and because the qualifying fee for this year's elections was raised from $50 to $500 in order to prevent most Negroes from becoming candidates. On May 3, five new county "freedom organizations" convened and nominated candidates for the offices of sheriff, tax assessor, members of the school boards. These men and women are up for election in November—if they live until then. Their ballot symbol is the black panther: a bold, beautiful animal, representing the strength and dignity of black demands today. A man needs a black panther on his side when he and his family must endure—as hundreds of Alabamians have endured—loss of job, eviction, starvation, and sometimes death, for political activity. He may also need a gun and SNCC reaffirms the right of black men everywhere to defend themselves when threatened or attacked. As for initiating the use of violence, we hope that such programs as ours will make that unnecessary; but it is not for us to tell black communities whether they can or cannot use any particular form of action to resolve their problems. Responsibility for the use of violence by black men, whether in self defence or initiated by them, lies with the white community.

This is the specific historical experience from which SNCC's call for "black power" emerged on the Mississippi march last July. But the concept of "black power" is not a recent or isolated phenomenon: It has grown out of the ferment of agitation and activity by different people and organizations in many black communities over the years. Our last year of work in Alabama added a new concrete possibility. In Lowndes County, for example, black power will mean that if a Negro is elected sheriff, he can end police brutality. If a black man is elected tax assessor, he can collect and channel funds for the building of better roads and schools serving black people—thus advancing the move from political power into the economic arena. In such areas as Lowndes, where black men have a majority, they will attempt to use it to exercise control. This is what they seek: control. Where Negroes lack a majority, black power means proper representation and sharing of control. It means the creation of power bases from which black people can work to change statewide or nationwide patterns of oppression through pressure from strength—instead of weakness. Politically, black power means what it has always meant to SNCC: the coming-together of black people to elect representatives and *to force those representatives to speak to their needs.* It does not mean merely putting black faces into office. A man or woman who is black and from the slums cannot be automatically expected to speak to the needs of black people. Most of the black politicians we see around the country today are not what SNCC means by black power. The power must be that of a community, and emanate from there.

SNCC today is working in both North and South on programs of voter registration and independent political organizing. In some places, such as Alabama, Los Angeles, New York, Philadelphia, and New Jersey, independent organizing under the black panther symbol is in progress. The creation of a national "black panther party" must come about; it will take time to build, and it is much too early to predict its success. We have no infallible master plan and we make no claim to exclusive knowledge of how to end racism; different groups will work in their own different ways. SNCC cannot spell out the full logistics of self-determination but it can address itself to the problem by helping black communities define their needs, realize their strength, and go into action along a variety of lines which they must choose for themselves. Without knowing all the answers, it can address itself to the basic problem of poverty; to the fact that in Lowndes County, 86 white families own 90 per cent of the land. What are black people in that county going to do for jobs, where are they going to get money? There must be reallocation of land, of money.

Ultimately, the economic foundations of this country must be shaken if black people are to control their lives. The colonies of the United States—and this includes the black ghettos within its borders, north and south—must be liberated. For a century, this nation has been like an octopus of exploitation, its tentacles stretching from Mississippi and Harlem to South America, the Middle East, southern Africa, and Vietnam; the form of exploitation varies from area to area but the essential result has been the same—a powerful few have been maintained and enriched at the expense of the poor and voiceless colored masses. This pattern must be broken. As its grip loosens here and there around the world, the hopes of black Americans become more realistic. For racism to die, a totally different America must be born.

This is what the white society does not wish to face; this is why that society prefers to talk about integration. But integration speaks not at all to the problem of poverty, only to the problem of blackness. Integration today means the man who "makes it," leaving his black brothers behind in the ghetto as fast as his new sports car will take him. It has no relevance to the Harlem wino or to the cotton-picker making three dollars a day. As a lady I know in Alabama once said, "the food that Ralph Bunche eats doesn't fill my stomach."

Integration, moreover, speaks to the problem of blackness in a despicable way. As a goal, it has been based on complete acceptance of the fact that *in order to have* a decent house or education, blacks must move into a white neighborhood or send their children to a white school. This reinforces, among both black and white, the idea that "white" is automatically better and "black" is by definition inferior. This is why integration is a subterfuge for the maintenance of white supremacy. It allows the nation to focus on a handful of Southern children who get into white schools, at great price, and to ignore the 94 per cent who are left behind in unimproved all-black schools. Such situations will not change until black people have power—to control their own school boards, in this case. Then Negroes become equal in a way that means something, and integration ceases to be a one-way street.

Then integration doesn't mean draining skills and energies from the ghetto into white neighborhoods; then it can mean white people moving from Beverly Hills into Watts, white people joining the Lowndes County Freedom Organization. Then integration becomes relevant.

Last April, before the furor over black power, Christopher Jencks wrote in a *New Republic* article on white Mississippi's manipulation of the anti-poverty program:

> The war on poverty has been predicated on the notion that there is such a thing as *a community* which can be defined geographically and mobilized for a collective effort to help the poor. This theory has no relationship to reality in the Deep South. In every Mississippi county there are *two* communities. Despite all the pious platitudes of the moderates on both sides, these two communities habitually see their interests in terms of conflict rather than cooperation. Only when the Negro community can muster enough political, economic and professional strength to compete on somewhat equal terms, will Negroes believe in the possibility of true cooperation and whites accept its necessity. En route to integration, the Negro community needs to develop greater independence—a chance to run its own affairs and not cave in whenever "the man" barks . . . Or so it seems to me, and to most of the knowledgeable people with whom I talked in Mississippi. To OEO, this judgment may sound like black nationalism . . .

Mr. Jencks, a white reporter, perceived the reason why America's anti-poverty program has been a sick farce in both North and South. In the South, it is clearly racism which prevents the poor from running their own programs; in the North, it more often seems to be politicking and bureaucracy. But the results are not so different: in the North, non-whites make up 42 per cent of all families in metropolitan "poverty areas" and only 6 per cent of families in areas classified as not poor. SNCC has been working with local residents in Arkansas, Alabama, and Mississippi to achieve control by the poor of the program and its funds; it has also been working with groups in the North, and the struggle is no less difficult. Behind it all is a federal government which cares far more about winning the war on the Vietnamese than the war on poverty; which has put the poverty program in the hands of self-serving politicians and bureaucrats rather than the poor themselves; which is unwilling to curb the misuse of white power but quick to condemn black power.

To most whites, black power seems to mean that the Mau Mau are coming to the suburbs at night. The Mau Mau are coming, and whites must stop them. Articles appear about plots to "get Whitey," creating an atmosphere in which "law and order must be maintained." Once again, responsibility is shifted from the oppressor to the oppressed. Other whites chide, "Don't forget— you're only 10 per cent of the population; if you get too smart, we'll wipe you out." If they are liberals, they complain, "What about me?—don't you want my help any more?" These are people supposedly concerned about black Americans, but today they think first of themselves, of their feelings of rejection. Or they admonish, "You can't get anywhere without coalitions," without considering the problems of coalition with whom; on what terms (coalescing from weakness can mean absorption, betrayal); when? Or they accuse us of "polarizing the races" by our calls for black unity, when the true responsibility for polarization lies with whites who will not accept their responsibility as the majority power for making the democratic process work.

White America will not face the problem of color, the reality of it. The well-intended say: "We're all human, everybody is really decent, we must forget color." But color cannot be "forgotten" until its weight is recognized and dealt with. White America will not acknowledge that the ways in which this country sees itself are contradicted by being black—and always have been. Whereas most of the people who settled this country came here for freedom or for economic opportunity, blacks were brought here to be slaves. When the Lowndes County Freedom Organization chose the black panther as its symbol, it was christened by the press "the Black Panther Party"—but the Alabama Democratic Party, whose symbol is a rooster, has never been called the White Cock Party. No one ever talked about "white power" because power in this country is white. All this adds up to more than merely identifying a group phenomenon by some catchy name or adjective. The furor over that black panther reveals the problems that white America has with color and sex; the furor over "black power" reveals how deep racism runs and the great fear which is attached to it.

Whites will not see that I, for example, as a person oppressed because of my blackness, have common cause with other blacks who are oppressed because of blackness. This is not to say that there are no white people who see things as I do, but that it is black people I must speak to first. It must be the oppressed to whom SNCC addresses itself primarily, not to friends from the oppressing group.

From birth, black people are told a set of lies about themselves. We are told that we are lazy—yet I drive through the Delta area of Mississippi and watch black people picking cotton in the hot sun for fourteen hours. We are told, "If you work hard, you'll succeed"—but if that were true, black people would own this country. We are oppressed because we are black—not because we are ignorant, not because we are lazy, not because we're stupid (and got good rhythm), but because we're black.

I remember that when I was a boy, I used to go to see Tarzan movies on Saturday. White Tarzan used to beat up the black natives. I would sit there yelling, "Kill the beasts, kill the savages, kill 'em!" I was saying: Kill *me*. It was as if a Jewish boy watched Nazis taking Jews off to concentration camps and cheered them on. Today, I want the chief to beat hell out of Tarzan and send him back to Europe. But it takes time to become free of the lies and their shaming effect on black minds. It takes time to reject the most important lie: that black people inherently can't do the same things white people can do, unless white people help them.

The need for psychological equality is the reason why SNCC today believes that blacks must organize in the black community. Only black people can convey the revolutionary idea that black people are able to do things themselves. Only they can help create in the community an aroused and continuing black consciousness that will provide the basis for political strength. In the past, white allies have furthered white supremacy without the whites involved realizing it—or wanting it, I think. Black people must do things for themselves; they must get poverty money they will control and spend themselves, they must conduct tutorial programs themselves so that black children can identify with black people. This is one reason Africa has such importance: The reality of black men ruling their own nations gives blacks elsewhere a sense of possibility, of power, which they do not now have.

This does not mean we don't welcome help, or friends. But we want the right to decide whether anyone is, in fact, our friend. In the past, black Americans have been almost the only people whom everybody and his momma could jump up and call their friends. We have been tokens, symbols, objects—as I was in high school to many young whites, who liked having "a Negro friend." We want to decide who is our friend, and we will not accept someone who comes to us and says: "If you do X, Y, and Z, then I'll help you." We will not be told whom we should choose as allies. We will not be isolated from any group or nation except by our own choice. We cannot have the oppressors telling the oppressed how to rid themselves of the oppressor.

I have said that most liberal whites react to "black power" with the question, What about me?, rather than saying: Tell me what you want me to do and I'll see if I can do it. There are answers to the right question. One of the most disturbing things about almost all white supporters of the movement has been that they are afraid to go into their own communities—which is where the racism exists—and work to get rid of it. They want to run from Berkeley to tell us what to do in Mississippi; let them look instead at Berkeley. They admonish blacks to be nonviolent; let them preach nonviolence in the white community. They come to teach me Negro history; let them go to the suburbs and open up freedom schools for whites. Let them work to stop America's racist foreign policy; let them press this government to cease supporting the economy of South Africa.

There is a vital job to be done among poor whites. We hope to see, eventually, a coalition between poor blacks and poor whites. That is the only coalition which seems acceptable to us, and we see such a coalition as the major internal instrument of change in American society. SNCC has tried several times to organize poor whites; we are trying again now, with an initial training program in Tennessee. It is purely academic today to talk about bringing poor blacks and whites together, but the job of creating a poor-white power bloc must be attempted. The main responsibility for it falls upon whites. Black and white can work together in the white community where possible; it is not possible, however, to go into a poor Southern town and talk about integration. Poor whites everywhere are becoming more hostile—not less—partly because they see the nation's attention focussed on black poverty and nobody coming to them. Too many young middle-class Americans, like some sort of Pepsi generation, have wanted to come alive through the black community; they've wanted to be where the action is— and the action has been in the black community.

Black people do not want to "take over" this country. They don't want to "get Whitey", they just want to get him off their backs, as the saying goes. It was for example the exploitation by Jewish landlords and merchants which first created black resentment toward Jews—not Judaism. The white man is irrelevant to blacks, except as an oppressive force. Blacks want to be in his place, yes, but not in order to terrorize and lynch and starve him. They want to be in his place because that is where a decent life can be had.

But our vision is not merely of a society in which all black men have enough to buy the good things of life. When we urge that black money go into black pockets, we mean the communal pocket. We want to see money go back into the community and used to benefit it. We want to see the co-operative concept applied in business and banking. We want to see black ghetto residents demand that an exploiting landlord or store keeper sell them, at minimal cost, a building or a shop that they will own and improve co-operatively; they can back their demand with a rent strike, or a boycott, and a community so unified behind them that no one else will move into the building or buy at the store. The society we seek to build among black people, then, is not a capitalist one. It is a society in which the spirit of community and humanistic love prevail. The word love is suspect; black expectations of what it might produce have been betrayed too often. But those were expectations of a response from the white community, which failed us. The love we seek to encourage is within the black community, the only American community where men call each other "brother" when they meet. We can build a community of love only where we have the ability and power to do so: among blacks.

As for white America, perhaps it can stop crying out against "black supremacy," "black nationalism," "racism in reverse," and begin facing reality. The reality is that this nation, from top to bottom, is racist; that racism is not primarily a problem of "human relations" but of an exploitation maintained—either actively or through silence—by the society as a whole. Camus and Sartre have asked, can a man condemn himself? Can whites, particularly liberal whites, condemn themselves? Can they stop blaming us, and blame their own system? Are they capable of the shame which might become a revolutionary emotion?

We have found that they usually cannot condemn themselves, and so we have done it. But the rebuilding of this society, if at all possible, is basically the responsibility of whites—not blacks. We won't fight to save the present society, in Vietnam or anywhere else. We are just going to work, in the way *we* see fit, and on goals *we* define, not for civil rights but for all our human rights.

JAMES P. COMER

The Social Power of the Negro

The concept of "black power" is an inflammatory one. It was introduced in an atmosphere of militancy (during James Meredith's march through Mississippi last June) and in many quarters it has been equated with violence and riots. As a result the term distresses white friends of the Negro, frightens and angers others and causes many Negroes who are fearful of white disapproval to reject the concept without considering its rationale and its merits. The fact is that a form of black power may be absolutely essential. The experience of Negro Americans, supported by numerous historical and psychological studies, suggests that the profound needs of the poorest and most alienated Negroes cannot be met—and that there can therefore be no end to racial unrest—except through the influence of a unified, organized Negro community with genuine political and economic power.

Why are Negro efforts to achieve greater unity and power considered unnecessary and even dangerous by so many people, Negro as well as white, friends as well as enemies? I believe it is because the functions of group power—and hence the consequences of political and economic impotence—are not understood by most Americans. The "melting pot" myth has obscured the critical role of group power in the adjustment of white immigrant groups in this country.

When immigrants were faced with discrimination, exploitation and abuse, they turned in on themselves. Sustained psychologically by the bonds of their cultural heritage, they maintained family, religious, and social institutions that had great stabilizing force. The institutions in turn fostered group unity. Family stability and group unity—plus access to political machinery, jobs in industry and opportunities on the frontier—led to group power:

immigrants voted, gained political influence, held public office, owned land and operated businesses. Group power and influence expanded individual opportunities and facilitated individual achievement, and within one or two generations most immigrants enjoyed the benefits of first-class American citizenship.

The Negro experience has been very different. The traumatic effects of separation from Africa, slavery, and the denial of political and economic opportunities after the abolition of slavery created divisive psychological and social forces in the Negro community. Coordinated group action, which was certainly appropriate for a despised minority, has been too little evident; Negroes have seldom moved cohesively and effectively against discrimination and exploitation. These abuses led to the creation of an impoverished, under-educated, and alienated group—a sizable minority among Negroes, disproportionately large compared with other ethnic groups. This troubled minority has a self-defeating "style" of life that leads to repeated failure, and its plight and its reaction to that plight are at the core of the continuing racial conflict in the U.S. Only a meaningful and powerful Negro community can help members of this group realize their potential, and thus alleviate racial unrest. The importance of "black power" becomes comprehensible in the light of the interrelation of disunity, impotence, and alienation.

The roots of Negro division are of African origin. It is important to realize that the slave contingents brought out of Africa were not from a single ethnic group. They were from a number of groups and from many different tribes with different languages, customs, traditions, and ways of life. Some were farmers, some hunters and gatherers, some traders. There were old animosities, and these were exacerbated by the dynamics of the slave trade itself. (Today these same tribal animosities are evident, as in Nigeria, where centuries-old conflict among the Ibo, Hausa, and Yoruba tribes threatens to disrupt the nation. A significant number of slaves came from these very tribes.)

The cohesive potential of the captives was low to begin with, and the breakup of kinship groupings, which in Africa had defined people's roles and relations, decreased it further. Presumably if the Africans had been settled in a free land, they would in time have organized to build a new society meeting their own needs. Instead they were organized to meet the needs of their masters. The slaves were scattered in small groups (the average holding was only between two and five slaves) that were isolated from one another. The small number and mixed origins of each plantation's slaves made the maintenance of any oral tradition, and thus of any tribal or racial identity and pride, impossible. Moreover, any grouping that was potentially cohesive because of family, kinship, or tribal connections was deliberately divided or tightly controlled to prevent rebellion. Having absolute power, the master could buy and sell, could decree cohabitation, punishment or death, could provide food, shelter, and clothing as he saw fit. The system was engraved in law and maintained by the religious and political authorities and the armed forces; the high visibility of the slaves and the lack of places to hide made escape almost inconceivable.

The powerless position of the slave was traumatic, as Stanley M. Elkins showed in his study of Negro slavery. The male was not the respected provider, the protector and head of his household. The female was not rearing her child to take his place in a rewarding society, nor could she count on protection from her spouse or any responsible male. The reward for hard work was not material goods and the recognition of one's fellow men but only recognition from the master as a faithful but inferior being. The master—"the man"—became the necessary object of the slave's emotional investment, the person whose approval he needed. The slave could love or hate or have ambivalent feelings about the relationship, but it was the most important relationship of his life.

In this situation self-esteem depended on closeness or similarity to the master, not on personal or group power and achievement, and it was gained in ways that tended to divide the Negro population. House slaves looked down on field hands, "mixed-bloods" on "pure blacks," slaves with rich and important masters on slaves whose masters had less prestige. There was cleavage between the "troublemakers" who promoted revolt and sabotage and the "good slaves" who betrayed them, and between slave Negroes and free ones. The development of positive identity as a Negro was scarcely possible.

It is often assumed that with the end of the Civil War the situation of the free Negroes was about the same as that of immigrants landing in America. In reality it was quite different. Negroes emerging from slavery entered a society at a peak of racial antagonism. They had long since been stripped of their African heritage; in their years in America they had been unable to create much of a record of their own; they were deeply marked by the degrading experience of slavery. Most significant, they were denied the weapons they needed to become part of American life: economic and political opportunities. No longer of any value to their former masters, they were now direct competitors of the poor whites. The conditions of life imposed by the "Black codes" of the immediate postwar period were in many ways as harsh as slavery had been. In the first two years after the end of the war many Negroes suffered violence and death at the hands of unrestrained whites; there was starvation and extreme dislocation.

In 1867 the Reconstruction Acts put the South under military occupation and gave freedmen in the 11 Southern states the right to vote. (In the North, on the other hand, Negroes continued to be barred from the polls in all but nine states, either by specific racial qualifications or by prohibitive taxation. Until the Fifteenth Amendment was ratified in 1870, only some 5 per cent of the Northern Negroes could vote.) The Reconstruction Acts also provided some military and legal protection, educational opportunities, and health care. Reconstruction did not, however, make enough land available to Negroes to create an adequate power base. The plantation system meant that large numbers of Negroes remained under tight control and were vulnerable to economic reprisals. Although Negroes could outvote whites in some states and did in fact control the Louisiana and South Carolina legislatures, the franchise did not lead to real power.

This lack of power was largely due to the Negro's economic vulnerability, but the group divisions that had developed during slavery also played a part. It was the "mixed-bloods" and the house slaves of middle- and upper-class whites who had acquired some education and skills under slavery; now many of these people became Negro leaders. They often had emotional ties to whites and a need to please them, and they advanced the cause of the Negroes as a group most gingerly. Moreover, not understanding the causes of the apathy, lack of achievement, and asocial behavior of some of their fellows, many of them found their Negro identity a source of shame rather than psychological support, and they were ready to subordinate the needs of the group to personal gains that would give them as much social and psychological distance from their people as possible. The result was that Negro leaders, with some notable exceptions, often became the tools of white leaders. Throughout the Reconstruction period meaningful Negro power was being destroyed, and long before the last Negro disappeared from Southern legislatures Negroes were powerless. Under such circumstances Negro economic and educational progress was severely inhibited. Negro-owned businesses were largely dependent on the impoverished Negro community and were operated by people who had little education or experience and who found it difficult to secure financing; they could not compete with white businesses. Negroes were largely untrained for anything but farm labor or domestic work, and a white social structure maintaining itself through physical force and economic exploitation was not likely to provide the necessary educational opportunities. Minimal facilities, personnel and funds were provided for the "Negro schools" that were established, and only the most talented Negroes were able—if they were lucky—to obtain an education comparable to that available to whites.

As John Hope Franklin describes it in *Reconstruction after the Civil War,* the Reconstruction was ineffective for the vast majority of Negroes, and it lasted only a short time: Federal troops had left most Southern states by 1870. While Negroes were still struggling for a first foothold, national political developments made it advisable to placate Southern leaders, and the Federal troops were recalled from the last three Southern states in 1877. There was a brief period of restraint, but it soon gave way to violence and terror on a large scale. Threats and violence drove Negroes away from the polls. Racist sheriffs, legislators, and judges came into office. Segregation laws were passed, buttressed by court decisions and law enforcement practices, and erected into an institution that rivaled slavery in its effectiveness in excluding Negroes from public affairs—business, the labor movement, government, and public education.

At the time—and in later years—white people often pointed to the most depressed and unstable Negro and in effect made his improvement in education and behavior a condition for the granting of equal opportunities to all Negroes. What kind of people made up this most disadvantaged segment of the Negro community? I believe it can be shown that these were the Negroes who had lived under the most traumatic and disorganized conditions as slaves. Family life had been prohibited, discouraged or allowed to exist only under precarious conditions, with no recourse from sale, separation, or sexual violation. Some of these people had been treated as breeding stock or work animals; many had experienced brutal and sadistic physical and sexual assaults. In many cases the practice of religion was forbidden, so that even self-respect as "a child of God" was denied them.

Except for running away (and more tried to escape than has generally been realized)' there was nothing these slaves could do but adopt various defense mechanisms. They responded in various ways, as is poignantly recorded in a collection of firsthand accounts obtained by Benjamin A. Botkin. Many did as little work as they could without being punished, thus developing work habits that were not conducive to success after slavery. Many sabotaged the master's tools and other property, thus evolving a disrespect for property in general. Some resorted to a massive denial of the reality of their lives and took refuge in apathy, thus creating the slow-moving, slow-thinking stereotype of the Southern Negro. Others resorted instead to boisterous "acting out" behavior and limited their interests to the fulfillment of such basic needs as food and sex.

After slavery these patterns of behavior persisted. The members of this severely traumatized group did not value family life. Moreover, for economic reasons and by force of custom the family often lacked a male head, or at least a legal husband and father. Among these people irresponsibility, poor work habits, disregard for conventional standards, and anger toward whites expressed in violence toward one another combined to form a way of life—a style—that caused them to be rejected and despised by whites and other Negroes alike. They were bound to fail in the larger world.

When they did fail, they turned in on their own subculture, which accordingly became self-reinforcing. Children born into it learned its way of life. Isolated and also insulated from outside influences, they had little opportunity to change. The values, behavior patterns and sense of alienation transmitted within this segment of the population from generation to generation account for the bulk of the illegitimacy, crime, and other types of asocial behavior that are present in disproportionate amounts in the Negro community today. This troubled subgroup has always been a minority, but its behavior constitutes many white people's concept of "typical" Negro behavior and even tarnishes the image many other Negroes have of themselves. Over the years defensive

Negro leaders have regularly blamed the depressed subgroup for creating a bad image; the members of the subgroup have blamed the leaders for "selling out." There has been just enough truth in both accusations to keep them alive, accentuating division and perpetuating conflicts, and impeding the development of group consciousness, cooperation, power, and mutual gains.

It is surprising, considering the harsh conditions of slavery, that there were any Negroes who made a reasonable adjustment to freedom. Many had come from Africa with a set of values that included hard work and stability of family and tribal life. (I suspect, but I have not been able to demonstrate, that in Africa many of these had been farmers rather than hunters and gatherers.) As slaves many of them found the support and rewards required to maintain such values through their intense involvement in religion. From this group, after slavery, came the God-fearing, hardworking, law-abiding domestics and laborers who prepared their children for responsible living, in many cases making extreme personal sacrifices to send them to trade school or college. (The significance of this church-oriented background in motivating educational effort and success even today is indicated by some preliminary findings of a compensatory education program for which I am a consultant. Of 125 Negro students picked for the program from 10 southeastern states solely on the basis of academic promise, 95 per cent have parents who are regular churchgoers, deeply involved as organizers and leaders in church affairs.)

For a less religious group of Negroes the discovery of meaning, fulfillment, and a sense of worth lay in a different direction. Their creative talents brought recognition in the arts, created the blues and jazz, and opened the entertainment industry to Negroes. Athletic excellence provided another kind of achievement. Slowly, from among the religious, the creative, and the athletic, a new, educated, and talented middle class began to emerge that had less need of white approval than the Negroes who had managed to get ahead in earlier days. Large numbers of Negroes should have risen into the middle class by way of these relatively stable groups, but because of the lack of Negro political and economic power and the barriers of racial prejudice many could not. Those whose aspirations were frustrated often reacted destructively by turning to the depressed Negro subgroup and its way of life; the subculture of failure shaped by slavery gained new recruits and was perpetuated by a white society's obstacles to acceptance and achievement.

In the past 10 years or so the "Negro revolt"—the intensified legal actions, nonviolent demonstrations, court decisions, and legislation—and changing economic conditions have brought rapid and significant gains for middle-class Negroes. The mass of low-income Negroes have made little progress however; many have been aroused by civil rights talk but few have benefited. Of all Negro families, 40 per cent are classified as "poor" according to Social Security Administration criteria. (The figure for white families is 11 per cent.) Low-income Negroes have menial jobs or are unemployed; they live in segregated neighborhoods and are exploited by landlords and storekeepers; they are often the victims of crime and of the violent, displaced frustrations of their friends and neighbors. The urban riots of the past few years have been the reaction of a small segment of this population to the frustrations of this daily existence.

Why is it that so many Negroes have been unable to take advantage of the Negro revolt as the immigrants did of opportunities offered them? The major reason is that the requirements for economic success have been raised. The virtually free land on the frontier is gone. The unskilled and semiskilled jobs that were available to white immigrants are scarce today, and many unions controlled by lower-middle-class whites bar Negroes to keep the jobs for their present members. The law does not help here because Negroes are underrepresented in municipal and state legislative bodies as well as in Congress. Negroes hold few policy-making positions in industry and Negro small businesses are a negligible source of employment.

Employment opportunities exist, of course—for highly skilled workers and technicians. These jobs require education and training that many Negroes, along with many white workers, lack. The training takes time and requires motivation, and it must be based on satisfactory education through high school. Most poor Negroes lack that education, and many young Negroes are not getting it today. There are Negro children who are performing adequately in elementary school but who will fail by the time they reach high school, either because their schools are inadequate or because their homes and subculture will simply not sustain their efforts in later years.

It is not enough to provide a "head start"; studies have shown that gains made as the result of the new preschool enrichment programs are lost, in most cases, by the third grade. Retraining programs for workers and programs for high school dropouts are palliative measures that have limited value. Some of the jobs for which people are being trained will not exist in a few years. Many students drop out of the dropout programs. Other students have such self-defeating values and behavior that they will not be employable even if they complete the programs.

A number of investigators (Daniel P. Moynihan is one) have pointed to the structure of the poorer Negro family as the key to Negro problems. They point to an important area but miss the crux of the problem. Certainly the lack of a stable family deprives many Negro children of psychological security and of the values and behavior patterns they need in order to achieve success. Certainly many low-income Negro families lack a father. Even if it were possible to legislate the father back into the home, however, the grim picture is unchanged if his own values and conduct are not compatible with achievement. A father frustrated by society often reacts by mistreating his children. Even adequate parents despair and are helpless in a subculture that leads their children astray. The point of intervention must be the subculture that impinges on the family and influences its values and style of behavior and even its structure.

How, then, does one break the circle? Many white children who found their immigrant family and subculture out of step with the dominant American culture and with their own desires were able to break away and establish a sense of belonging to a group outside their own—if the pull was strong enough. Some children in the depressed Negro group do this too. A specific pull is often needed: some individual or institution that sets a goal or acts as a model.

The trouble is that racial prejudice and alienation from the white and Negro middle class often mean that there is little pull from the dominant culture on lower-class Negro children. In my work in schools in disadvantaged areas as a consultant from the Child Study Center at Yale I have found that many Negro children perceive the outside culture as a separate white man's world. Once they are 12 or 14 years old—the age at which a firm sense of racial identity is established—many Negroes have a need to shut out the white man's world and its values and institutions and also to reject "white Negroes," or the Negro middle class. Since these children see their problems as being racial ones, they are more likely to learn how to cope with these problems from a middle-class Negro who extends himself than from a white person, no matter how honest and free of hostility and guilt the white person may be.

Unfortunately the Negro community is not now set up to offer its disadvantaged members a set of standards and a psychological refuge in the way the white immigrant subcultures did. There is no Negro institution beyond the family that is enough in harmony with the total American culture to transmit its behavioral principles, and is meaningful enough to Negroes to effect adherence to those principles, and sufficiently accepted by divergent elements of the Negro community to act as a cohesive force. The church comes closest to performing this function, but Negroes belong to an exceptional number of different denominations, and in many cases the denominations are divided and antagonistic. The same degree of division is found in the major fraternal and civic organizations and even in civil rights groups.

There is a special reason for some of the sharp divisions in Negro organizations. With Negroes largely barred from business, politics and certain labor unions, the quest for power and leadership in Negro organizations has been and continues to be particularly intense, and there is a great deal of conflict. Only a few Negroes have a broad enough view of the total society to be able to identify the real sources of their difficulties. And the wide divergence of their interests often makes it difficult for them to agree on a course of action. All these factors make Negro groups vulnerable to divide-and-conquer tactics, either inadvertent or deliberate.

Viewing such disarray, altruistic white people and public and private agencies have moved into the apparent vacuum—often failing to recognize that, in spite of conflict, existing Negro institutions were meeting important psychological needs and were in close contact with their people. Using these meaningful institutions as vehicles for delivering new social services would have strengthened the only forces capable of supporting and organizing the Negro community. Instead, the new agencies, public and private, have ignored the existing institutions and have tried to do the job themselves. The agencies often have storefront locations and hire some "indigenous" workers, but the class and racial gap is difficult to cross. The thong-sandaled, long-haired white girl doing employment counseling may be friendly and sympathetic to Negroes, but she cannot possibly tell a Negro youngster (indeed, she does not know that she should tell him): "You've got to look better than the white applicant to get the job." Moreover, a disadvantaged Negro—or any Negro—repeatedly helped by powerful white people while his own group appears powerless or unconcerned is unlikely to develop satisfactory feelings about his group or himself. The effects of an undesirable racial self-concept among many Negroes have been documented repeatedly, yet many current programs tend to perpetuate this basic problem rather than to relieve it.

A solution is suggested by the fact that many successful Negroes no longer feel the need to maintain psychological and social distance from their own people. Many of them want to help. Their presence and tangible involvement in the Negro community would tend to balance the pull—the comforts and the immediate pleasures—of the subculture. Because the functions of Negro organizations have been largely preempted by white agencies, however, no Negro institution is available through which such people can work to overcome a century of intra-Negro class alienation.

Recently a few Negroes have begun to consider a plan that could meet some of the practical needs, as well as the spiritual and psychological needs, of the Negro community. In Cleveland, New York, Los Angeles, and some smaller cities new leaders are emerging who propose to increase Negro cohesiveness and self-respect through self-help enterprises: cooperatives that would reconstruct slums or operate apartment buildings and businesses providing goods and services at fair prices. Ideally these enterprises would be owned by people who mean something to the Negro community—Negro athletes, entertainers, artists, professionals, and government workers—and by Negro churches, fraternal groups, and civil rights organizations. The owners would share control of the enterprises with the people of the community.

Such undertakings would be far more than investment opportunities for well-to-do Negroes. With the proper structure they would become permanent and tangible institutions on which the Negro community could focus without requiring a "white enemy" and intolerable conditions to unify it. Through this mechanism Negroes who had achieved success could come in contact with the larger Negro group. Instead of the policy king, pimp, and prostitute being the models of success in the subculture, the Negro athlete, businessman, professional, and entertainer might become the models once they could be respected because they were obviously working for the Negro community. These leaders would then be in a position to encourage and promote high-level performance in school and on the job. At the same time broad measures to "institutionalize" the total Negro experience would increase racial pride, a powerful motivating force. The entire program would provide the foundation for unified political action to give the Negro community representatives who speak in its best interests.

That, after all, has been the pattern in white America. There was, and still is, Irish power, German, Polish, Italian, and Jewish power—and indeed white Anglo-Saxon Protestant power—but color obviously makes these groups less clearly identifiable than Negroes. Churches and synagogues, cultural and fraternal societies, unions, business associations, and networks of allied families and "clans" have served as centers of power that maintain group consciousness, provide jobs and develop new opportunities, and join to form pressure and voting blocs. The "nationality divisions" of the major parties and the balanced ticket are two reminders that immigrant loyalties are still not completely melted.

The idea of creating Negro enterprises and institutions is not intended as a rejection of genuinely concerned white people or as an indictment of all existing organizations. White people of good will with interest, skills, and funds are needed and—contrary to the provocative assertions of a few Negroes—are still welcome in the Negro community. The kind of "black power" that is proposed would not promote riots; rather, by providing constructive channels for the energies released by the civil rights movement, it should diminish the violent outbursts directed against the two symbols of white power and oppression: the police and the white merchants.

To call for Negro institutions, moreover, is not to argue for segregation or discrimination. Whether we like it or not, a number of large cities are going to become predominantly Negro in a short time. The aim is to make these cities places where people can live decently and reach their highest potential with or without integration. An integrated society is the ultimate goal, but it may be a second stage in some areas. Where immediate integration is possible it should be effected, but integration takes place most easily among educated and secure people. And in the case of immediate integration an organized and supportive Negro community would help its members to maintain a sense of adequacy in a situation in which repeated reminders of the white head start often make Negroes feel all the more inferior.

The power structure of white society—industry, banks, the press, government—can continue, either inadvertently or deliberately, to maintain the divisions in the Negro community and keep it powerless. Social and economic statistics and psychological studies indicate that this would be a mistake. For many reasons the ranks of the alienated are growing. No existing program seems able to meet the needs of the most troubled and troublesome group. It is generally agreed that massive, immediate action is required. The form of that action should be attuned, however, to the historically determined need for Negro political and economic power that will facilitate Negro progress and give Negroes a reasonable degree of control over their own destiny.

VINCENT HARDING

Black Power and the American Christ

The mood among many social-action-oriented Christians today suggests that it is only a line thin as a razor blade that divides sentimental yearning over the civil rights activities of the past from present bitter recrimination against "Black Power." As is so often the case with reminiscences, the nostalgia may grow more out of a sense of frustration and powerlessness than out of any true appreciation of the meaning of the past. This at least is the impression one gets from those seemingly endless gatherings of old "true believers" which usually produce both the nostalgia and the recriminations. Generally the cast of characters at such meetings consists of well-dressed, well-fed Negroes and whites whose accents almost blend into a single voice as they recall the days "when we were all together, fighting for the same cause." The stories evoke again the heady atmosphere, mixed of smugness and self-sacrifice, that surrounded us in those heroic times when nonviolence was our watchword and integration our heavenly city. One can almost hear the strains of "our song" as men and women remember how they solemnly swayed in the aisles or around the charred remains of a church or in the dirty southern jails. Those were the days when Martin Luther King was the true prophet and when we were certain that the civil rights movement was God's message to the churches—and part of our smugness grew out of the fact that *we* knew it while all the rest of God's frozen people were asleep.

A Veil Between Then and Now

But as the reminiscences continue a veil seems to descend between then and now. The tellers of the old tales label the veil

Black Power, and pronounce ritual curses on Stokely Carmichael and Floyd McKissick and their followers.

The trouble with these meetings is that they are indeed becoming ritual, cultic acts of memory that blind us to creative possibilities. Because that "veil" may be a wall, not primarily for separating but for writing on—both sides of it. Or it may be a great sheet "let down from heaven"; or a curtain before the next act can begin. Most of us appear totally incapable of realizing that there may be more light in blackness than we have yet begun to glimpse.

Such possibilities should be pondered especially by those of us who combine the terrible privileges of blackness and Christian commitment within a single life. We are driven to see not only what was happening in our warm, genteel days of common black-white struggle, but to grasp clearly what is happening now. We have no choice but to hold Black Power in our black arms and examine it, convinced that Christ is Lord of this too. Anyone who is black and claims to be a part of the company of Christ's people would be derelict if he failed to make such an examination and to proclaim with fear and trembling and intimations of great joy what he has discovered.

Perhaps the first and central discovery is also the most obvious: there is a strong and causative link between Black Power and American Christianity. Indeed one may say with confidence that whatever its other sources, the ideology of blackness surely grows out of the deep ambivalence of American Negroes to the Christ we have encountered here. This ambivalence is not new. It was ours from the beginning. For we first met the American Christ on slave ships. We heard his name sung in hymns of praise while we died in our thousands, chained in stinking holds beneath the decks, locked in with terror and disease and sad memories of our families and homes. When we leaped from the decks to be seized by sharks we saw his name carved on the ship's solid sides. When our women were raped in the cabins they must have noticed the great and holy books on the shelves. Our introduction to this Christ was not propitious. And the horrors continued on America's soil. So all through the nation's history many black men have rejected this Christ—indeed the miracle is that so many accepted him. In past times our disdain often had to be stifled and sullen, our anger silent and self-destructive. But now we speak out. Our anger is no longer silent; it has leaped onto the public stage, and demands to be seen and dealt with—a far more healthy state of affairs for all concerned.

If the American Christ and his followers have indeed helped to mold the Black Power movement, then might it not be that the God whom many of us insist on keeping alive is not only alive but just? May he not be attempting to break through to us with at least as much urgency as we once sensed at the height of the good old "We Shall Overcome" days? Perhaps he is writing on the wall, saying that we Christians, black and white, must choose between death with the American Christ and life with the Suffering Servant of God. Who dares deny that God may have chosen once again the black sufferers for a new assault on the hard shell of indifference and fear that encases so many Americans?

If these things are difficult to believe perhaps we need to look more closely both at the American Christ and the black movement he has helped to create. From the outset, almost everywhere we blacks have met him in this land, this Christ was painted white and pink, blond and blue-eyed—and not only in white churches but in black churches as well. Millions of black children had the picture of this pseudo-Nazarene burned into their memory. The books, the windows, the paintings, the film-strips all affirmed the same message—a message of shame. This Christ shamed us by his pigmentation, so obviously not our own. He condemned us for our blackness, for our flat noses, for our kinky hair, for our power, our strange power of expressing emotion in singing and shouting and dancing. He was sedate, so genteel, so white. And as soon as we were able, many of us tried to be like him.

Glad to Be Black

For a growing edge of bold young black people all that is past. They fling out their declaration: "No white Christ shall shame us again. We are glad to be black. We rejoice in the darkness of our skin, we celebrate the natural texture of our hair, we extol the rhythm and vigor of our songs and shouts and dances. And if your American Christ doesn't like that, you know what you can do with him." That is Black Power: a repudiation of the American culture-religion that helped to create it and a quest for a religious reality more faithful to our own experience.

These young people say to America: "We know your Christ and his attitude toward Africa. We remember how his white missionaries warned against Africa's darkness and heathenism, against its savagery and naked jungle heart. We are tired of all that. This Africa that you love and hate, but mostly fear—this is our homeland. We saw you exchange your Bibles for our land. We watched you pass out tracts and take in gold. We heard you teach hymns to get our diamonds, and you control them still. If this is what your Christ taught you, he is sharp, baby, he is shrewd; but he's no savior of ours. We affirm our homeland and its great black past, a past that was filled with wonder before your white scourge came. You can keep your Christ. We'll take our home." That is Black Power: a search for roots in a land that has denied us both a past and a future. And the American Christ who has blessed the denial earns nothing but scorn.

The advocates of Black Power know this Christ well. They see his people running breathlessly, cursing silently, exiting double-time from the cities with all their suffering people. They see this white throng fleeing before the strangled movement of the blacks out of the ghettos, leaving their stained-glass mausoleums behind them. This very exodus of the Christians from the places where the weak and powerless live has been one of the primary motivating forces of Black Power.

The seekers of Black Power, seeing their poorest, most miserable people deserted by the white American Christians, have come to stand with the forlorn in these very places of abandonment. Now they speak of Black Unity, and the old Christian buildings are filled with Negroes young and old studying African history. The new leaders in the ghettos tell them: "Whites now talk about joining forces, but who has ever wanted to join forces with you? They only want to use you—especially those white American Christian liars. They love you in theory only. They love only your middle-class incarnations. But they are afraid of you—you who are black and poor and filled with rage and despair. They talk about 'progress' for the Negro, but they don't mean *you*."

These young people whose names we old "true believers" intone in our nightly litanies of frustrated wrath have listened with the perception born of alienation to white Christians speaking to Negroes of "our people and your people, our churches and your churches, our community and your community, our schools and your schools." And they hear this hypocrisy crowned with the next words from bleeding Christian hearts: "Of course some of your most spiritual (and quiet) people may come to our churches, and your wealthiest (and cleanest) people may move into our communities, and your brightest children may come to our schools. But never forget: we expect regular hymns of gratitude for our condescension. Always remember that they are still ours and not yours—people and communities and schools and churches." And as an afterthought: "But of course we all love the same Christ."

Sensitized by Apprehension

To this the angry children of Malcolm X shout fiercely: "To hell with you and your Christ! If you cannot live where we live, if your children cannot grow where we grow, if you cannot suffer what we suffer, if you cannot learn what we learn, we have no use for you or your cringing Christ. If we must come to where you are to find quality and life, then this nation is no good and integration is irrelevant."

Then Black Power leaders turn to the people of the ghettos. "Let us use the separateness that the white Christians have imposed upon us," they say to the black brothers. "Let us together find our own dignity and our own power, so that one day we may stand and face even those who have rejected us, no longer begging to be accepted into their dying world, but showing them a world transformed, a world where we have shaped our own destiny. We shall build communities of our own, where men are truly brothers and goods are really shared. The American Christ is a Christ of separation and selfishness and relentless competition for an empty hole. We want no part of him."

Let there be no mistake. These evangels of a new movement are not deaf. They hear all the American words. They listen when good Christians ask: "Why should we pay our taxes to support those lazy deadbeats, those winos, those A.D.C. whores? Our money doesn't belong to them. Our money . . . our money . . ." Sensitized by long years of apprehension, the blacks need only look into the mirror to know who those "deadbeats" and "winos" are and what the "A.D.C. whores" look like. At the same time they wonder why the same white Christians sing no sad songs about tax rebates for General Motors' investments in South Africa's apartheid, and why they raise no complaints about the tax money given to farmers for planting nothing.

Groveling No More

They open that American family magazine the *Saturday Evening Post* and find an enlightened northern editor saying to rebellious blacks that all whites are Mississippians at heart. He adds: "We will do our best, in a half-hearted way, to correct old wrongs. [Our] hand may be extended grudgingly and patronizingly, but anyone who rejects that hand rejects his own best interests." To those who live in the realm of Black Consciousness this snarling voice is the voice of the people of the American Christ. Out of their anguished indignation the black rebels reply: "We reject your limp, bloodied hand and your half-hearted help. We shall use our own black hands and lives to build power. We shall love our own people. We shall lead them to a new justice, based on the kind of power that America respects—not nonviolence and forgiveness, but votes and money and violent retaliation. We shall beg no more. You shall define our best interests no longer. Take your Mississippi hand and your Cicero Christ and may both of them be damned." That is Black Power.

As black men they have long seen into the heart of American darkness. They have no patriotic illusions about this nation's benevolent intentions toward the oppressed nonwhite people of the world, no matter how often the name and compassion of divinity are invoked. With eyes cleared by pain they discern the arrogance beneath the pious protestations. The American Christ leads the Hiroshima-bound bomber, blesses the Marines on their way to another in the long series of Latin American invasions, and blasphemously calls it peace when America destroys an entire Asian peninsula. And as black men they know from their own hard experience that these things can happen because this nation, led by an elder of the church, is determined to have its way in the world at any cost—to others. How often have the white-robed elders led the mob thirsting for the black man's blood!

Black people are not fooled by the churchly vestments of humility. They hear arrogant white pastors loudly counting dollars and members, and committees smugly announcing the cost of their new modern churches—hollow tombs for Christ. They hear the voices: "Negroes, oh Negroes, you must be humble, like Christ. You must be patient and long-suffering. Negroes, don't push so hard. Look at all we've given you so far." And the voices trail off: "Negroes, dear Negroes, remember our Lord taught how good it is to be meek and lowly." And then a whisper: "'Cause if you don't, niggers, if you don't, we'll crush you."

So the Black Power advocates sanely shout, "Go to hell, you whited sepulchers, hypocrites. All you want is to cripple our will and prolong our agony, and you use your white Christ to do it." To the black people they say: "Don't grovel, don't scrape. Whether you are 1 per cent or 50 per cent or 100 per cent black, you are men, and you must affirm this in the face of all the pious threats. You must proclaim your manhood just as the white Christians do—in arrogance, in strength and in power. But the arrogance must be black, and the strength must be black, and black must be the color of our power."

Christian Blasphemers

Then comes the sharpest of all moments of truth, when Christian voices are raised in hostility and fear, directing their missionary chorus to the young men drained of hope by the ghetto. "Black boys," they say, "rampaging, screaming, laughing black boys, you must love—like Christ and Doctor King. Black boys, please drop your firebombs. Violence never solved anything. You must love your enemies—if they're white and American and represent law and order. You must love them for your rotting houses and for your warped education. You must love them for your nonexistent jobs. Above all, you must love them for their riot guns, their billy clubs, their hatred and their white, white skin."

It would be terrifying enough if the voices stopped on that emasculating note. But they go on: "Just the same, black boys, if the enemies have been properly certified as such by our Christian leaders, and if they're poor and brown and 10,000 miles away, you must hate them. You must scream and rampage and kill them, black boys. Pick up the firebombs and char them good. We have no civilian jobs for you, of course, but we have guns and medals, and you must kill those gooks—even if some of them do resemble the image reflected in the night-black pool of your tears."

What can a nation expect in response to such vicious words? It gets the truth—far more than it deserves. For the black men reply: "Hypocrites, white hypocrites, you only want to save your skin and your piled-up treasure from the just envy-anger of your former slaves, your present serfs and your future victims. In the name of this Christ you deny our past, demean our present and promise us no future save that of black mercenaries in your assaults upon the world's dark and desperate poor."

Their rage cries out: "Give us no pink, two-faced Jesus who counsels love for you and flaming death for the children of Vietnam. Give us no blood-sucking savior who condemns brick-throwing rioters and praises dive-bombing killers. That Christ stinks. We want no black men to follow in *his* steps. Stop forcing our poor black boys into your legions of shame. We will not go."

"If we must fight," they say, "let it be on the streets where we have been humiliated. If we must burn down houses, let them be the homes and stores of our exploiters. If we must kill, let it be the fat, pious white Christians who guard their lawns and their daughters while engineering slow death for us. If we must die, let it be for a real cause, the cause of black men's freedom as black men define it. And may all the white elders die well in the causes they defend." This is Black Power—the response to the American Christ.

Unbelievable words? If any Christian dare call them blasphemous, let him remember that the speakers make no claims about Christ or God. Only we Christians—black and white—do that. If the just creator-father God is indeed alive, and if Jesus of Nazareth was his Christ, then we Christians are blasphemers. We are the ones who take his name in vain. We are the ones who follow the phony American Christ and in our every act declare our betrayal of the resurrected Lord.

If judgment stands sure it is not for Stokely Carmichael alone but for all of us. It is we Christians who made the universal Christ into an American mascot, a puppet blessing every mad American act, from the extermination of the original possessors of this land to the massacre of the Vietnamese on their own soil—even, perhaps, to the bombing of the Chinese mainland in the name of peace.

If judgment stands sure it is not primarily upon SNCC that it will fall, but upon those who have kidnaped the compassionate Jesus—the Jesus who shared all he had, even his life, with the poor—and made him into a profit-oriented, individualistic, pietistic cat who belongs to his own narrowly-defined kind and begrudges the poor their humiliating subsistence budgets. These Christians are the ones who have taken away our Lord and buried him in a place unknown.

We shall not escape by way of nostalgia or recrimination. For if he whom we call the Christ is indeed the Suffering Servant of God and man, what excuse can there be for those who have turned him into a crossless puppet, running away from suffering with his flaxen locks flapping in the wind?

If God is yet alive we cannot afford time to reminisce about the good old days of the civil rights movement when everybody knew the words of the songs. The time of singing may be past. It may be that America must now stand under profound and damning judgment for having turned the redeeming lover of all men into a white, middle-class burner of children and destroyer of the revolutions of the oppressed.

Chance for Redemption

This may be God's message for the church—through Black Power. It is a message for all who claim to love the Lord of the church. If this reading is accurate, our tears over the demise of the civil rights movement may really be tears over the smashing of an image we created or the withdrawal of a sign we were no longer heeding. Therefore if we weep, let it not be for the sins of SNCC and CORE but for our own unfaithfulness and for our country's blasphemy. And let us begin to pray that time may be granted us to turn from blond dolls to the living, revolutionary Lord who proclaimed that the first shall be last and the last, first.

If this message can break the grip of self-pity and nostalgia on us, the power of blackness may yet become the power of light and resurrection for us all. Has it not been said that God moves in mysterious ways his wonders to perform? I can conceive of nothing more wonderful and mysterious than that the blackness of my captive people should become a gift of light for this undeserving nation —even a source of hope for a world that lives daily under the threat of white America's arrogant and bloody power. Is that too much to hope for? Or is the time for hoping now past? We may soon discover whether we have been watching a wall or a curtain—or both.

ALVIN F. POUSSAINT

The Negro American: His Self-Image and Integration

Most psychiatrists and psychologists would agree that the Negro American suffers from a marred self-image, of varying degree, which critically affects his entire psychological being. It is also a well-documented fact that this negative self-concept leads to self-destructive attitudes and behavior that hinder the Negro's struggle toward full equality in American life.[1] Civil rights leaders have long been aware of the need to build a positive sense of identity in the Negro masses. Today, however, there are widening schisms among these leaders as to how this can best be accomplished.

For the past decades civil rights groups have vigorously pursued the ideal that the integration of Negroes into "all phases of American life" combined with the teaching of a bit of "Negro History" would solve most of the Negro's identity problems. Exceptions have been the Black Muslims and other nationalist groups who have insisted upon separation of the races as the ultimate solution to the racial problem. In recent years, however, some of these same civil rights groups have begun to lose faith in the virtues of integration. A few militants have described integration as "a subterfuge for white supremacy," i.e., as always involving only a token number of Negroes integrated into "white institutions on the white man's terms." They believe that integration as presently conceived and practiced in America will lead eventually to a greater crisis in identity for the mass of American Negroes, especially the poor, unless there are counter-measures. Therefore, some have advocated "black consciousness" and different forms of racial solidarity as the way to the Negro's eventual psychological salvation and dignity.

Before we attempt to explore in detail some of the above ideas and approaches, it is necessary to review briefly the historical factors that have led to the Negro's chronic identity crisis.

Historical Background

To understand the Negro's self-image, self-concept, and "Who am I?" problems we must go back to the time of the birth and creation of the "American Negro." Over 300 years ago black men, women, and children were extracted from their native Africa, stripped bare both psychologically and physically, and placed in an alien white land. They were to occupy the most degraded of human conditions: that of a slave, a piece of property, a non-person. For inhumane economic reasons, the Negro family was broken up and scattered from auction block to auction block all over America. The Negro male was completely emasculated, and the Negro woman systematically exploited and vilely degraded. The plantation system implanted a subservience and dependency in the psyche of the Negro that made him forever dependent upon the good will and paternalism of the white man.

By 1863, when slavery was abolished, the Negro had been stripped of his culture and left with this heritage: an oppressed black man in a hostile white man's world. In the late 1800's and early 1900's the systematized racist and sometimes psychotic propaganda of the white man, haranguing about the inferiority of the Negro, increased in intensity. He was disenfranchised, terrorized, mutilated and lynched. The Negro became every unacceptable, pernicious idea and impulse that the white man's psyche wished to project, i.e., the black man was animal with a violence to murder, ravaging sexual impulses, etc. The intensity of the white man's psychological need that the Negro be shaped in the image of this projected mental sickness was such as to inspire the whole system of organized discrimination, segregation and exclusion of Negroes from society.

In the resulting color caste system, while people made certain that any wares they allotted to the Negro were inferior. The Caucasian American socialized the black man to internalize and believe all of the many vile things he said about him. They encouraged and rewarded behavior and attitudes in Negroes that substantiated their indicting stereotypes. Black men were happy-go-lucky, lazy, stupid, irresponsible, etc. Our mass media disseminated these images with vigor on radio, in movies, etc., and like unrelenting electric shocks conditioned the mind of the Negro to say, "Yes, I am inferior."

Not only have black men been taught that blackness is evil and Negroes "no-good," they have, in addition, been continually brainwashed that only "white is right." It was the light-skinned Negroes with straight hair who were allowed to elevate themselves in America. Of course, the white people suggested, and Negroes came to believe, that such Negroes were better because they had much "white blood." And there are still cliques of light-skinned Negroes in our communities who reject their darker brothers. Black men were taught to despise their kinky hair, broad nose, and thick lips. Our "black" magazines pushed the straightening of hair and bleaching cream as major weapons in the Negro's fight for social acceptability and psychological comfort.

Current Situation

The most tragic, yet predictable, part of all this is that the Negro has come to form his self-image and self-concept on the basis of what white racists have prescribed. Therefore, black men and women learn quickly to hate themselves and each other because they are Negroes. And, paradoxically, some black men tend to distrust and hate each other more than their white oppressor.[1,2] There is abundant evidence that racism has left almost irreparable scars on the psyche of Afro-Americans that burden them with an unrelenting, painful anxiety that drives the psyche to reach out for a sense of identity and self-esteem.[1,2,3]

Although the Negro's self-concept is determined in part by factors associated with poverty and low economic class status, being a Negro has many implications for the ego development of black people that are not inherent in lower-class membership. The black child develops in a color caste system and inevitably acquires the negative self-esteem that is the natural outcome of membership in the lowest stratum of such a system. Through contacts with institutionalized symbols of caste inferiority such as segregated schools, neighborhoods, etc., and more indirect negative indicators such as the reactions of his own family, he gradually becomes aware of the social and psychological implications of racial membership. He may see himself as an object of scorn and disparagement, unwanted by the white high caste society, and as a being unworthy of love and affection. Since there are few counterforces to this negative evaluation of himself, he develops conscious or unconscious feelings of inferiority, self-doubt, and self-hatred.

From that point in early life when the Negro child learns self-hatred, it molds and shapes his entire personality and interaction with his environment. In the earliest drawings, stories, and dreams of Negro children there appear many wishes to be white and a rejection of their own color. They usually prefer white dolls and white friends, frequently identify themselves as white, and show a reluctance to admit that they are Negro.[1,2,3] Studies have shown that Negro youngsters assign less desirable roles and human traits to Negro dolls.[2,3] One study reported that Negro children in their drawings tend to show Negroes as small, incomplete people and whites as strong and powerful.[4]

In Mississippi or any northern city ghetto, one has only to visit Head Start schools with three to five year olds to see that these children already suffer damaged self-esteem. You hear the children shouting at each other in anger, "Black pig," "Dirty nigger," etc. Much of this negative self-image is passed to them directly by parents who themselves have been conditioned by racism to hate their blackness. And thus, a vicious circle is perpetuated from generation to generation.

Sometimes this self-hatred can be quite subtle. Some black people may retreat into their own world and actually be more afraid of success than they are of failure because too often failure has come to be what they know and expect. It is all too frequent that Negroes with ability, intelligence and talent do not aspire to higher levels because they fear the responsibility that will be needed to handle success. Many Afro-Americans tend to have lower aspirations and shy away from competition, particularly with white people. One study showed that even when Negroes were given objective evidence of their equal intellectual ability in an interracial situation they typically continued to feel inadequate and react submissively.[5]

The Negro community's high rate of crimes of violence, illegitimacy, and broken homes can be traced in part to the Negro's learned self-hatred as well as to poverty. Black crime rates are particularly elevated for crimes involving aggression, such as assault and homicide, and these acts are usually committed against other Negroes, and for escapist deviations such as gambling, drug addiction and alcoholism.[2] Many Negroes are caught up in a vicious circle of self-destructive behavior as if to say to the world, "Yes, I am inferior and I hate myself for it."

Discussion

Many of the civil rights gains in the past decade and especially in the 1960's have done, one can surmise, a great deal to modify the negative self-concept of the Negro. The civil rights movement itself has brought a new sense of dignity and respect to those blacks most severely deprived by poverty and oppression in the rural south and northern ghetto. One factor that may have been important in the movement that helped to improve the self-image of the masses of Negroes was that black men were leading the struggle, and not white men. This fact in itself probably made Negroes, through the process of identification, take a pride in their group and feel less helpless knowing that they could bring about positive change in their environment. The feeling that one can have "control" over social forces is crucial to one's feelings of ego-strength and self-esteem. Thus, the movement brought to the Negro a new sense of power in a country dominated by a resistant white majority. Beyond this achievement, however, civil rights leaders tended to see total integration of the black and white races as the final step in destroying the Negro's negative self-image.

In stark contrast to this position, and not without a salutary influence on the Negro's self-image, was that of the Black Muslims. This was the one major Negro group that called for separation of the races and black supremacy as an alternative approach to the black man's problems of identity and self-esteem. Observers generally agree that the Muslims were quite effective in rehabilitating many anti-social and criminal types by fostering in them a positive self-image and pride in their blackness.[6,7] The significant fact is that the Muslims were able to alleviate much of the individual Negro's self-hatred without holding up or espousing integration or "full acceptance" of the black man into American white society.

Now we see slowly emerging in segments of the civil rights movement a disenchantment with the social and psychological consequences of integration. This disenchantment is due at least in part to the fact that integration has moved at a snail's pace and has been marked by white resistance and tokenism. The

Negro has found himself in the uncomfortable position of asking and demanding the white man to let him in his schools, restaurants, theatres, etc., even though he knew the white man did not want him. In the south and north, many Afro-Americans resented the indignity of being in the eternal position of "begging for acceptance" into the white man's institutions. And it was further demoralizing to the mass of Negroes that the recent civil rights laws did not effectively change this pattern. It became apparent that integration was not to be integration in a real sense at all, particularly in the schools. Negro parents in the south never speak of sending their children to the "integrated school"; they say, "My child is going to the *white* school." No white children are "integrated" into Negro schools. Since integration is only a one-way street that Negroes travel to a white institution, then inherent in the situation itself is the implied inferiority of the black man.

Parents who fear psychological harm to their children are not anxious to send them to "integrated" schools. Some of the college-aged young people in the movement state frankly that they find this type of integration personally degrading and do not want to go to any school where they have to be "accepted by Southern white racists."

Since the Negro numbers at any white school are token, particular hardships are created for them because they are placed in a school with children who are generally the products of white racists' homes. The black child must withstand abundant psychological abuse in this situation as well as be an "experimental laboratory" for bigoted whites "to learn to live with Nigras." Since all children want to belong, the Negro must become an expert at "being liked and accepted." If such a child's self-esteem grows in such a situation it is not from a greater comfortness in being Negro but more likely because of his own conditioned belief that "white is right," or because he is successfully being a true martyr or pioneer.

Assimilation by definition always takes place according to the larger societal (white) model of culture and behavior, and thus the Negro must give up much of his black identity and subculture to be comfortably integrated. Many Negroes who seek complete assimilation become preoccupied with "proving" themselves to white people and trying to show them that "we are just like all other human beings," that is, that they are really *not* Negro.

Many Afro-Americans expend a great deal of internal energy trying to seek "individual freedom" in a white man's world. But it is a vain effort because "personal acceptability" has to be repeatedly proven to each new white group. The Negro group's vigorous pursuit of middle-class status symbols is frequently an overdetermined attempt to demonstrate to the white man, as well as to themselves, that they can be successful, worthwhile human beings. White America, however, has lumped all Negroes together in one collective image and hence, for no Negro can there be "individual freedom" unless there is "group freedom," which means undoing racial self-hatred. The Negro too often aspires to and gets entangled in the perverse situation where he feels that the most flattering compliment his white friends can pay him is: "You don't act like all the other Negroes," or "You don't seem Negro to me."

Many Negroes, including segments of the civil rights movement and nationalists, are beginning to fear that this type of "token integration" may augment the identity problems of the Negro. Little has been done to study the changes in self-concept of Negro children who attend "desegregated" schools in the south. Clearly, much more research has to be done in this field. But we do know that such integration as has existed in the north has not substantially helped to solve the Negro's identity problems.[3] In any event, there is a growing sense of racial solidarity and pride in Negroes both in the north and south. Afro-Americans are beginning to feel that it is through their strength as a group that they will win human dignity and power.

"Black consciousness," including the call for "black power," movement supporters argue that as long as Negroes are powerless politically and do not have their own sense of pride and worth as black men, they are psychological beggars in a white man's house. As has been pointed out, there are many negative implications of "token integration" for the Negro. On the other hand, would all-black institutions provide Negroes with a more stable, positive sense of identity and self-esteem?

It is known that such groups as the Black Muslims have frequently had many positive and constructive effects on the black community.[6,7] This group has brought greater self-reliance and dignity to the Negro community. They have also instilled pride and esteem in Negroes by emphasizing Negro history and achievements. "Black consciousness" programs can build Negro self-confidence by calling upon the black man to think and do for himself. They may also provide the stimulus for more independent thought and grass-roots problem-solving and the development of community leadership. Such programs seem to have the potential for undoing much of the Negro's learned self-hatred that leads to self-destructive behavior. Finally, such groups could constructively channel Negro frustrations and anger that lead to destructive violence and riots.

The question must be raised, however, whether such "all black" programs will in some way lead to more identity and self-esteem problems for the Negro since such groups would always exist within the pervading dominant white culture. There is some chance for such negative effects to develop, but if Negroes are truly *equals* in the larger society, a black subculture could exist much in the same way that America has subcultures of other national and racial groups such as the Jews, Irish, Chinese, etc. It is also clear that despite the drive for racial integration this is being vigorously resisted by the white population and we can expect to have isolated, predominantly black communities for a long time to come.

Since the Negro's self-concept problems cannot be solved through token integration, it is important that black men turn to the development of their own communities as an alternative and supplementary approach for building the Afro-American's self-image and -esteem. Unfortunately, the white man cannot give Negroes "black consciousness," Negro Americans must give it to each other. This means that black people must undo the centuries of brain-washing by the white man, and substitute in its stead a positive self-image and positive concepts of oneself—and that self happens to be the black, dispossessed, disenchanted, and particularly poverty-stricken Negro.

Summary

The Negro suffers from many problems of identity and negative self-image because of the racism, discrimination, and segregation in American life. The civil rights movement has generated some changes, but integration as presently practiced does not seem to offer the mass of Negroes a solution to problems of negative self-concept. It has been suggested in this paper that token integration into "white institutions" may lead to greater identity crises for Afro-Americans. "Black consciousness" movements appear to be able to contribute a great deal to the Negroes' sense of identity and self-esteem, and could mobilize the black community for positive political and social action. The development of "black consciousness" could serve as an alternative and supplementary approach to the building of the Negroes' self-image along with the present drive toward complete racial integration.

Literature Cited

1. KVARACEUS, W. C. et al. Negro Self-Concept: Implications for School and Citizenship. McGraw-Hill, Inc., New York, 1965.
2. PETTIGREW, T. F. A Profile of the Negro American. D. Van Nostrand Co., Inc., Princeton, 1964.
3. GROSSACK, M. M. Mental Health and Segregation. Springer Publishing Co., Inc., New York, 1965.
4. COLES, R. "When I Draw the Lord He'll be a Real Big Man," The Atlantic, May, 1966, p. 69.
5. KATZ, I. and L. BENJAMIN. Effects of White Authoritarianism in Biracial Work Groups. J. Abnormal and Soc. Psych., 61:448, 1960.
6. LINCOLN, C. E. The Black Muslims in America. Beacon Press, Boston, 1961.
7. HALEY, A. The Autobiography of Malcolm X. Grove Press, New York, 1964.

NATHAN WRIGHT, Jr.

The Crisis Which Bred Black Power

The current focus on Black Power may be seen as a logical result of a crisis which had been developing for more than a decade in the black communities across America.

I
The So-Called "Decade of Progress"

There have been at least several interrelated developments which brought about our current crisis.

For one thing, there had been—since the early 1950's—a growing official commitment throughout the nation to what was defined as civil rights. The historic Supreme Court school desegregation decision in 1954 was seen as symbolic of the new official attitude of America in the area of civil rights. Indeed, so jubilant and optimistic were many black Americans concerning the import of the 1954 school desegregation ruling that some national civil rights organizations at the time contemplated their own imminent extinction. In the mid 1950's a great debate took place in black and white academic circles as to the new role of the now seemingly anachronistic Negro colleges.

With the delayed (and presently questionable) implementation of the 1954 school desegregation ruling, it soon became clear that the battles of black America had not yet quite been won. By the late 1950's it was seen that there was at least some distance more to go.

Because of the intransigent attitude to school desegregation in the South, the focus of the civil rights forces turned southward. This fortunately threatened little the life patterns of northern whites, and so in the name of democracy and fair play in the

Southland, eager and dedicated white northern ambassadors for southern freedom were enlisted. Then began a period of dramatic awakening and witness. It was staged in the late 1950's and early 1960's in such a magnificent and compelling manner that the very grandeur of the action seemed at least an appropriate substitute for a critical appraisal of the current goals.

Throughout the 1955-1965 "decade of progess" the dollar income gap between black and white Americans moved steadily toward a perilous proportion, relief roles mounted, northern school and residential segregation increased, and the economic control by black people of their local environments continued to decrease. Meanwhile the civil rights movement hailed a human rights revolution as black and white people fought and won fresh skirmishes over front seats on the buses and won the right to eat hamburgers at the corner coffee shop.

That black Americans were entitled to the enjoyment of full desegregation should have been clear to all. This, of course, gave the unquestionable stamp of validity for the increased pace of and massive involvement by white and black Americans in the sit-ins, the rallies and the marches which became the popular pattern in civil rights in the decade prior to 1965. Gains needed to be made in civil rights areas, as these were seen both by the leaders and by the masses. The national response to the program of the movement was evidenced in the glorious finale of the events leading up to and culminating in the great Civil Rights Act of 1964.

From the Montgomery Bus Boycott Movement started by Mrs. Rosa Parks in 1957, through the college student sit-ins in the early 1960's, the Birmingham demonstrations and the unforgettable "Letter from a Birmingham Jail" by Dr. Martin Luther King, and on to the moments of the monumental March on Washington, the civil rights movement had captured the hearts and the imagination of the land.

Yet assuredly all was not well in the now seen to be critical area of civil rights. In the late 1950's and early 1960's Malcolm X, militant young former prisoner and self-taught leader of the Muslims, grew in stature from an apparently minor menace to something of an enigmatic black hero. He haunted the nation's mind and dampened the gala mood of the marches and demonstrations as he posed an increasing challenge to the seeming certainty of the nation's perceived path of racial progress.

Malcolm X died early in 1965. He was cut down as his star took on an acknowledged brilliance and suddenly began to soar to national and international heights. His message contradicted the integrationist spirit and the mood of "making progress" on the part of the leaders for civil rights.. Civil rights leaders, on the one hand, called upon the nation to be colorblind. Malcolm X spoke, on the other hand, of the need for racial self-awareness and for increased pride in blackness. The leaders of the civil rights movement called for increased help from white people. Malcolm X spoke contrarily of the need for at least a sense of sufficiency and self-respect. White people had come to lead, as well as control, much of the movement for civil rights. Malcolm X, against this state of affairs, demanded that organizations for black men's improvement—like those of the Jews by Jews and Irish by Irish—be black supported and black led. Civil rights leaders courted the friendship of white people. Malcolm X was unequivocal in his perception of each and every white man as being, whether consciously or unconsciously, by historical and cultural circumstance none other than the oppressor of black people.

With the demise of Malcolm X, other voices rose to echo repeatedly his crisp refrains. They were the voices of outraged black parents in the inner city and semi-suburban areas of New York, Boston, Washington, Chicago, Oakland, and in almost any other major American city which one might name. Black young people were not learning to read. Job opportunities were lost; college entrance was often barred to the children of chagrined black professional parents; and the mounting drop-out rate by black teenagers posed itself as a mushroom cloud to threaten the peace of our northern cities.

By the many signs the helping hand had not performed its ostensibly intended work. So beneath the surface of seeming success in the area of civil rights the ripples of restless uncertainty began to mount towards the proportions of a tidal wave.

To the voices of frustrated black parents, there were added other echoes of the late Malcolm X. They were heard in such cries as "Negro Removal," "War on the Poor," "Operation False-start," and the expressed alarm at what was seen to be the "Widening Gap" between black and white Americans in the economic sphere. Summer riots in the black urban ghettos in the early and mid 1960's seemed to be becoming a way of life. As the Anti-Poverty Program increased in its endeavors, relief rolls throughout the black sectors of the nation continued to mount.

By 1966, the gala festivities of the rallies, the marches, and the sit-ins were over. The Civil Rights Act of 1964 had effectively opened eating, sleeping, and recreational places to black Americans. Some relatively small and well publicized handfuls of black men had been elevated to new positions of higher visibility than ever before. Yet upon calm assessment the predicament of the overwhelming numbers of the black masses was one of growing economic attrition and a mounting inability to control or have investment in the local environment of their communities.

Despair and growing desperation were the unveiled products of ten years of deepening commitment to programs in civil rights which were largely uncritically assessed as to their priorities for the good of black people and the nation as a whole.

The 1967 Report of the United States Commission on Civil Rights, entitled *Racial Isolation in the Public Schools* tells in sober language the ever saddening story:

"The persistence of disparities in educational attainment has been accompanied by continuing and even widening social and economic disparities between Negro and white Americans.

True, there has been improvement in absolute terms in the position of Negroes. Levels of income are substantially higher now than before. More Negroes are attending college and entering professions; more skilled jobs are being filled by Negroes than ever before.

Despite this improvement, however, when the social and economic gains of Negroes are measured against the gains of white Americans, the gap is as wide as ever. The income of Negroes has risen over the years, but their situation relative to white Americans has worsened. In the 15-year period between 1949 and 1964, the median annual income for nonwhite families increased from $1,650 to $3,800. Median annual income for white families rose during the same period from $3,200 to more than $6,800. The disparity between white and nonwhite annual income in 1949 had been less than $1,600. By 1964, the gap was more than $3,000.

The distribution of occupations for Negroes and whites reveals much the same situation. The proportion of the total Negro labor force in white-collar occupations increased by one-third—to 11 percent—between 1950 and 1960. For whites, however, 33 percent were in white-collar jobs in 1950, three times the percentage attained by Negroes 10 years later.

Within the Negro population, there also is a growing gap separating the poor from the relatively affluent. For a comparatively small percentage of the urban Negro population, the decade of the 1950's brought real economic progress and even relative affluence. For the great majority of Negro Americans, however, there was little economic change in relation either to whites or to more affluent Negroes.

The great majority of Negroes still are "have-not" Americans. Small advances in their overall economic and social position have not altered significantly their situation relative to whites. The closer the promise of equality seems to come, the further it slips away. In every American city today, most Negroes inhabit a world largely isolated from the affluence and mobility of mainstream America."

II
Signs of Crisis

There were no clearer concrete signs of a state of crisis for those in the black ghettos and for the nation as a whole than in the forecast revealed in the statistics of the 1965 report of the President's Commission on Technology, Automation, and Economic Progress.

The Commission's report depicts what is no less than a charted pathway toward peril, if the nation continues in the decade between 1965-1975 in the so-called pattern of progress adopted for the previous decade.

The report states in part:

If nonwhites continue to hold the same proportion of jobs in each occupation as in 1964, the non-white unemployment rate in 1975 will be more than five times that for the labor force as a whole. In 1964, the unemployment rate for non-whites was 9.8 percent, about twice that for whites. *If trends in upgrading the jobs of nonwhites continue at the same rate as in recent years,* the non-white unemployment rate in 1975 would still be about 2½ times that for the labor force as a whole. Thus nonwhites must gain access to the rapidly growing higher skilled and white-collar occupations at a faster rate than in the past 8 years if the unemployment rate is to be brought down to the common level.

(Technology and the American Economy, page 31)

One may ask: can the nation as a whole, or its black community, hold still for such a situation as this to come to pass? It is clearly unthinkable that black people would not come to wholesale riot and revolution long before such a state of affairs would be realized.

According to trends even then apparent, some government economists predicted in the late 1950's that come 1972-73, this nation would experience the greatest racial conflagration this hemisphere has ever known. If the ominous facts in the report of the President's Commission on Technology, Automation, and Economic Progress do not confirm this forboding thesis, then the supposition cannot stand.

The use of the term "progress" as we have used it over the past decade may be an exercise in illusion. Jobs for Negroes, a special report from Business Week, dated June 12, 1965 cites the following measures of progress in defense jobs and in general business. Tables I and II respectively below.

Table I
Progress In Defense Jobs

	1962	1964	% Increase
All employees			
Total	2,049,064	2,111,864	3.1%
White-collar	775,033	832,774	7.5%
Blue-collar	1,274,031	1,279,090	0.4%
Negro employees			
Total	136,613	146,880	7.5%
White-collar	12,079	15,782	30.7%
Blue-collar	124,534	131,098	5.3%

The interpretation for Table I is as follows:
Only a few of the statistical pictures of the progress of Negroes

toward new and better jobs are reliable. The President's Committee on Equal Employment Opportunity is a prime source. It gets reports from prime contractors and first-level subcontractors who hold government contracts for $50,000 or more and employ 50 or more workers. Reports from 3,471 plants show [the above] progress from 1962 to 1964.

Table II
Progress in General Business

	1963	1964	% Increase
All employees			
Total	3,969,748	4,090,361	3.0%
White-collar	1,887,437	1,905,144	0.9%
Blue-collar	2,082,311	2,185,217	4.9%
Non-white employees			
Total	232,692	266,317	14.5%
White-collar	40,553	47,134	16.2%
Blue-collar	192,139	219,183	14.1%

The interpretation for Table II is as follows:

Plans for Progress is another program run by the same committee. It's a voluntary program in which 308 companies with 8.6 million employees have promised to go beyond legal requirements in giving employment opportunities to non-whites. [The above] is the picture of progress from 1963 to 1964 shown in reports from 100 of these companies with about 4 million employees.

The Report of the President's Commission on Technology, Automation, and Economic Progress details the "Employment by

Major Occupation Groups, 1964, and Projected Requirements, 1975" in Table III following:

Table III*

Major occupation group	Number (in millions)	Per- cent	Number (in- millions)	Per- cent	Percent change 1964-75
Total employment	70.4	100.0	88.7	100.0	26
White-collar workers	31.1	44.2	42.8	48.3	38
Professional, technical, & kindred workers	8.6	12.2	13.2	14.9	54
Managers, officials, and proprietors, except farm	7.5	10.6	9.2	10.4	23
Clerical and kindred workers	10.7	15.2	14.6	16.5	37
Sales workers	4.5	6.3	5.8	6.5	30
Blue-collar workers	25.5	36.3	29.9	33.7	17
Craftsmen, foremen, and kindred workers	9.0	12.8	11.4	12.8	27
Operatives & kindred workers	12.9	18.4	14.8	16.7	15
Laborers, except farm & mine	3.6	5.2	3.7	4.2	**
Service Workers	9.3	13.2	12.5	14.1	35
Farmers, farm managers, laborers, and foremen	4.4	6.3	3.5	3.9	–21

*Projections assume a national unemployment rate of 3 percent in 1975. The choice of 3 percent unemployment as a basis for these projections does not indicate an endorsement or even a willingness to accept that level of unemployment.
**Less than 3 percent.

Note: Because of rounding, sums of individual items may not equal totals.

Source: U.S. Department of Labor, Bureau of Labor Statistics, America's Industrial and Occupational Manpower Requirements, 1964-75.

From the foregoing charts it seems clear that major efforts of an unprecedented nature must be made in the future, if black Americans are to be dealt into the economic life of the nation in such a manner as to preserve or extend the nation's peaceable and ordered life. "Equal" opportunity will not suffice to make "progress" as black Americans start from a position of gross disadvantage.

Further, the nation's social and economic well-being call for the black American's being dealt into the nation's economic life with immediate equity *at all levels and according to existing potentialities.* This means, in effect, that no reasonable "progress" may be made in the employment patterns for black Americans unless some form of restitution or preferential device is employed to create a condition of equity. The staggering crippling effects of past and present discrimination must be overcome.

Far too often in the past have unrealistic pictures of Negro economic progress been painted. The painting of such pictures and the gross and repeated misuse of the term "progress" undoubtedly have played a major role in creating our present crisis in civil rights.

To be helpfully realistic all "progress" must be defined in relation to at least two considerations. Progress must be gauged in part to economic trends and in part to the social needs of the nation as a whole. In regard to the painting of pictures in the light of economic trends, Table IV below is informative. Its heading is "Labor Force: Percentage Distribution over Broad Occupation Categories, 1900-1959." It shows the percentage change by ten-year periods in the labor force of three categories of workers. These are white-collar workers, manual and service workers, and farm workers.

The percentage of workers in the manual and service category remained relatively constant over a sixty-year period. The approximately sixty-year percentage change was only 3.1, from 44.9 percent in 1900 to 48.0 percent in 1959. Meanwhile the percentage of farm workers moved downward from 37.5 in 1900 to 9.9 in 1959. This represented a drop within the total labor force of 25.6 percent. To turn the statistics around, there were approximately 4 times as many workers on the farms in 1900 as there were in 1959. The overwhelming majority of all Negroes lived on the farm in 1900. By 1959 the vast preponderance of farm jobs occupied in 1900 simply did not exist. Negroes moved to the city during this sixty-year period. (See Table V.) Farm workers have lower visible income than do non-farm workers. The shift by Negroes to the city would suggest an apparent economic upgrading for Negroes. In fact the seemingly higher echelon and higher income jobs which Negroes came to occupy in the cities had now become by a simple change in economic patterns the lower echelon jobs of 1959.

Table IV
Labor Force: Percentage Distribution over Broad Occupation Categories, 1900-1959

Category	1900	1910	1920	1930	1940	1950	1959
White-collar	17.6	21.3	24.9	29.4	31.1	36.6	42.1
Manual and service	44.9	47.7	48.1	49.4	51.5	51.6	48.0
Farm	37.5	30.9	27.0	21.2	17.4	11.8	9.9
TOTAL	100.0	99.9	100.0	100.0	100.0	100.0	100.0

Source: Fritz Machlup, The Production and Distribution of Knowledge in the United States (Princeton, NJ: University Press, 1962), p. 381. Reprinted by permission of Princeton University Press. Copyright 1962, Princeton University Press; all rights reserved. Data for 1900 to 1950: US Bureau of the Census, Working Paper No. 5, "Occupational Trends in the United States, 1900-1950"; for 1959: Current Population Reports, Series P-60, No. 33, pp. 40-41.

Note: Figures do not always add up to total because of rounding. The 1959 data contain almost 4 million unemployed not distributed amoung occupation groups. In order to make the series comparable, these unemployed are here distributed among the three categories in the proportion in which the figures for "economically active" for 1950 exceeded those for "employed" in 1950, according to the Current Population Report, Series P-60, No. 9 (April 1951) p. 36.

The most visible sign of apparent economic success on the part of black Americans has been the entry of this group into the ranks of white-collar workers. This category of workers represented 17.6 percent of all workers in 1900. By 1959 this category had more than doubled to 42.1 percent. This represented an inroad of 24.4 percent into the total employment force of the nation. Here again, with automation and technology, nearly half of the employment force came to be represented in the white collar category. The movement of the black American into this category by itself may not represent, as often we have been led to believe, upgrading for black workers, so much as it may reflect a relative downgrading or extension of white-collar category jobs.

Table V

Percentage of Negro and White Population living in Urban Areas, by Region, Conterminous United States, 1910-1960

Year	United States		South		North & West	
	Negro	White	Negro	White	Negro	White
1910	27.4	48.7	21.2	23.2	77.5	57.3
1920	35.4	53.3	27.0	28.5	84.3	61.6
1930	43.7	57.6	31.7	35.0	88.1	65.5
1940	48.6	59.0	36.5	36.8	89.1	67.4
1950	62.4	64.3	47.7	48.9	93.5	70.1
1960	73.2	69.6	58.4	58.6	95.3	73.7

Sources:

1920-40:   Sixteenth Census of the United States: 1940 Population, Vol. II, Characteristics of the Population, Pts. 1-7, tables 4, 5, for each State (US Bureau of the Census).

1950:   Census of Population, 1950, Vol. II, Characteristics of the Population, Pt. 1, United States Summary, table 145 (US Bureau of the Census).

1960:   Census of Population, Detailed Characteristics, United States Summary, Final Report PC(1) 1D, tables 158, 233; 1910: Abstract of the Thirteenth Census (1910), table 28, p. 103 (US Bureau of Census).

The fact that we are in our imminently dire predicament today in spite of a pattern of seeming progress should be fair warning to us not to make uncritical assessments of apparent progress in the future. Progress must be made in relation to circumstances which bear clear comparison. If the overall economic picture has changed, simple percentages of Negro changes do not necessarily tell a tale of progress.

Again, the social needs of the nation as a whole must be a major factor in any assessment of employment progress by black Americans. Because black people have been isolated economically for so long a period in the nation's life, a black economic problem has become a social problem of major proportions for the nation as a whole. An entire ethnic group is perilously isolated in an arbitrary way from the economic and social mainstream of American life. Progress in the future must be gauged in substantial measure by the demands of the nation's internal peace and order. Social controls are aways operative in ordering every aspect of the nation's life. The increasingly crucial concern for the future must be that social controls be exercised with the wisest possible judgement in the clear light of critically assessed priorities. That such judgements had not been made in the decade from 1965-1975 has played perhaps the most significant part in precipitating both the present crisis in civil rights and the perilously darker days which appear to lie ahead.

III
The Question of Power

The present crossroads or crisis in civil rights—and its possible resolution—must be associated with the issue of power.

The call on the part of black people for Black Power represents an unmistakable turnabout in both mood and direction in the area once appropriately described as civil rights.

There are certain clear differences between the civil rights movement and the impetus towards Black Power. The civil rights movement has asked for what was due to the Negro. The thrust toward Black Power does not ask what the black American is due. It seeks inherently to add the power, the latent and preciously needed potential, of black people for the enrichment of the life of the nation as a whole.

Black Power is not a negative concept. It is a positive, creative concept, seeking to bring a wanted maturity to our too long adolescent nation's life. To produce growth and a wholesome sense of maturity there must be equitable relationships of power. The gross imbalance between the power of black and white

Americans has effectively subverted our democratic goals, blurred the nation's vision of the pathway towards the great destiny of which it dreams, and perverted its moral sense as an apparently all-powerful white America has confronted its seemingly powerless major ethnic minority.

Black Power, seeks to bring to the nation's life the saving necessity of equitable and growth-producing power tension and extension.

Vice President Hubert Humphrey recently remarked that in spite of apparent disagreements concerning Black Power among some civil rights leaders, it should be clear to all familiar with American history that Black Power is within the basic American traditions. Black Americans, he asserted, need Black Power to achieve political, civic, and economic goals even as other ethnic groups have used the weight of their ethnic numbers to achieve their goals. In this way America has come thus far towards its own self-realization and fulfillment.

Black Power reflects the failure of the civil rights movement in at least several significant respects.

Above all else, black Americans have needed the power which comes from pride in one's own accomplishments. Black people have throughout this nation's history been *dependent* on other people. At first, this was due to necessity. Later it was due to long-standing cultural conditioning.

In the civil rights movement to a not inconsiderable degree the slave mentality of looking to others for direction and support is seen to have been kept in force. Black people manifestly must have the sense of pride and self-respect which can only come through the tradition of self-directed efforts at self-sufficiency. Black organizations and efforts for black self-improvement—as with Jewish organizations led by Jews and Italian organizations, by Italians—must be black led.

Black leadership must be able leadership. But the substitute of white competence for blackness in leadership cannot be said to have a clear advantage. White technical competence in educational matters, for example, may take Negroes much further down the road than black incompetence. But it will have—as the evidence in our inner cities plainly attests—a well-nigh impossible task in taking our youngsters over the bridge at the river or bringing them across the finish line. The ideal that is needed is the kind of black competence which affords pride and holds onto hope in uniquely saving ways. For these precious qualities there can be no effective substitute. We cannot and must not, as black men or white, settle for less, if we are to have the latent potential of our hopeless and increasingly desperate black masses come to its best flower.

Black Power does not negate the value of friendship and cooperation on the part of others. It speaks basically to the role of leadership. The basic American tradition is for each rising ethnic group to devise and execute its own plan for economic, political, and civic freedom and development. So it must be with the black people of our land. They have been the most assisted and the most greatly benighted. The civil rights movement focused upon cooperation and, in a way foreign to the American tradition and to all rising ethnic groups, accepted direction and leadership from outside its ranks. However wise it may be, no outside leadership has that crucially significant ingredient of that inner drive and urgency to be free which can come only from one who is a part of the oppressed.

The proof of the civil rights movement pudding has been in its eating. It has been tested severely especially in the decade ending in 1965; and the clear record of its sad legacy after a gloriously executed decade of battle tells its own sad story. We have seen that the black people of America are—as a whole— more benighted than ever in relation to the nation as a whole, and a white America faces a black future in which its rehabilitative and policing costs will stagger our minds and threaten the security of our institutions and our way of life.

Black Power speaks for a new day of candor and integrity. Integration, as we have sought to work it out over the past decade and more, has clearly failed. There can be no meaningful integration between unequals. Thus as black men have turned toward an illusive integrationist goal, with white men holding the reins of power, black men have lost both their identity and their self-respect.

No black man needs the presence of a white man to have a sense of worth. Increasingly black men are saying today that if they never saw white men in their lives, their being would not be diminished one bit. Nor is it necessary, as our government statistics seem daily to insist, for black children to have the presence of white children in order to learn as they should.

Where white children are present there is a pervasive sense that one has a future, that one might share in the shaping of the conditions of one's life. Black children, through the impetus toward Black Power, may have by themselves those same horizons. No one seeing life as one dark vast cavern of uncertainty would or could be moved or impelled to learn. But give a child hope, and his life may suddenly come to flower.

The integrationist mood of the civil rights movement has led to what some see as a dead-end street. White people in America overwhelmingly are not quite yet ready for open and honest friendship and brotherhood with black Americans. The integrationist mood of the civil rights movement asked black Americans to play a game of brotherhood where, almost universally, white men have welshed on the rules. If men and women will not be open and honest and fair and free when their children are of the age of courtship and marriage, how can they ask others to make full and free counter-commitments? In all fairness, black Americans cannot be asked to make emotional commitments to white friendships into which white people have historically built a guarantee of soon or late frustration.

No rising ethnic group in this nation has, on its own, asked for integration. All have asked simply for desegregation. Desegregation involves some integration as a means to an end but not as an end in itself. Desegregation involves the clearing of the decks of all barriers to free choice relationships which do not interfere with the rights of others. It is permissive of growth and is not negative in its implications.

Black men, at this hour in our nation's life, need solidarity. They need pride in what they are. This means pride in blackness. They need the power implicit in their rising from their sitters and their standing on their feet. Black men want desperately to do just this. They want to pull themselves up by their own bootstraps, but where even bootstraps are so often lacking, some substitute must be supplied.

Because the black American's moving into self-sufficiency and pride and self-realization are the only means by which the mounting desperation of black people may be averted, Black Power is in the clear self-interest of all white Americans.

White Americans can and must facilitate Black Power by converting their neighbors and by encouraging in many creative ways the solidarity and self-respect which black Americans so sorely need. They can help also in the removal of many specific devices which debilitate black people. Black people are effectively barred from access not only to loans for large business properties, but also to many home ownership loans. Banks are threatened almost daily if they lend to Negroes in a way that breaks the unspoken racist code. Negroes are barred from consideration for many higher echelon civil or public service jobs vital to the well-being of the black and white community by screening committees with prevailing cultural perceptions and by non-objective oral examinations. White people concerned with the development of Black Power may help to insure that competent black men direct the human resources administrations of our states and shape the Model Cities plans at the local level. What most often appears to be black apathy is in substantial measure a black time-ingrained cynicism at the systematic way in which cards are stacked against black people.

Black Power, actively developed, and espoused and facilitated by all, may thus break through the present crisis and inaugurate a new day of hope. Peril may be averted when the powerless command a sense of power to find some semblance of fulfillment.

The current crisis in civil rights came about through an honorable, but faulty intent. Black Power now seeks a better way. It should be our purpose—for the sake of all who comprise and will come to comprise America—to encourage power for growth and for fulfillment on the part of all.

LeROI JONES

The Need For a Cultural Base to Civil Rites & Bpower Mooments

The civilrighter is usually an american, otherwise he would know, if he is colored, that that concept is meaningless fantasy. Slaves have no civil rights. On the other hand, even integration is into the mobile butcher shop of the devil's mind. To be an american one must be a murderer. A white murderer of colored people. Anywhere on the planet. The colored people, negroes, who *are* Americans, and there are plenty, are only colored on their skin. They are white murderers of colored people. Themselves were the first to be murdered by them; in order to qualify.

The blackpower seeker, if connected to civilrights mooment can be bourgeois meaning. He wants the same civilrights/power white people have. He wants to be a capitalist, a live-gooder, and a deathfreak. In whatever order. There is the difference Frantz Fanon implies in *BlkSkin-WhiteMask*. Black Bourgeoisie can be white or black. The difference is critical only if Black Black Bourgeoisie can be used for good, possibly. White ones are examples of shadow worship, and are deathfreaks and American.

Black Power cannot mean ONLY a black sheriff in the sovereign state of Alabama. But that is a start, a road, a conceptualizing on heavier bizness. Black Power, the power to control our lives ourselves. All of our lives. Our laws. Our culture. Our children. Their lives. Our total consciousness, black oriented. We do not speak of the need to live in peace or universal humanity, since we are peaceful humanists seeking the spiritual resolution of the world. The unity of all men will come with the evolution of the species that recognizes the need for such. The black man does. The black man is a spirit worshiper as well. The religious-science and scientific-religion is the black man's special evolutional province. He will reorder the world, as he finds his own rightful place in it. The world will be reordered by the black man's finding such place. Such place is, itself, the reordering. Black Power. Power of the majority is what is meant. The actual majority in the world of colored people.

Census

BLACK PEOPLE BLACK PEOPLE BLACK PEOPLE
YELLOW PEOPLE YELLOW PEOPLE YELLOW PEOPLE
BROWN PEOPLE BROWN PEOPLE BROWN
RED PEOPLE RED PEOPLE RED PEOPLE
POOR PEOPLE POOR PEOPLE POOR PEOPLE POOR
PEOPLE POOR PEOPLE POOR PEOPLE POOR PEOPLE
. . . .
& others.

Bourgeois black power seeks mostly to get in on what's going down now. The implication or murdermembership is clear. Of course the form of Bourgeois black power can be harnessed for heavier ends. The control by black people for their own benefit CAN BE set up similar to bourgeois black power, but if the ends are actually to be realized, you are talking again about nationalism, nationalization. Finally the only black power that can exist is that established by black nationalism. We want power to control our lives, as separate from what americans, white and white oriented people, want to do with their lives. That simple. We ain't with yuall. Otherwise you are talking tricknology and lieconjuring. Black power cannot exist WITHIN white power. One or the other. There can only be one or the other. They might exist side by side as separate entities, but never in the same space. Never. They are mutually exclusive.

"Might exist," because that is theoretically possible, except the devils never want to tolerate any power but their own. In such cases they want to destroy what is not them. However, the power of the majority on the planet will exist, this is an evolutional fact. The adjustment, what the world must go through because of this, is current events.

The socio-political workers for black power must realize this last fact. That the black and white can never come to exist as equals within the same space. Side by side perhaps, if the devils are cool, but the definition of devil is something uncool.

This means that any agitation within the same space for Black Power is for control of the space you *can* control called part of the society, but in reality in black enclaves, cities, land, black people are usually already in control in terms of population. Further control must be nationalization, separation. Black power cannot exist except as itself, power, to order, to control, to legalize, to define. There are wars going on now to stop black power, whether in Sinai, Vietnam, Angola, or Newark, New Jersey. The difference is that in Newark, New Jersey, many colored people do not even *know* they are in this war (tho they might realize, on whatever level of consciousness, that they are losing).

Black power is nationalization. Absolute control of resources beneficial to a national group. It cannot come to exist in areas of white control. Neither Harlem nor Hough nor Watts &c. are really America. They are controlled by America . . . this is the sickness. Black power is the cure for this sickness. But it must be the alternative to what already exists, i.e., white power. And to be an actual alternative it must be complete.

Black power cannot be complete unless it is the total reflection of black people. Black power must be spiritually, emotionally, and historically in tune with black people, as well as serving their economic and political ends. To be absolutely in tune, the seekers of black power must know what it is they seek. They must know what is this power-culture alternative through which they bring to focus the world's energies. They must have an understanding and grounding in the cultural consciousness of the nation they seek to bring to power. And this is what is being done, bringing to power a nation that has been weak and despised for 400 years.

That is, to provide the alternative, the new, the needed strength for this nation, they must proceed by utilizing the complete cultural consciousness of this black nation's people. We should not cry black power unless we know what that signifies. We must know full well what it is we are replacing white power with, in all its implications. We are replacing not only a white sheriff, for the values that sheriff carries with him are, in fact, an extension of the white culture. *That black sheriff had better be an extension of black culture, or there is NoChange!* (In the sense that Edward Brooke, so-called Negro Senator from Massachusetts, as a representative of white culture, could never signify in any sense, Black Power. He is, for all intents and purposes, a white man.)

There are people who might cry BlackPower, who are representatives, extensions of white culture. So-called BlackPower advocates who are mozartfreaks or Rolling Stones, or hypnotized by Joyce or Hemingway or Frank Sinatra, are representatives, extensions, of white culture, and can never therefore signify black power. Black power, as black, must be, is in reality, the total realization of that nation's existence on this planet from the year one until this moment. All those experiences which have been this lost nation's must be brought to bear upon all its righteous workings; especially for Power. (And with Power will come Freedom.) Black Power is the Power first to be Black. It is better, in America, to be white. So we leave America, or we never even go there. (It could be twelve miles from New York City (or two miles) and it would be the black nation you found yourself in. That's where yourself was, all the time.)

The very failure of the civil rights and blackpower organizations (collecting memberships on strictly socio-political grounds) to draw more membership is due to the fact that these organizations make very little reference to the totality of black culture. The reason Mr. Muhammad's Nation of Islam has had such success gathering black people from the grass roots is that Mr. Muhammad offers a program that reflects a totality of black consciousness. Islam is a form of spirit worship (a moral guide) as well as a socio-economic and political program. Religion as the total definer of the world. (This is as old as the world, and finally will be the only Renewal possible for any of us to submit to the Scientific-Religious reordering of the world, through black eyes and black minds.) It must be a culture, a way of feeling, a way of living, that is replaced with a culture, feeling, way of living and being, that is black, and, yes, finally, more admirable.

Hence, the socio-political must be wedded to the cultural. The socio-political must be a righteous extension of the cultural, as it is, legitimately, with National groups. The american negro's culture, as it is, is a diphthong with the distortions of the master's hand always in back or front ground, not real but absolutely concrete and there; . . . the culture, the deepest black and the theoretical . . . socio-politico (and art &c.) must be wedded. A culturally aware black politics would use all the symbols of the culture, all the keys and images out of the black past, out of the black present, to gather the people to it, and energize itself with their strivings at conscious blackness. The Wedding . . . the conscious-unconscious. The politics and the art and the religion all must be black. The social system. The entirety of the projection. Black Power must mean a black people with a past clear back to the beginning of the planet, channeling the roaring energies of black to revive black power. If you can dig it???. Not to discover it now . . . but to revive. Our actual renaissance (Like the devils pulled themselves out of their "dark ages" by re-embracing the "classics," or Classicism: what they could see as the strengths and beauties of a certain kind of "pure" Europeanism (whiteness). And with that went to the source! Eastern Thought . . . black african-middle eastern, also the re-embracing of the Far East via Marco Polo, &c., like *Trade*.)

So that no man can be "cultured" without being *consciously* Black. Which is what we're talking about all the time, in any Rising (Evolutional) Pitch. *Consciousness.*

The Civil Righters are not talking about exchanging a culture. They are, no matter what moves they make, layin' in the same place, making out. Black Power, as an actuality, will only exist in a Black-oriented, Black-controlled space. It is White Culture that rules us with White Guns. Our only freedom will be in bringing a Black Culture to Power. We Cannot Do This Unless We Are Cultured. That is, Consciously Black. (The Consciousness of Black Consciousness must know & Show itself as well.)

The erection of large schools teaching Black Consciousness. Wherever there are Black People in America. This should be one definite earnest commitment of any Black Power group. Even the rundown schools full of black children deep in the ghettos are white schools. The children are taught to value white things more than themselves. All of them are white-controlled, and the quality of education suffers because white people want the quality of our education to suffer, otherwise something else would be the case. We will have no quality education for our children until we administer it ourselves. You *must* know this!

There is no black power without blackness conscious of itself. "Negro History" is not what we must mean, but the absolute reordering of our Education Systems. In other words the philosophy of blackness, the true consciousness of our world, is what is to be taught. The understanding of the world as felt and analyzed by men and women of soul.

The Black Student Union of San Francisco State College has started moving toward a "Black Studies Program" at that school. A Black Studies Program on departmental status at the school, where students could spend all of their time recreating our black past, and understanding, and creating the new strong black nation we all must swear to bring into existence.

The black power groups must help to create the consciousness of who we black people are, and then we will be driven to take power, and be faithful to our energies as black people with black minds and hearts, quite a *different* people from the species that now rules us.

Afro-American History, African History, Realistic World History, Eastern Philosophies-Religion, Islam-Arabic-African Religion and Languages, Black Art-past and contemporary, The Evolving Patterns of the Colored World, Black Psychology, Revolutionary Consciousness, Socio-Political Evolution of Afro-Americans, Africans, Colored Peoples, War, The Placement of the New Culture, Eastern Science, Black Science, Community Workshops (How To) in Black Power, Business and Economics: Keys to a new black world, given the strengths our studies into times of the black man's power will build for us. Black Studies is to make us cultured, i.e., consciously black.

The so-called Negro Colleges ought to be the first to be forced into Blackness. The consciousness of the self, without which no righteous progress is possible. Instead the Negro Colleges are "freak factories," places where black children are turned into white-oriented schizophrenic freaks of a dying society. But many of the students have already shown that they are not willing to be misused by the whiteminds of their puppet professors.

A cultural base, a black base, is the completeness the black power movement must have. We must understand that we are *Replacing* a dying culture, and we must be prepared to do this, and be absolutely conscious of what we are replacing it with. We are sons and daughters of the most ancient societies on this planet. The reordering of the world that we are moving toward cannot come unless we are completely aware of this fact, and are prepared to make use of it in our day-to-day struggle with the devil.

E.G.: Black Art—The recreation of our lives, as black . . . to inspire, educate, delight and move black people.

It is easier to get people into a consciousness of black power, what it is, by emotional example than through dialectical lecture. Black people seeing the recreation of their lives are struck by what is wrong or missing in them.

Programmatic application of what is learned through black art is centrally the black power movement's commitment.

The teaching of colored people's languages, including the ones we speak automatically, moves the student's mind to other psychological horizons. European language carries the bias of its inventors & users. *You must be* anti-black, speaking in their language, except by violent effort. The masses of black people, for instance, have never spoken the European's languages. Or let me say, they have never spoken them to such degree that the complete bias of that "competence" would dull their natural tuning.

The teaching of Black History (African and African-American) would put our people absolutely in touch with themselves as a nation, and with the reality of their situation. You want them to move to take power, they must know how they can deserve this power.

Black Power must be a program of Consciousness. The consciousness to Act. (Maulana Ron Karenga and the US group in Los Angeles work very successfully at making black consciousness cultural and of course socio-political.) It should all be one thing. Blackness.

Voting nor picketing nor for that matter fighting in the streets means anything unless it is proposed by a black consciousness for the aggrandizement and security of the Black culture and Black people. Each of our "acts of liberation" must involve the liberation of the Black man in every way imaginable.

Black Power movements not grounded in Black culture cannot move beyond the boundaries of Western thought. The paramount value of Western thought is the security and expansion of Western culture. Black Power is inimical to Western culture as it has manifested itself within black and colored majority areas anywhere on this planet. Western culture is and has been destructive to Colored People all over the world. No movement shaped or contained by Western culture will ever benefit Black people. Black power must be the actual force and beauty and wisdom of Blackness . . . reordering the world.

ADELAIDE CROMWELL HILL

What is Africa to Us?

Any discussion of Black Power ultimately requires an assessment
of the identity of the Negro American. The elements of this
identity, among other things, reflect some expression of it as a
state of being and some awareness of its relation to the color of
the Negro, which in turn is reminiscent of his African ancestry.
This ancestry, in spite of the attempts at degradation, depreciation,
or denial, is woven into the Negro's sense of self.

In 1927, before most Negro Americans knew how to express
this fact freely, Countee Cullen, with the sensitivity a poet must
have, was able to do so in his poem, "Heritage." Cullen wrote:

> What is Africa to me
> Copper Sun or scarlet sea
> Jungle star or jungle track
> Strongblack men or regal black
> Women from whose loins I sprang
> When the birds of Eden sang?
> One three centuries removed
> From the scenes his father told
> Spring grove, cinnamon tree,
> What is Africa to me?

. . . . .

The answers to this question come from an understanding of
what the Negro American thinks of himself and what he wants
for himself. As the Negro's presence on the American scene has
rarely been fully acknowledged and never fully welcomed, little
serious attention has been given to either question until quite
recently.

In considering the question of identity—even in what some more present-oriented persons insist on calling its newer form, it is necessary for me to return to earlier days—at least in my own career—and to reiterate what I have come to believe are some of the basic ingredients in Negro identity.

Almost thirty years ago, in 1939 to be precise, in the research necessary for my senior thesis in college, I questioned a group of high school girls about certain aspects of their lives. These girls were all Negroes, lived in Washington, D.C., and were attending the Negro schools of that city. I put the question to them bluntly: Are you glad you are colored? Seventy-nine percent said they were and when asked why, they gave such explanations as— because coloreds are prettier than whites; whites look like witches when they grow old; or God made me colored and that is the way I am going to stay; or because I will be able to help the race progress.

These admittedly were the days before self-conscious African nationalism or the Negro Revolution and the answers have a kind of simplistic ring in content. And of course these were also the days before we were preoccupied with the psychological concept of identity having neither the theories of Erikson nor those of Fanon on which to draw. And yet in Washington, away from the excitement of Renaissance Harlem or strident Garveyism, in an environment of respectable scholarship and the security of government jobs, these young girls were aware of their identity— an identity formed and perpetuated within the restrictive features of their society.

Admittedly I was not in the position of probing their unconscious or even unravelling the complex layers of their conscious, and further, this was not a unanimous assessment. Not all of the girls were glad they were colored. Furthermore one could have uncovered other prevalent patterns—the rejection of race and the passing phenomenon so popular in Washington on one extreme, and the weak but clear strain of Africa for the Africans, meaning also American Negroes, the rallying cry of Garvey and his followers, on the other. But at this time, these were the extremes—the main stream was an acceptance of one's identity and an acceptance that was neither necessarily passive nor negative, although it could be either. The feeling at that time, however, did not have the fire and international content that later years would supply.

Before examining the changing content of this identity, a brief word on naming or labelling is appropriate. This too is a subject that has intrigued me because naming or nomenclature is a most important way of defining and *controlling* relations between people. "Native" and "foreigner" imply something quite different about the relation and status of the native from "native" and "European," for example. Also as language is so important to our species, each communal group has generally named itself and in turn has been named by other groups. Depending on the character of the relationship, the names do not necessarily coincide. Even in the most modern context this is clear; we call ourselves Americans; foreigners call us Yanks.

Against these generalizations, a rather unique situation has occurred with the Negro. On this soil, the Negro has never been given an opportunity to name himself. Denied full inclusion in the terms designated by whites for whites, lacking such tribal terms as American Indians have, or the genuine nationality-based terms of the so-called hyphenated Americans, the Negro has been given such terms as American society feels are appropriately descriptive—for a brief time in the North, they were called Africans, but more generally for the country as a whole, slaves (slave-black, slave-mulatto, slave-quadroon) but always slave or free men. After the Civil War, briefly, they were called freedmen. Gradually, however, seemingly in an endeavor to please all sections of the country by maintaining in the definition a decent separatism but reflecting an improved status, the term "Negro" was bestowed upon us. And what variant forms it has undergone, what subtleties of meaning it has been able to encompass—"nigger" meaning still slave and evil, "niggrah" meaning still slave but compliant, "negro" with a lower case "n" meaning not slave or non-slave—but never citizen, or truly a free man—or even respected individual!

While being named, counted and classified according to these categories, the "so-called Negroes" (and here especially Malcolm X's adjective seems appropriate) began to react to what they felt as their position reflected in their name. Some preferred colored as a gentle reminder of the true description of race relations as it really had been in this country, others preferred Afro-American in order to join the other large ethnic hyphenated American communities in this country and some were so imaginative and creative as to suggest Negrosaxon. Gradually, however, reflective of the time—the period between the end of Reconstruction and World War II and the rise of Independent Africa—most Negroes settled for the term Negro, insisting only that the first letter be capitalized.

This term then defined or prescribed the limits of their identity —not equal but deserving of some respect. This was the identity of the high school girls I questioned so long ago. And let me say that in the context of the time, I think it was a solid base from which to develop. I do not feel, regrettably, that Negro high school students in Boston or Detroit or New York or perhaps even Jackson or Durham would necessarily have felt this way. Although it is quite likely, as Horace Mann Bond has indicated, that the basis for identity and motivation would even then have been greater in Durham, Jackson or Dallas than in Boston, Chicago or New York. Bond writes in his study of Negro holders of doctorates that "among the high schools definitely known to be segregated, whether in the North or South, the high schools that either had been private, or operated on private or state college campuses as laboratory high schools, hold a far higher doctoral production rate than the large urban high schools, and especially higher than the large urban de facto segregated high schools in northern slums. . . . Yet the evidence is that there have been superior high schools in large segregated city school systems: Dunbar in Washington, D.C., Sumner in St. Louis, Mo., where the doctoral productivity was much higher than in such high schools as Du Sable in Chicago, Benjamin Franklin in Philadelphia and Attucks in Indianapolis, Indiana." (See Horace Mann Bond, *A Study of Factors Involved in the Identity and Encouragement of Unusual Academic Talent among Underprivileged Populations, Final Report,* Contract No. SAF8028, Project No. 5-0859, Bureau of Research, Office of Education, U.S. Department of Health, Education and Welfare, January 1967.)

We are saying that a strength and awareness of group potential are essential for the most minimal form of identity to emerge. Or to quote Fanon, "Without a Negro past, without a Negro future, it was impossible for me to live my Negrohood. Not yet white, no longer wholly black, I was damned."

This identification was nourished and shaped, ostensibly at

least, within the context of the American experience. It grouped under the same umbrella the wide variety of people from those white in appearance to those of the blackest hues, from those of substantial or comfortable means according to any standards to those for whom welfare payments not only meant survival but advancement, from those whose search for God occurred in the most formal of settings to those whose religious outlet took place in tents or abandoned city stores. So diverse were they that superficially the only bond they seemed to have was the common ability to speak English and almost total inability to speak any other language than English. There was obviously one additional and crucial common fact. According to the social and political rules of this country they were *not* white. These NOT WHITES as opposed to other not whites usually referred to in the census as "Other" were not white because some or all of their ancestors had come from Africa. Slavery or the fact of having been slaves is only a secondary factor. Realizing it or not, this group of Not Whites, the so-called Negroes, derived their identity from their relation to Africa.

Now as the American Negro begins to understand these facts, he sees himself vaguely and always hesitantly as part of the world's Not White peoples. This makes him, forces him, to look at India's independence in a way different from that of whites of this planet. It also affects his view of China, of Japan, of Vietnam. But in a more direct and meaningful way it determines and it must determine the view he has of Africa.

There is not the time, nor, I feel, at this period of history, the necessity to review the traditional image of Africa as presented to the Western world in general and to the Negro in particular. It is important only to recall that this image, as just one of the many ways of educating Negroes, was always, with a few weak and spasmodic exceptions, left entirely in the hands of whites; so Negroes saw Africa as whites saw Africa . . . black, savage, unhealthy, and heathen. Of course Americans did not generally view with favor their countries of origin . . . as a nation of immigrants we were a people who had for one reason or another left our old countries to improve our lot here, to do better than we could have done in the land of our birth. This is true of course for all except Africans who were torn and snatched from their land of birth. It is a bit ironic then that as a "country" of origin Africa has assumed the least favorable image of all the other countries of origin vis-à-vis America. To white Americans in "the land of the brave and the home of the free," no country, not China, not Italy, not Russia, not even France and England and most assuredly not Africa is as fair and desirable or beautiful and wonderful as America . . . otherwise why would we have come here? It would then have been totally out of character for Americans to single out Africa as a continent of charm and beauty. But of course we know that is not the entire story—that is not why Africa was described as a dark continent—we know that there was in addition a deliberate effort to deny the culture, the tradition, the wealth and the beauty of that continent in order to perpetuate the rational basis for colonialism there and slavery here. But for Negroes the image was made even more negative and repulsive by the frequent threat of racists to send us *back* to Africa!—such forced returns to any country of origin, but especially Africa had the impact of a life sentence on Alcatraz.

However since Africa was indeed the basis of our non-white status, it provided from the beginning a fragile source for our identity . . . which we never completely denied. The naming of our earliest schools, African schools, our mutual aid societies, African societies and the first of our important religious bodies, African Methodist Episcopal, are but a few examples to prove that Africa was never absent from our self-image—symbolic and remote as it was for so many decades. It was left to Marcus Garvey however not only to make us view Africa as potentially merely a boat-ride away but to admit, yes even to proclaim, that our status and our identity was not a negative value but a positive one; we were not just not white, not just Negroes, however that was defined, we were black.

It has taken almost a half a century, and let it be regrettably admitted, a changed attitude first by the whites rather than by the Negro for us really to accept what Garvey was saying. We have witnessed a radical change in the attitude of the larger society toward Africa and coincidentally toward black.

To many people black and Africa are in a sense synonymous terms—in spite of the range in color types found there. But our identity in its present form requires that the image of both black and Africa be made positive. Africa could and did change from a continent of *dependent* peoples to a continent of *independent* peoples. Black cannot be changed; we can only change our attitude about it—it cannot be rubbed off or washed off or wished off, and black as a value—except perhaps for the basic black dress once thought so essential for style—has rarely had a positive connotation—in conjunction with Africa or separately. . . . A black lie, the black hole of Calcutta, black death, etc., all illustrate the added strength black gives to whatever is already a bad situation.

But Garvey said we were black, not Negro or brown or colored or some other white euphemism but black:

> The Black Race, like the white, is proud of its own society and will yield nothing in the desire to keep it pure and ward off a monstrous subjugation of its original and natural type, by which creation is to be judged, as a race responsible for its own, and held accountable in the final analysis for the presentation of itself, before the Judgement seat of God. The Ethiopian cannot change his skin; and we shall not.
> —Philosophy and Opinions of Marcus Garvey; ed. by Amy Jacques-Garvey . . . 1st ed. Registered in the name of Amy Jacques-Garvey, under A 704742; May 5, 1923; p. 62.

Meanwhile Black Africa began to stretch forth her hands—on her own continent, to the capitals of the world and to the United Nations, fortuitously for us located in the front yard of our own Negro capital, Harlem. From then on it's been smooth sailing. The community we always had, the identity we always had, were both broadened and enriched by the reality of Africans. We say that black, not just mulatto, high yellow or what have you people, could succeed in this world—and succeed at points of power and decision-making. No longer was the expectation complete to think that only a light-brown skinned boy could become a doctor or a lawyer. Now quite clearly a black man could be a king— and a black woman a real queen.

The feedback on this realization has been tremendously exciting. African heroes and tradition bulwark our long concern with Negro heroes and traditions. It has almost become better to be black than brown or yellow. White society, long accustomed even from the days of slavery to favoring those closer to them in appearance and indeed passing this value on to us as a group, even the ineligible us, now having to associate with and view the power of black kings and queens, no longer favors browns and yellows. To get real credit for pushing civil rights, one must give a black man a visible job, make a black girl your secretary and welcome a black family into your neighborhood.

This brings us, I feel, to where we are today. Our sense of community has not appreciably changed. We have a separate identity which has been strengthened by having its most basic ingredients, Africa and our blackness, viewed positively . . . by the white world and by us. Africa is no longer the land we never knew. . . . And we here are becoming real people to Africans. It is interesting that this broadening of the base of our identity is emerging at a time in American history when group identity rather than amalgamation or group disappearance is viewed as the more positive value. We are "Beyond the Melting Pot." We no longer proclaim our advancement as one superior people but as one varied people, enriched by our variety. It may be that at last Negroes can be accused of the sin of having a dual identity, of seeing our roots so vehemently that we do not see our homes. I doubt that this will happen except for an occasional person, because Africa is our continental home not our national home and Africa is a continent of many nations. Yet we are indeed free, as few Americans are, to decide from what part of that vast continent we want to think our ancestors came. Other nationalities cannot do this. You are either a Southern Italian or not, a Cantonese or not, an Irishman or a Scotsman. We can say, and with some documentation to substantiate it, that our slave forebears could have been kings or prophets or farmers or fishermen from Nigeria or from Ghana, from Mozambique or from Kenya. And for the purposes of identity, it does not make much difference which group we choose—they were all black and they all came from Africa. We can glory in the past and present achievement of all Black Africans and we can cry bitter tears of despair over the flagrant injustices anywhere in Africa . . . from Cape to Cairo and especially from the Sahara to the sea. And let me parenthetically warn you not to forget that in its traditional usage Black Africa, a term we did not invent, meant Africa from the Sahara to the Cape, not Africa from the Sahara to the Kalahari or the Zambesi.

We can learn the languages, understand the cultures of that vast area. And we can accept the responsibility of being a block of informed citizens speaking out within our society on matters of foreign policy especially as they affect those areas. This identification in turn will make our young people see a greater need for exercising their suffrage, getting an education, seeking positions of power. The strength to achieve these goals will come from within our communities revitalized by strengths from Africa. This seems to me to be the basis of our new identity. The identity itself is old; its roots are merely spreading and strengthening.*

*Paper delivered at the National Conference on Black Power, Newark, New Jersey, 1967.

LAWRENCE P. NEAL

Black Power in the International Context

The struggle for black liberation has come to a significant turning point. Currently, the most advanced elements of the Black Power movement are beginning to understand the international implications of the struggle for black liberation. It is becoming increasingly clear that the struggle cannot be contained within the bounds of national life. As a matter of fact, to continue to do so is a tendency that must be strongly fought. The African-American struggle is inextricably linked to the world-wide struggles of oppressed peoples against decadent political and economic systems.

The present-day attempts to put the struggle on an international basis have their roots in the writings of such nineteenth century thinkers as Martin R. Delaney who was the first Afro-American to raise the question of self-determination for the Africans. In the twentieth century, Garvey, Du Bois, Malcolm X, and Harold Cruse have examined the relationship between the Afro-American struggle and the international situation in more precise details.

During the twenties, Garvey used Delaney's slogan "Africa for the Africans" as the rallying cry for the United Negro Improvement Association. Du Bois wrote in *The Souls of Black Folk*: "The problem of the twentieth century is the problem of the color line—the relation of the darker to the lighter races of men in Asia and Africa, the Americas, and the islands of the seas." Malcolm X, extracting from both Garvey and Du Bois, constantly urged the movement to internationalize itself.

Therefore, the current internationalist tendencies of groups like SNCC, CORE, and RAM should not come as a surprise. They are perfectly consistent, given an understanding of the history of the black man's struggle in America. The present movement is part of an historical process that began with Garvey and the NAACP. It was Garvey who first posed a concrete threat to European colonial interests in Africa. And it was the NAACP, under Du Bois' direction, which established a viable Pan-Africanism—a Pan-Africanism which greatly influenced nationalist leaders like Dr. Kwame Nkrumah and Jomo Kenyatta. As late as 1949, the NAACP was supporting wars of national liberation: "We stretch our hand across the sea to the new independent state of India. We hail the Indonesians in their struggle for liberty. We are one with the Africans in their effort to throw off the yoke of colonialism. We offer them every assistance within our power. The race problem is bigger than the few prejudiced men who influence the United States Congress. It is bigger than a few states in the deep South. It has assumed world-wide proportions and the American Negro is prepared to take his place in the world-wide struggle."

This statement was made by Roy Wilkins at the fortieth annual convention of the NAACP on July 12, 1949. Wilkins' statement is essentially a reworking of Du Bois' remarks concerning the color question in *The Souls of Black Folk*. Since then Roy Wilkins has tended to de-emphasize the international role of the NAACP. This de-emphasis is directly related to the general manner in which the NAACP has now come to see the struggle in this country.

The main thrust of the NAACP is now directed towards assimilating blacks into the present socio-economic structure of white America. But in the present political and economic context this is neither possible nor desirable. On the national level, it means the destruction of potential pockets of black resistance to white America's decadent political structure. On the international level, it means that Black America becomes aligned with the racist power structure in the destruction of the Third World (Africa, Asia, and Latin America). Therefore, the NAACP and similarly oriented Negro leaders display strong acceptance of United States foreign policy. And American foreign policy is essentially reactionary.

Consequently, one of the things separating Black Power militants from the traditional wing of the movement is a basic difference in the way history is viewed. Roy Wilkins and Whitney Young are both descended from slaves; as were Malcolm X and Marcus Garvey. But there are profound differences in orientation between these two groups of men. Their political orientations undoubtedly play a role in their style of action. Whitney Young would not *act* like Malcolm because Malcolm's assessment of the world and Young's are vastly different. Young's style is perfect for the manner in which he perceives the attainment of freedom in America. That is, he moves in corporate structures; he moves in the financial world of Wall Street. Consequently, he has been forced to develop a different set of priorities; and these priorities (goals) must be consistent within his operating framework. It is impossible for Young to act like a Malcolm in that corporate framework. It is foolish to expect him to.

The present-day Negro leadership has no independent international position because it does not see the struggle in nationalist terms. And that is why it is dangerous. It is important not to fall into the trap of simply labeling these leaders as "Uncle Toms." It is imperative that we have a clear understanding of the manner in which they view the world. This is the only way to fight them. They speak for thousands of black people, and the failure of the militants to understand the reasons for that appeal would be disastrous. Psychologically, Black America is divided between seeing itself as a separate nation and seeing itself as an integral part of American society. Du Bois referred to this phenomenon as "double consciousness." This double consciousness has been implicit in the black man's history since the first slaves were brought here four hundred years ago. The struggle within the race has centered around the correct manner in which to destroy this double consciousness. Or in more precise political terms, it has been an internal struggle between the nationalists and the integrationists.

The integrationists do not believe that the basic socio-economic structure must be destroyed. But rather, that Negroes must simply be given a greater slice of the capitalistic action. They believe in reform not revolution. They are men who are essentially awed by the power of the Establishment. They have weighed the issues and decided that the best course lies in seeking some kind of rapprochement with the "system." The system is not bad at heart, they say, it just does not have enough black people in key jobs and fine houses.

Further, more in line with our topic, they believe that the struggle must be confined simply to giving Negroes rights as

American citizens. Therefore, when King linked the struggle in Vietnam with the human rights struggle here in the United States, Wilkins, Young, and Rustin vehemently denounced him. They stated emphatically that not only was King's action tactically incorrect, but that there was no relationship between our struggle and the war in Vietnam. But it became clear in the months following Dr. King's remarks that the black man's relationship to that war is one of the key issues surrounding it. The rebellions in the cities further helped to illustrate the explicit relationship between the status of Afro-Americans and the war itself. While Whitney Young consistently made statements geared to assure the Johnson administration that the "War on Poverty" and the Vietnam War could be conducted with the same degree of intensity, there were rebellions in over fifty American cities. It became increasingly clear that the massive aid demanded in the cities and the massive resources necessary for waging war in Vietnam were at odds with each other.

Even though Young has never stated it, his trip last year to Vietnam for the apparent reason of speaking to Negro G. I.s strongly implies, in and of itself, that there is a functional relationship between those soldiers and the society to which they must return. And recently, almost ironically, we find Mr. Young a member of the unofficial fact-finding tour on the Vietnam elections. If Stokely Carmichael and King are wrong about the moral relationship of the war to Black America, why did the President select a civil rights leader as a member of the fact-finding committee? Johnson was simply attempting to convince black people that they have a vital interest in the political and military conduct of the war. Further, he made a hypocrite of Young.

Thus, the established Negro leadership is forced to continue waging the fight for total liberation within the limits set by the oppressor. Or more precisely, it has constructed an ideology that naturally limits the contours of the struggle. This is a bad position for an oppressed minority to be in. It means that we are limited to alternatives imposed by a decadent government. It further means or assumes that the over-all needs of Black America can be fully satisfied within the framework of the American body politic. It assumes that the long-range interests of Black America coincide with those of the white power structure.

The only way out of this trick-bag is to begin from the position that black people constitute a would-be nation apart from that of white America. Therefore, there are *two* Americas — a Black one and a white one; and Black America very clearly must decide its own destiny. It must independently decide what its interests are, both in the national and the international context. Consequently, it is no longer a question of civil rights for Negroes; but rather, it is a question of national liberation for Black America. That means that we see ourselves as a "colonialized" people instead of as disenfranchised American citizens. That means that our struggle is one with the struggles of oppressed people everywhere, and we alone must decide what our stance will be towards those nations struggling to liberate themselves from colonial and neo-colonial domination.

Currently, America is the chief neo-colonist power, exercising control over the resources of most of Africa and Latin America, while keeping the props under the politically stale regime of Thieu and Ky in Vietnam. There has been increased activity in the Third World. The forces fighting for national liberation have had to increase the tempo of the struggle. But ultimately none of them can succeed, as long as the United States remains the reactionary giant that it is. Finally the United States itself must have a total and complete revolution; and Black America is the key to that revolution, and its potential vanguard. American foreign policy is essentially predicated on the maintenance of a stable society at home. But we are here, and the conditions under which we exist do not lend themselves to stability. We will have to struggle on every possible level to survive. And because of the nature of our historical experience, it is foolish to speak in terms of *individual* survival.

The civil rights movement spoke in terms of individual survival. Hence, it failed to understand the implicit nationalism of the masses of Black America. All of the nationalistic elements were there, but the Negro leadership refused to see or to acknowledge them. Therefore, when Whitney Young expresses a desire to discard the blues for Bach, or the "jitter bug" for the ballet, he is advocating the destruction of an identifiable Afro-American culture. He is advocating the destruction of the Black Nation. In European terms, the Negro leaders are intelligent men, but their failure to understand the revolutionary possibilities of Black culture doomed the civil rights movement to oblivion.

Black Power is a natural response to the nationalistic strivings of the masses of Black America. It is implicitly based on the concept of nationhood. With this understanding, the attempts by Garvey, Du Bois, Malcolm X, Robert Williams, and Stokely Carmichael to internationalize our struggle are dialectically consistent with the thrust of Afro-American history. For example, as a member of a national liberation front, Brother Stokely's recent trip to Havana, North Vietnam, Algeria, and the Middle East is perfectly logical. It connects the Afro-American nation to the larger context of the world-wide revolution; and at the same time, it breaks down the ideological walls which have contained the struggle thus far. It supplies the black theorist and activist with a new set of political alternatives. Like the guerilla fighter, we have at our disposal the advantage of greater and more flexible tactical mobility. Only in this case the initial thrust of the movement is more political than military. It is important, therefore, that the political goals of the movement be expanded. The slogan Black Power should be more explicitly connected with the question of nationhood. The movement in the United States must become more consolidated; and national priorities must be advanced along with international priorities.

In order for this kind of strategy to bear fruit, the progressive wing of the Black Power movement must attack the narrowness that has plagued the struggle in recent years. This is within both camps, the nationalists' and the integrationists'. We have already discussed the narrow ideology of the integrationists. But the nationalists have also displayed a limited view of the struggle. Here I refer specifically to the "back-to-Africa" advocates. Many of them have no revolutionary program, and therefore, see unity with Africa in purely racial terms. Consequently, there is a nationalist movement in Chicago now being organized to send thousands of people back to Liberia, which is itself in need of a revolution. Very few nationalists of this variety have ever analyzed the diversity of political systems in Africa. Very few of them have voiced a desire to join the liberation movements in Angola, Mozambique, and Zimbabwe (Southern Rhodesia). This latter is one of the most valid forms of support that we can offer our brothers and sisters in these regions.

The best course, internationally, is the linking together of all spheres of revolutionary activity in the Third World. This is the course recently taken by SNCC, RAM, and to a lesser degree by CORE. For example, SNCC sent delegates to the recent conference of Latin American revolutionaries and to key parts of

Africa and Asia.

Wilkins' criticism of Carmichael's Havana trip deserves comment here. He attacked Stokely in what must be called essentially "nationalistic" terms, pointing out that the Havana trip betrayed the concept of an "all black" movement. But SNCC has never claimed that a strictly all black movement was consistently relevant in an international context. Theoretical magazines like *Soulbook* and *Black America* had been saying this for quite some time. Wilkins betrays his reluctance to see the international ramifications of the black liberation movement when he writes:

> Now comes a public acknowledgment by spoken and written word, by picture and by physical presence that the 'black' creation of these earnest young people is but a tail to another's kite. It is tied to Castro, to Chile and to South America, to Peking and to God knows what else. *It is not a movement by black people for the improvement of black Americans here in America,* but a movement whose direction depends upon people (not black) far from Rolling Fork, Miss., Terrell County, Ga., and the slums of Roxbury, Mass.
>
> This does not prove of course, that the Negro militants are Communists or that the drive of *Negro Americans for their citizenship rights* is communist. But the development sparked by Chief Black Power himself certainly suggests strongly that devotees of blackism may have been delivered into the orbit, if not into the actual hands, of non-blacks who are motivated by much more than singleminded dedication to the advancement of black people. (all emphasis mine)
>
> —New York Post, August 19, 1967

It is clear that Wilkins' vision of freedom is radically different from Stokely's. The former envisions freedom in the simple context of American national life. The latter sees the contradiction between freedom in the United States and freedom gained at the expense of continued United States aggression abroad. Carmichael is aware of an implicit connection between a liberation movement in Terrell County and one in Angola and Chile. While Wilkins would make Black America a party to white America's neo-colonialist designs in Africa and Latin America, Carmichael is a revolutionary. Wilkins is a reformist. As such they see social and economic configurations quite differently.

Our choices must be separate ones. If it is important to have an independent black movement in this country which fights for the human rights of black people, then that same movement must itself determine where it stands in the context of international affairs.

The movement is greatly in need of international allies. It must have what Maulana Karenga calls "functional unity." That is, it would seek a concrete coordination of political and military activities with the Third World. The first level of this functional unity would operate towards methods of destroying the psychology of colonialism. This level also involves a high degree of organization and communication between theorists and activists here and abroad. The political consciousness of Black America must be broadened to give black people a deeper understanding of its role in the destruction of oppression both here and abroad. Although military power is the foundation of the beast's power, we must understand the role of information and media as methods of controlling the oppressed. Internationally the United States Information Service determines how the Afro-American struggle will be seen. Black America must establish a unified information service in Africa, Asia, and Latin America. There can be no unity without communication.

The propaganda apparatus of the movement must become much more sophisticated than it is now. The recent Arab-Israeli war is a case in point. The Negro leadership voiced strong support of the Israelis during the conflict and they were given a great deal of exposure in the racist press. But the nationalists had no adequate means of presenting the Arab side of the conflict. So powerful was the pro-Israeli propaganda that most pro-Arab militants were labelled as racist "anti-semites." Popular approval of Zionist aspirations in the Middle East is not based on Biblical mysticism, but on the cumulative results of good propaganda for over forty years.

An analysis of international realities clearly indicates that Zionist interests are decidedly pro-Western, and that these interests are neo-colonialist in nature and design. In Africa, for example, a notable amount of the resources of the continent is controlled by Zionist-oriented Jews like the Rothschilds and Harry F. Oppenheimer whom Kwame Nkrumah calls the "king of mining in South Africa." It is the duty of the progressive elements of the movement to educate the community about these facts. Further, it is tactically dangerous to fall prey to emotional invective, and especially so on such matters as the Arab-Israeli conflict. Propaganda is most emotionally effective when it is precise, and based on facts that can be easily substantiated. The role of the revolutionary is to educate his people as he makes a revolution. And we can not simply educate our people about domestic matters. Modern technology has made the factor of distances obsolete. There are no far-off places any more. Angola, Vietnam, and Chile are here, and we must deal with that reality in a manner that is understandable to the masses of Black America.

Therefore, in the spirit of revolutionary concreteness, I put forth the following suggestions:

The U.S. War of Aggression in Vietnam

The attack against the Negro G. I.s who are fighting in the war should be better directed. The movement must not only criticize the "brothers' " involvement in that war, but it must offer meaningful alternatives. It must be first made clear to them that a national liberation army is needed at home. It should also be stressed that dignity for the black man cannot come at the expense of suppressing the legitimate aspirations of the Vietnamese people. We should advise these black soldiers to join the national liberation movements in Angola, Mozambique, and Zimbabwe (Southern Rhodesia). There they can fight the white colonialist honkie. The war in Vietnam should be contrasted with the liberation struggles in Africa. Some of us should give up our American citizenship to fight in these places. In this way the unity that we seek is more functional than symbolic.

The United Nations

The question of the status of Black America should be brought before the United Nations. Not because we have faith in that body, but for educational reasons. We should also attempt to maintain a permanent representative of Black America at the United Nations. Contact between Afro-Americans and delegates to the U. N. must be broadened.

Liberation Front Offices

There should be liberation front offices (agencies) in all countries friendly to the cause of black liberation. These offices would counteract the activities of the CIA and the USIA. They could keep the lines of communication open between revolutionaries throughout the world. Their functions could be expanded as the situation worsens in America.

Cultural Exchange Programs

There should be cultural exchange programs between independent black institutions and the Third World. Black artists armed with the power of Black Culture should fan out all over the world spreading the soul message of Black America. Recently, the CIA-controlled AMSAC (American Society for the Study of African Culture) participated in the "Negro Arts festival" in Senegal, one of the most reactionary countries in Africa. Many Negro artists were thus exploited by the CIA by way of AMSAC. It is very important that the artistic community organize. Or it will find itself being manipulated in the propaganda war against the Third World. Black film makers should develop exchange programs. Films produced by black artists should be distributed all over the world. The same is true for tapes, photos, magazines and revolutionary recordings.

All of these suggestions presuppose that Black Power is a revolutionary slogan. They also presuppose that strong independent organizations are now being developed in the black community. Without viable black organization here in the United States none of these things is possible. So the building of strong black institutions here in America must be the first consideration. These suggestions represent a tentative approach to the international implications of the Afro-American struggle. If the drift towards state-condoned fascism continues in the United States, many of these suggestions will have to be radically altered. We must be psychologically and physically prepared in the event that happens. But even a start in the direction outlined here will help develop the strength and resources necessary for liberation. The nature of what lies ahead is unknown. But the realities of the present give clear evidence that we must establish viable links with our brothers and sisters struggling in the Third World. We must develop revolutionary black institutions and be ready to defend them with our lives. We have no choices. *All praise is due the Black Man.*

READINGS

I
Books

W. E. B. Du Bois, *The Souls of Black Folk,* New York, Fawcett World Library, 1961.

Frantz Fanon, *The Wretched of the Earth,* New York, Grove Press, 1965.

————. *Toward The African Revolution,* New York, Monthly Review Press, 1967.

Marcus Garvey, *Philosophy and Opinions,* Vols. I & II, San Francisco, Richardson, 1967.

Kwame Nkrumah, *Neo-Colonialism: The Last Stage Of Imperialism,* London, Nelson, 1965.

George Padmore, *Pan-Africanism or Communism,* London, Dennis Dobson, 1956.

Lin Piao, *Long Live The Victory of People's War,* Peking, Foreign Languages Press, 1965.

E. U. Essien-Udom, *Black Nationalism,* New York, Dell, 1964.

II
Articles & Papers

Black America, Summer-Fall, 1965.

James Boggs, "Black Power: A Scientific Concept," *Liberator,* April, 1967.

Harold Cruse, "Revolutionary Nationalism and the Afro-American," *Studies on the Left,* Spring, 1963.

Willie Green, "The World is the Black Man's Land," *Soulbook,* Winter-Spring, 1967.

Lawrence P. Neal, "Open Letter to Roy Wilkins," *Liberator,* August, 1967.

Student Nonviolent Coordinating Committee, in the International Seminar on Apartheid, "Racial Discrimination and Colonialism in South Africa".

III

BLACK

POWER

IN

ACTION

ROBERT F. WILLIAMS

from Negroes with Guns

In 1957, Mr. Williams led a black community in Monroe, North Carolina, to organize armed self-defense against the racist violence of the Ku Klux Klan. Chapter 7 from his book follows:

The stranglehold of oppression cannot be loosened by a plea to the oppressor's conscience. Social change in something as fundamental as racist oppression involves violence. You cannot have progress here without violence and upheaval, because it's struggle for survival for one and a struggle for liberation for the other. Always the powers in command are ruthless and unmerciful in defending their position and their privileges. This is not an abstract rule to be meditated upon by Americans. This is a truth that was revealed at the birth of America, and has continued to be revealed many times in our history. The principle of self-defense is an American tradition that began at Lexington and Concord.

Minds Warped by Racism

We have come to comprehend the nature of racism. It is a mass psychosis. When I've described racial conditions in the United States to audiences of foreign newsmen, Cubans and other Latin Americans, they have been shocked to learn of the depths of American race hatred. When I have cited as illustrations such extreme situations as the segregation of telephone party-lines in Union County, or the segregated pet-animal cemetery in Washington, D.C., where an Afro-American cannot bury his dog, they find such things comic as well as pathetic.

Such extreme examples of the racist mentality only appear comic when looked upon as isolated phenomena. In truth they are perfectly logical applications of the premises that make up the racist mentality. Look at the phenomena this way and they are the logical inventions of a thoroughly diseased mind. The racist is a man crazed by hysteria at the idea of coming into equal human contact with Negroes. And this mass mental illness called racism is very much a part of the "American Way of Life."

When Afro-American liberation is finally achieved in the U.S.A., one of the many new developments in such a society will be some sort of institution that will correct those Americans whose minds are thoroughly warped by racism. Somehow a way will be found so that these insane people will be made whole, will be made well again.

"We Must Create a Black Militancy . . ."

This is the time for the Afro-American to act. Our sense of national consciousness and militancy is growing. I speak of the masses of people, the masses of Afro-Americans that I know and have visited; in Jacksonville, Florida; in Atlanta, in Savannah, and in Macon, Georgia; in Columbia, in Charleston, and in Greenville, South Carolina. The oppressed and exploited black men that I've met on the streets of Harlem, on the streets of Detroit, and in Chicago. And I speak of the people in Monroe where five years ago, when I started talking about self-defense, I would walk through the streets and many of my black neighbors would walk away to avoid me. Today, despite the FBI manhunt and my exile, despite the frame-up arrests and the shootings since, despite the intimidation campaigns like the one to drive Mrs. Johnson of *The Crusader* staff from Monroe, despite all of this, black Monroe continues its struggle.

As editor of *The Crusader,* I went south in the fall of 1960, deep into Jim Crowland, to observe the freedom struggle. I was confronted with this new wonderful spirit rising throughout Dixie —this determination to break the chains of bondage and the spirit of valor of a people who just a few years ago were submissive peons in civilization's no-man's-land. Daily, I saw the old myth about Afro-Americans being incapable of unity and action exploded.

In Savannah an NAACP leader had contributed $30,000 to the local branch. The branch has a full-time worker and a suite of office space. Pickets and sit-iners have been beaten, and jobs have been lost, but the struggle goes on. The leader is not afraid of violence to himself because the people are with him. In that city an Afro-American union leader said that it had come to pass that the masses of Afro-Americans can see that "We must defend ourselves against violence with violence." That many of them now say that the American white racist needs a good "whipping" to bring him down to earth and to break his white supremacy mania.

I learned in Atlanta that Mr. Elijah Muhammad had made quite an impression and that many Afro-Americans are learning, to the consternation and embarrassment of the black respectable leadership, that he has more to offer than weak prayers of deliverance. A prominent minister in South Carolina said, "Our biggest stumbling block is the Uncle Tom minister — the people must stop paying these traitors." In Atlanta, a university professor, energetic about the new spirit on the part of the Negroes, was very hopeful that new militant leadership would replace the old Uncle Toms, whose days, he was confident, were numbered.

There are exceptions among us. The Uncle Toms, the Judases, and the Quislings of the black "elite" would deny this rising consciousness. They do everything possible to make white Americans think that it is not true, while apologizing to us for the very people who oppress us. Some of these "responsible" Negroes are afraid that militant action damages "amiable race relations." They complain that race relations may deteriorate to a point that many Negroes may lose jobs. What they mean is that they may lose *their* jobs. For the black workers, who are the first to be fired, and last, if ever, to be hired, the situation is so bad it can't deteriorate.

We realize that there must be a struggle within our own ranks to take the leadership away from the black Quislings who betray us. Then the white liberals who are dumping hundreds of thousands of dollars into our struggle in the South to convert us to pacifism will have to accept *our* understanding of the situation or drop their liberal pretensions.

Why do the white liberals ask us to be non-violent? We are not the aggressors; we have been victimized for over 300 years! Yet nobody spends money to go into the South and ask the racists to be martyrs or pacifists. But they always come to the downtrodden Negroes, who are already oppressed and too submissive as a group, and they ask them not to fight back. There seems to be a pattern of some sort of strange coincidence of interest when whites preach a special doctrine to Negroes. Like the choice of theology when the plantation-owners saw to the Christianization of the slaves. Instead of the doctrines which produced the rugged aggressively independent and justice-seeking spirit that we associate with Colonial America as the New England Conscience, the slaves were indoctrinated in the most submissive "trust-your-master" pie-in-the-sky after-you-die form of Christianity.

It is because our militancy is growing that they spend hundreds of thousands of dollars to convert us into pacifists. Because our militancy is growing they come to us out of fear.

Of course, the respectable Negro leadership are the most outspoken exponents of non-violence. But if these people, especially the ministers, are such pure pacifists, why is it that so few, if any, criticize the war preparations of this country? Why is it that so few speak out against the Bomb? Isn't that the sort of preaching one expects and *hears* from sincere pacifists? The responsible Negro leadership is pacifist in so far as its one interest is that we do not fight white racists; that we do not "provoke" or enrage them. They constantly tell us that if we resort to violent self-defense we will be exterminated. They are not stopping violence — they are only stopping defensive violence against white racists out of a fear of extermination.

This fear of extermination is a myth which we've exposed in Monroe. We did this because we came to have an active understanding of the racist system and we grasped the relationship between violence and racism. The existence of violence is at the very heart of a racist system. The Afro-American militant is a "militant" because he defends himself, his family, his home, and his dignity. He does not *introduce* violence into a racist social system — the violence is already there, and has always been there. It is precisely this unchallenged violence that allows a racist social system to perpetuate itself. When people say that they are opposed to Negroes "resorting to violence" what they really mean is that they are opposed to Negroes defending themselves and challenging the exclusive monopoly of violence practiced by white racists. We have shown in Monroe that with violence working *both ways* constituted law will be more inclined to keep the peace.

When Afro-Americans resist and struggle for their rights they also possess a power greater than that generated by their will and their hands. With the world situation as it is today, the most racist and fascist United States government conceivable could not succeed in exterminating 20,000,000 people. We know there is a great power struggle going on in the world today, and the colored peoples control the true balance of power. We also know, from the statistics of the Detroit race riots, that production in this country would fall in forty-eight hours. People everywhere in the world would be ready to support our struggle.

Nor should we forget that this same deceiving pacifist-preaching well-to-do southern blacks profit from the struggle, living lives of luxury while most Afro-Americans continue to suffer. Are they any better than the Negro Quisling in neighboring Charleston, North Carolina—a black man who rode around in a new pink Cadillac with anti-NAACP and anti-integration literature, a huge roll of money, and an expense account, all the blessings of the White Citizens' Council? It is an ironic sign that black Judases are becoming more expensive as the white racist becomes desperate— though it is a small consolation to those of us who suffer from his betrayals.

In Monroe, where we fought the Klan, we were being penalized. There are children there growing up without any education, children without shoes, children without food. Old people without medical attention. For the Monroe Negro, there is no work; there is no welfare. From all the money raised in the North by the official black leadership, no one would send a penny to Monroe, because the white liberals who gave this money considered us to be outlaws and thugs. They preferred to let us suffer rather than to identify themselves with our position. They sent truck convoys into other places in the South, but penalized us because we took a militant stand.

But our children who are growing up without shoes are also growing up with a sense of direction they cannot obtain in the Jim Crow schools. There once was a threat, in Monroe, of Negro teen-age gang war. It abated as the teen-agers resolved their difficulties by coming to understand the problem. It is only natural to expect the black youth to be infected with a desire to do something. Frustrated by less active adults, this desire may be projected in the wrong direction. The vigor of the youth can be channeled into constructive militant actions. It is simply a matter of common sense to have these young Negroes constructively fight racial injustice rather than fight among themselves. Danger is not a respecter of color lines; it is better to bleed for a just cause than to bleed just for the thrill of the sight of blood. Rebellion ferments in modern youth. It is better that it expend itself against its true enemies than against teen-age schoolmates who can't even explain the reasons for their dangerous skirmishes.

The Montgomery bus boycott was perhaps the most successful example of completely pacifist action. But we must remember that in Montgomery, where Negroes are riding in the front of buses, there are also Negroes who are starving. The Montgomery bus boycott was a victory—but it was limited. It did not raise the Negro standard of living; it did not mean better education for Negro children, it did not mean economic advances.

Just what was the issue at hand for the white racists? What sacrifice? Remember that in Montgomery most of the white Americans have automobiles and are not dependent on the buses. It's just like our own experience in Monroe when we integrated the library. I just called the chairman of the board in my county. I told him that I represented the NAACP, that we wanted to integrate the library, and that our own library had burned down. And he said, "Well, I don't see any reason why you can't use the same library that our people use. It won't make any difference. And after all, I don't read anyway." Now, this is the attitude of a lot of white Southerners about the Montgomery bus boycott. The white people who control the city didn't ride the buses anyway; they had their own private cars, so it didn't make any difference to them.

But when Afro-Americans get into the struggle for the right to live as human beings and the right to earn the same amount of money, then they'll meet the greatest amount of resistance, and out of it will come police-condoned or -inspired violence. When that happens, the racist must be made to realize that in attacking us he risks his own life. After all, his life is a white life, and he considers the white life to be superior; so why should he risk a superior life to take an inferior one?

Now I believe, and a lot of other Negroes do too, that we must create a black militancy of our own. We must direct our own struggle, achieve our own destiny. We must realize that many Afro-Americans have become skeptical and extremely suspicious of the so-called white liberals who have dominated "Negro" freedom movements. They just feel that no white person can understand what it's like to be a suppressed Negro. The traditional white liberal leadership in civil rights organizations, and even white radicals, generally cannot understand what our struggle is and how we feel about it. They have always made our struggle secondary and after all these years we really never got any place.

They have a patient sense for good public relations. But we're not interested in a good press. We're interested in becoming free. We want to be liberated. To me, oppression is harmful. It is painful. I would wake up in the morning as a Negro who was oppressed. At lunchtime, I would eat as a Negro who was oppressed. At night, I would go to bed as a Negro who was oppressed. And if I could have been free in thirty seconds, it would not have been too soon.

"Too long have others spoken for us," began the first editorial in the first Afro-American newspaper, which began publication in 1827. The truth of these words has not dimmed in the century and a half since they first appeared in *Freedom's Journal*. They are more appropriate than ever.

There *are* white people who are willing to give us aid without strings attached. They are willing to let us direct our own struggle; they are genuinely interested in the liberation of the Negroes. I wouldn't have been able to remain in the South as long as I did if it had not been for the support that I got from some white people in the North. And I might never have succeeded in escaping the legal-lynching manhunt fomented by the FBI, nor have reached Cuban sanctuary but for the help of whites. They will be willing to continue helping us for the sake of justice, for the sake of human decency.

"Every Freedom Movement in the U.S.A.
Is Labeled 'Communist' "

I'm not a member and I've never been a member of the Communist Party. But most decent-minded Americans should realize by now that every movement for freedom that is initiated in the United States; every movement for human dignity, for decency; every movement that seeks fairness and social justice; every movement for human rights, is branded as "Communistic." Whenever a white person participates in a movement for black liberation, the movement is automatically branded as "under the domination of Moscow." I can't expect to be an exception.

This Communist-thing is becoming an old standard. An old standard accusation now. Anyone who uncompromisingly opposes the racists, anyone who scorns the religious fanatics and the super-duper American conservatives is considered a Communist.

This sort of thing gives the Communists a lot of credit, because certainly many people in my movement in the South don't know what a Communist is. Most of our people have never even heard of Marx. When you say Marx some of the people would think that maybe you were talking about a fountain pen or a New York City cab driver. Or the movie comedians.

But people aspire to be free. People want to be liberated when they are oppressed. No matter where the leadership comes from. The enslavement and suppression of Negroes in the American South were going on before Karl Marx was born, and Negroes have been rebelling against their oppression before Marxism came into existence. As far back as the 16th century, and the beginning of the 17th century, Negroes were even rebelling on the slave ships. The history of American Negro slavery was marked by very many conspiracies and revolts on the part of Negroes.

Certainly the Marxists have participated in the human rights struggle of Negroes, but Negroes need not be told by any philosophy or by any political party that racial oppression is wrong. Racial oppression itself inspires the Negro to rebellion. And it is on this ground that the people of Monroe protested; and on this ground that the people of Monroe refused to conform to the standard of Jim Crow life in a Jim Crow society. It is on this basis that they have struck out against the insanity of racial prejudice. We know that the Southern bigot, the Southern racist is mentally ill; that he is sick. The fact that Jim Crow discrimination and racial segregation may very well be based on economic exploitation is beside the point.

We are oppressed and no matter what the original cause or purpose of this oppression, the mind and personality of the racist doing the oppressing have been warped for so long that he is a mental case. Even if the economic situation is changed it will take quite a while, and it will require quite a shock, to cure this mental disease. I've read that one of the best treatments for some forms of mental illness is the shock treatment. And the shock treatment must come primarily from the Afro-American people themselves in conjunction with their white allies; in conjunction with the white youth.

This movement that I led was not a political organization. It had no political affiliations whatsoever. It was a movement of people who resented oppression. But I would say one thing about our movement. What happened in Monroe, North Carolina, had better become a lesson to the oppressors and the racists of America. Because it is symbolic of a new attitude, symbolic of a new era. It means that the Negro people are becoming restless. It means that there will be many more racial explosions in the days to come. Monroe was just the beginning. I dare predict that Monroe will become the symbol of the new Afro-American; a symbol of the Afro-American determined to rid himself of the stigma of race prejudice and the pain and torture of race hate and oppression at any cost.

Black Nationalism; Another Label

The label Black Nationalist is as meaningless as the Communist label. The Afro-American resents being set aside and oppressed, resents not being allowed to enter the mainstream of American society. These people who form their own groups, because they have been rejected, and start trying to create favorable societies of their own are called "Black Nationalists."

This is a misleading title. Because the first thing you must remember is that *I* am an Afro-American and *I've* been denied the right to enter the mainstream of society in the United States. As an Afro-American I am rejected and discriminated against. We are the most excluded, the most discriminated-against group in the United States; the most discriminated-against class. So it is only normal that I direct most of my energy toward the liberation of my people, who are the most oppressed class.

As for being a "Black Nationalist," this is a word that's hard to define. No, I'm not a "Black Nationalist" to the point that I would exclude whites or that I would discriminate against whites or that I would be prejudiced toward whites. I would prefer to think of myself as an *Inter-Nationalist*. That is, I'm interested in the problems of all mankind. I'm interested in the problems of

Africa, of Asia, and of Latin America. I believe that we all have the same struggle; a struggle for liberation. Discrimination and race hatred are undesirable, and I'm just as much against racial discrimination, in all forms, every place in the world, as I am against it in the United States.

What do we mean by "nationalism"? When you consider the present white American society it can be classified as nothing but a nationalistic society based on race. Yet as soon as an Afro-American speaks out for his people, and is conscious and proud of his people's historical roots and culture, he becomes a "nationalist." I don't mind these labels. I don't care what they call me. I believe in justice for all people. And because the Afro-American is the most exploited, the most oppressed in our society, I believe in working foremost for his liberation.

Non-Violence and Self-Defense

The tactics of non-violence will continue and should continue. We too believed in non-violent tactics in Monroe. We've used these tactics; we've used all tactics. But we also believe that any struggle for liberation should be a flexible struggle. We shouldn't take the attitude that one method alone is the way to liberation. This is to become dogmatic. This is to fall into the same sort of dogmatism practiced by some of the religious fanatics. We can't afford to develop this type of attitude.

We must use non-violence as a means as long as this is feasible, but the day will come when conditions become so pronounced that non-violence will be suicidal in itself. The day is surely coming when we will see more violence on the same American scene. The day is surely coming when some of the same Negroes who have denounced our using weapons for self-defense will be arming themselves. There are those who pretend to be horrified by the idea that a black veteran who shouldered arms for the United States would willingly take up weapons to defend his wife, his children, his home, and his life. These same people will one day be the loud advocates of self-defense. When violent racism and fascism strike at their families and their homes, not in a token way but in an all-out bloody campaign, then they will be among the first to advocate self-defense. They will justify their position as a question of survival. When it is no longer some distant Negro who's no more than a statistic, no more than an article in a newspaper; when it is no longer their neighbors, but it means them and it becomes a matter of personal salvation, then will their attitude change.

As a tactic, we use and approve non-violent resistance. But we also believe that a man cannot have human dignity if he allows himself to be abused; to be kicked and beaten to the ground, to allow his wife and children to be attacked, refusing to defend them and himself on the basis that he's so pious, so self-righteous, that it would demean his personality if he fought back.

We know that the average Afro-American is not a pacifist. He's not a pacifist and he has never been a pacifist and he's not made of the type of material that would make a good pacifist. Those who doubt that the great majority of Negroes are not pacifists, just let them slap one. Pick any Negro on any street corner in the U.S.A. and they'll find out how much he believes in turning the other cheek.

All those who dare to attack are going to learn the hard way that the Afro-American is not a pacifist; that he cannot forever be counted on not to defend himself. Those who attack him brutally and ruthlessly can no longer expect to attack him with impunity.

The Afro-American cannot forget that his enslavement in this country did not pass because of pacifist moral force or noble appeals to the Christian conscience of the slave-holders.

Henry David Thoreau is idealized as an apostle of non-violence, the writer who influenced Gandhi, and through Gandhi, Martin Luther King, Jr. But Thoreau was not dogmatic; his eyes were open and he saw clearly. I keep with me a copy of Thoreau's *Plea For Captain John Brown*. There are truths that are just as evident in 1962 as they were in 1859 when he wrote:

> . . . It was his [John Brown's] peculiar doctrine that a man has a perfect right to interfere by force with the slaveholder, in order to rescue the slave. I agree with him. They who are continually shocked by slavery have some right to be shocked by the violent death of the slaveholder, but such will be more shocked by his life than by his death. I shall not be forward to think him mistaken in his method who quickest succeeds to liberate the slave.
>
> I speak for the slave when I say, that I prefer the phil-

anthropy of Captain Brown to that philanthropy which neither
shoots me nor liberates me. . . . I do not wish to kill nor to be
killed, but I can foresee circumstances in which both these
things would be by me unavoidable. We preserve the so-called
peace of our community by deeds of petty violence every day.
Look at the policeman's billy and handcuffs! Look at the
jail! . . . We are hoping only to live safely on the outskirts of
this provisional army. So we defend ourselves and our hen-
roosts, and maintain slavery. I know that the mass of my
countrymen think that the only righteous use that can be made
of Sharpe's rifles and revolvers is to fight duels with them,
when we are insulted by other nations, or to hunt Indians, or
shoot fugitive slaves with them or the like. I think that for
once the Sharpe's rifles and the revolvers were employed in a
righteous cause. The tools were in the hands of one who could
use them.

The same indignation that is said to have cleared the temple
once will clear it again. The question is not about the weapon,
but the spirit in which you use it. No man has appeared in
America, as yet, who loved his fellowman so well, and treated
him so tenderly. He [John Brown] lived for him. He took up
his life and he laid it down for him. What sort of violence is
that which is encouraged, not by soldiers, but by peaceable
citizens, not so much by laymen as by ministers of the Gospel,
not so much by the fighting sects as by the Quakers, and not
so much by Quaker men as by Quaker women?

This event advertises me that there is such a fact as death;
the possibility of a man's dying. It seems as if no man had
ever died in America before; for in order to die you must first
have lived.

It is in the nature of the America Negro, the same as all other
men, to fight and try to destroy those things that block his path
to a greater happiness in life.

"The Future Belongs to Today's Oppressed"

Whenever I speak on the English-language radio station in
Havana (which broadcasts for an audience in the United States)
I hope in some way to penetrate the mental barriers and introduce
new disturbing elements into the consciousness of white America.

I hope to make them aware of the monstrous evil that they are party to by oppressing the Negro. Somehow, I must manage to clearly reflect the image of evil that is inherent in a racist society so that white America will be able to honestly and fully see themselves as they really are. To see themselves with the same clarity as foreigners see them and to recognize that they are not champions of democracy. To understand that today they do not really even *believe in* democracy. To understand that the world is changing regardless of whether they *think* they like it or not.

For I know that if they had a glimpse of their own reality the shock would be of great therapeutic value. There would be many decent Americans who would then understand that this society must mend its ways if it is to survive; that there is no place in the world now for a racist nation.

As an individual, I'm not inclined toward "politics." The only thing I care about is justice and liberation. I don't belong to any political party. But I think that as long as the present politics prevails the Negro is not going to be integrated into American society. There will have to be great political changes before that can come about.

Those Americans who most deny the logic of the future are the ones who have driven me into exile. Those people have been cruel. Yet cruel as it may be, this exile was not the end those people had planned for me. But it is not in the hands of today's oppressors to determine my end. Their role in history denies to them an understanding of this, just as their role will not allow them to understand that every true nationalist leader in Africa has been imprisoned or exiled, and that the future leaders of Latin American and Asian national liberation today are experiencing imprisonment, exile, or worse.

The future belongs to today's oppressed and I shall be witness to that future in the liberation of the Afro-American.

MAULANA RON KARENGA

from *The Quotable Karenga*

1. BLACK CULTURAL NATIONALISM

There is no such thing as individualism, we're all Black. The only thing that saved us from being lynched like Emmett Till or shot down like Medger Evers was not our economics or social status, but our absence.

The white boy is engaged in the worship of technology; we must not sell our souls for money and machines.

A Nationalist has a love of the people and values of his nation.

Cultural background transcends education. Having a scope is different from having a content.

We must address ourselves to needs, not desires. When we fill our concrete need then we will talk about desires.

Membership in the Black community requires more than just physical presence.

In terms of history, all we need at this point is heroic images; the white boy got enough dates for everybody.

US is a cultural organization dedicated to the creation, recreation and circulation of Afro-American culture.

Perhaps the teachings of *US* are harsh but it's better to work with hard facts than to play with pleasant but unproductive dreams.

A value system has three functions: it gives some predictability of behavior, it is an ultimate authority and it serves as a means of security.

If we could get a nigger to see how worthless, unimportant, ignorant and weak he is by himself, then we will have made a contribution.

I reject individualism for I am of all Black men. I am Joe the sharecropper, John the janitor and Mose the miner. When they catch hell, I catch hell!

The white man is a conglomeration of the Black man's contradictions.

The only real things *Negroes* produce are problems and babies.

Nationalism doesn't come in a day, it doesn't come in a week, or a month, not even a year—it takes a lifetime.

If by primitive you mean more natural, we need to be more primitive.

The *Negro* is made and manufactured in America.

Other people's approach to the problem is necessary but not sufficient. Our approach, the cultural approach, is both necessary and sufficient.

All *Negroes* want to be capitalists—and ain't none of them got any capital.

A Nationalist should be a man who saves his brothers from a leaking boat. But he should also teach them how to save themselves by being good swimmers.

The *Negro* works on a two-fold economy: he buys what he wants and begs what he needs.

Nationalism demands study. Show me a true Nationalist and I'll show you someone who studies.

The fact that we are Black is our ultimate reality. We were Black before we were born.

The white boy was teaching reverse racism when he taught us to hate ourselves.

Why is it so difficult for Black people to say I got this from Malcolm, I got this from Frederick Douglass, I got this from Muhammad? Why is this so difficult? We quote Shakespeare, Sartre, Camus. We quote everybody but Black people.

We're not for isolation but interdependence—but we can't become interdependent unless we have something to offer.

The difference between training and education is that in training you can't do anything by yourself; in education you can take that which you've learned and apply it to concrete needs.

Blacks must develop their own heroic images. To the white boy, Garvey was a failure—to us he was perfect for his time and context. To the white boy Malcolm X was a hate teacher—to us he was the highest form of Black Manhood in his generation.

We can live with whites interdependently once we have Black Power.

If you know you are Black then your purpose is to build Black.

We say *Negroes* are suffering from "mass insanity." Any man who burns his hair, bites his lips, or bleaches his skin has got to be insane.

Nationalism is not merely a response to white oppression, but a need for Black people to come together.

We must free ourselves culturally before we succeed politically.

Socially speaking, we want our effects to be collective or more clearly communal rather than collective. For, to be communalistic is to share willingly, but to be collectivistic is to force to share, which is a European concept.

You have to make a distinction between history writers and historians. History writers write what the power structure dictates. Historians create concrete images. Therefore Blacks must be their own historians and develop their own heroic images and heroic deeds.

All Nationalists believe in creativity in opposition to destruction. And a Nationalist must create for the Nation.

The purpose of a Nationalist should be to build and make the Black Nation eternal.

We say Blackness is three things—color, culture and consciousness.

Money is not the answer to the problem unless we have a value for spending it. There are some *Negro* millionaires but they ain't benefiting us. WHY? No values.

US doctrine is a shield to protect you, a weapon to attack with and a pillow of peace to rest your head on.

The Seven-fold path of Blackness is to Think Black, Talk Black, Act Black, Create Black, Buy Black, Vote Black, and Live Black.

To go back to tradition is the first step forward.

Nationalism in its primitive stage uproots people without giving them an alternative. We never take away what we can't replace and improve.

We must institute holidays which speak directly to the needs of Black people.

Nationalism is a belief that Black people in this country make up a cultural nation.

A cultural nation is a people with a common past, a common present and, hopefully, a common future.

Our society may be American, but our values must be Afro-American.

Yesterday we thought we were Negroes. Today we know we are Black men but we still have some Negro hang-ups.

We stress culture because it gives identity, purpose and direction. It tells us who we are, what we must do, and how we can do it.

If we can wear a French beret, a Russian hat and Italian shoes and not feel funny, we should be able to wear an Afro-American Buba.

Man is only man in a philosophy class or a biology lab. In the world he is African, Asian or South American. He is a Chinese making a cultural revolution, or an Afro-American with soul. He lives by bread and butter, enjoys red beans and rice, or watermelon and ice-cream.

No man is any more than the context to which he owes his existence.

Blacks can't be truly creative until they have a cultural context to create out of.

Culture is the basis of all ideas, images and actions. To move is to move culturally, i.e., by a set of values given to you by your culture.

The seven criteria for culture are:
1. Mythology
2. History
3. Social Organization
4. Political Organization
5. Economic Organization
6. Creative Motif
7. Ethos

Negroes have been copying white culture so long and are so mixed-up from doing so, they think it's theirs.

We don't borrow from Africa. We utilize that which was ours to start with.

Culture provides the bases for revolution and recovery.

To talk Black is to start talking "we" instead of "me."

2. REVOLUTION

The revolution being fought now is a revolution to win the minds of our people. If we fail to win this we cannot wage the violent one.

Sometimes brothers get so hung up in the myth of revolution that they talk about bringing America to her knees and can't even wipe out one police station.

A revolt is an attempt to overthrow the system; while the revolution is the complete overthrow of that system.

A lot of brothers play revolutionary; they read a little Fanon, a little Mao and some Marx. Although this information is necessary it is not sufficient for we must develop a new plan of revolution for Black people here in America.

You can't fight a revolution on a local level. It has to be fought through a national struggle.

We must fight for the right of self-determination, race pride and the pursuit of Blackness.

The only thing that will make us invincible is for us to fight— to fight for our freedom and not our personal selves—to fight to get back the freedom we lost in 1565.

Negroes who envy leaders who have an education don't understand revolution. Mao had an education; Nkrumah had an education; all people who have waged revolution have had an education. But the thing that keeps them revolutionary is that they are tired of the ways of the white man.

The more you learn, the more resentful you are of this white man. Then you see how he's tricking your people, emasculating your men, raping your women and using his power to keep you down.

The white boy has been waging a race war ever since he has been here. Now that we plan to retaliate he calls us racists.

Blacks live right in the heart of America. That is why we are best able to cripple this man. And once we understand our role we won't talk revolution, we'll make it.

The white boy knows if he moves against us he moves against himself. If he drops an A-bomb it's got to get some of them. If he drops poison gas the wind might change and it will go to his neighborhood.

When the word is given we'll see how tough you are. When it's "burn", let's see how much you burn. When it's "kill", let's see how much you kill. When it's "blow up", let's see how much you blow up. And when it's "take that white girl's head too", we'll really see how tough you are.

Whenever Blacks revolt, white people use every issue but racism as the cause.

The sad thing about revolution is that the strong brothers will be moved on first. It will be the dead brother who wakes up who will continue the revolution.

We are revolutionists. We believe in change. We believe in being realistic, but as for reality, we have come to change it.

We cannot have a revolution without direction, and that direction can only come through an ideology developed for our own situation.

To play revolution is to get put down.

We are the last revolutionaries in America. If we fail to leave a legacy of revolution for our children we have failed our mission and should be dismissed as unimportant.

Revolution to us is the creation of an alternative.

There must be a cultural revolution before the violent revolution. The cultural revolution gives identity, purpose and direction.

We must gear the money going from the church to the support of the revolution. Revolution cannot succeed without finance.

No revolt is isolated. When Blacks revolt in any section of the country it is an expression of the entire nation of Afro-America.

The American revolution is sacred to whites, and Black revolts are sacred to us.

If we fight we might be killed. But it is better to die as a man than live like a slave.

Black people must understand history and from historical knowledge we can evolve our own theory of revolution.

There are two kinds of violent movements. The first is defensive violence and the second is pre-emptive violence which means moving against the enemy if you know the enemy is going to move against you.

We say with Touré that for *US* there are no intellectuals, no students, no workers, no teachers; there are only supporters of the organization.

I remember my mother used to tell me—if you're bad the devil will get you. I didn't know that until the cops came.

He who convinces others appears to be together, but he who convinces himself is together.

We have to believe without reservation in our struggle, because there is so much we don't understand.

Failure is not bad in itself, only resignation is bad. For an African proverb says "to stumble is not to fall, but to go forward faster."

We as Black people must assume our "role" not our "place" for we must determine our own destiny and we will not be assigned any place.

We say that practice is better than theory, for we do not need any more ideas. If we could just practice the ones we have now we could answer the need of our struggle.

Talking general truisms is necessary but not sufficient. To say the white man is the devil is not enough. What are we going to do about it?

If we can't agree on who we are, then we can't agree on who our opposition is.

Sometimes a man moves by reason, but most of the time he moves by emotion. That's why we say that the first commitment is an emotional one.

Under the tactics of non-violence, politics have not become more moral. On the contrary, morality has become more political.

Violence in itself without consideration for time or circumstance is as inadequate as non-violence.

Non-violence gives the white man a license to destroy wherever and whenever he wishes.

As for the pacifist—you can't tell me you love your brother if you teach him a philosophy which will ultimately lead to his destruction.

Black people need a revolutionary school where we can be educated rather than trained.

The *Negro* is like the rat on a cylinder. The rat is running but he ain't going nowhere. He's got to keep running just in order to stand still!

It was necessary and revolutionary for the Muslims to come saying the white man is the devil because the *Negro* thought he was "God."

The emphasis on white oppression is no longer sufficient; we must also begin to praise Black achievement.

We must make warriors out of our poets and writers. For if all our writers would speak as warriors our battle would be half won. Literature conditions the mind and the battle for the mind is the first half of the struggle.

We must not be so busy showing our superiority as Nationalists that our audience leaves before we do.

We have an advantage in that the white boy doesn't take us seriously. The problem is neither does this *Negro*.

We must tell Blacks they are great and then make them so.

We have come to undermine the myth of white superiority.

Only thing non-violence proved was how savage whites were.

Racist minds created racist institutions. Therefore we must move against racism, not institutions. For even if we tear down the institutions, that same mind will build them up again.

The Black pacifist will have to give up his love for philosophy in order to satisfy his people's need for security. For phrases and formulas, quotes and quips, are poor protection in the street, or even at home, against bombs, bullets and beast-like men.

The white man tricked us into fighting to be given civil rights when all along we should have been fighting to exercise human rights. For human rights cannot be given, they can only be exercised.

If we can anticipate history, then we can make it.

We must not ask anything from the world but take something to it. We are not here to be taught by the world, but to teach the world.

CHARLES V. HAMILTON

Riots, Revolts and Relevant Response

The United States has experienced, as of 1967, its fourth consecutive summer season of major explosions in its cities' ghettos: burnings, lootings, killings, injuries and mass arrests. The mass media and public officials have consistently referred to these occurrences as riots—race riots. It is clear that the events have become virtually institutionalized; they have become part of what we might call "societal expectations." Around January and February of each year questions will be asked whether we can expect "another long hot summer," what cities we can expect to explode. Local mayors and others will get busy putting together remedial summer-time programs to occupy the potential "rioters": give them menial summer jobs; take them on little trips out of the ghettos to nice, green farms on week-ends; provide them with make-shift little swimming pools to splash around in in front of suffocating tenements. And in some places, when the inevitable happens, we can expect a "commission" of "blue-ribboned" persons to be appointed to "investigate" the causes. At times (as in Watts in '64 and Detroit in '67), we will hear great surprise expressed because those places "were not typical ghettos." They either were not like the tall-tenement-type of Harlem ghetto or had an "enlightened" mayor who had received Negro support (and had rewarded that support with Negro appointees to public office). Perhaps we will hear that a certain city was an unexpected target because the anti-poverty program there was "considered" a success.

Invariably, we can expect officials and private commentators to conclude: 1) these are riots having nothing to do with civil rights; 2) only a very small percentage of black people participate; 3) law and order must be maintained. There will be variations, but not too many.

This article will deal with various aspects of the above mentioned expectations. And it will suggest that:

1) what many official and unofficial decision-makers call "riots" is a serious misnomer in terms of understanding what is happening and for charting solutions;

2) the society is confronted with the overt manifestations of repetitive revolts (not *just* riots) against a presumed legitimacy of the system—a presumption held by the larger society. These are revolts born precisely out of a growing alienation from and rejection of many of the basically irrelevant premises and principles of the society;

3) a viable response demands that the decision-makers stop treating the problems solely as matters of control (anti-riot laws, maintaining law and order) or solely as matters of remedial distribution of goods and services (a few jobs here and there, a few housing units remodeled, etc.). It demands that we begin to accept the fact that this is a *systemic* problem, that is, the socio-political, economic system as it now stands is invalid for treating the causes of the revolts.

In other words, if absolutely tight control is clamped on the ghettos—curfews, armed guards, apartheid—this will only increase the danger, not alleviate it. Likewise, if black people are simply *given* more handouts, this will only perpetuate the present status of ghetto colonialism. Until black people actually have their full share in decision-making power, this society has not begun to address itself to its most crucial problem. And to provide for that, we are talking about the drastic transformation of the *nature* of the socio-political system itself, its values as well as its institutions. Let me deal with each of the three categories separately.

The Misnomer of Riots.

We may define an act of rioting as one constituting the unlawful and chaotic destruction of property, such as burning and looting, which, as has occurred in the racial explosions, frequently involves armed sniping at law enforcement and fire officials. In the riot situation, we see people, collectively in small or large groups and individually, breaking into stores, helping themselves to whatever merchandise they can carry, then perhaps applying a match to the premises. We see snipers from rooftops attempting to impede the work of firemen called to put out the fire, etc. These acts are clearly identified by the laws of the larger society as criminal acts. There are statutes on the books spelling out penalties. Invariably, then, we hear that the ghetto explosions are simply riots performed by "hoodlums," the riff-raff, by not more than two or three per cent of the total Negro community. We are told that the "right thinking" Negro community condemns these unlawful acts as much as the property owner whose store has been destroyed. And when the pronouncement is made (usually on the second day) that "law and order must be restored and chaos will not be tolerated," this means that the rioting will be suppressed by whatever military force is available and necessary.

The entire episode is interpreted as an event caused by "mad dogs" (California Governor Ronald Reagan's term) who are interested in getting something for nothing. This opinion is fortified by the view that while only the slightest incident ignited it (an arrest attempt, normally), the flames of excitement are fanned by agitators—inside and outside—who take advantage of mob frenzy to perpetuate the seemingly uncontrollable, emotional situation. Therefore, if the riot was not, in fact, caused by an organized group, it is perpetuated by organized bands who then effectively stir up the people and prolong it.

Thus, whatever effective remedies to end the situation are taken, those control remedies are sanctioned by the overall public. If it is "necessary" to shoot looters (or even those suspected of looting) in the back, this is acceptable. If a person does not respond readily to a national guardsman's command at bayonet point to "move on," the public sanctions the harshest solution to move him on—rifle butt or whatever other means.

The society's full attention is focussed on the acts of looting, burning and sniping. And the entire confrontation is thereby characterized as a "riot."

The fact is that this is a misnomer because the overt, observable acts are the least important of all. In whatever way the society's opinion-leaders decide to characterize the explosions, the fact that black people run through the streets with color television sets and other items on their shoulders is not at all the essence of the problem. It may well be that focussing on such things is the only way this society can relate to the question. But to label the situation as a "riot" and to proceed to deal with it solely in terms of effective control, solely in terms of criminal law enforcement, clearly blinds the decision-makers to the more fundamental problems involved. The goal of the political leaders becomes merely to end the riotous disturbance, to restore "law and order," to impose obedience to duly constituted authority.

Political Legitimacy and Revolts.

We cannot term these events riots precisely because, in the minds of many of the people breaking the windows and burning the property, that authority is not duly constituted. They are, in fact, revolts. By this we mean that they are acts which deny the very legitimacy of the system itself. The entire value structure which supports property rights over human rights, which *sanctions* the intolerable conditions in which the black people have been *forced* to live is questioned. They are revolts because the black people are saying that they no longer intend to abide by an oppressive notion of "law and order." That law and that order mean the perpetuation of an *intolerable* status quo. Imbedded in that status quo is an ingrained racist attitude which relegated the black people to a subordinated, suppressed status in the first place. That relegation was deliberate and conscious and vicious, having absolutely nothing to do with inaccurate views about the basic character of the black man. That status quo meant that black people would continue to be sacrificed to a more valued goal of maximizing profits from the colonized ghetto. That status quo meant that the traditional political procedures for alleviating one's ills were not sufficient.

Black people are told that if they have grievances they should take them to court or to the "bargaining table." Occasionally they are told that they must pursue the traditional political processes of the ballot.

But we know that these accepted principles of legitimacy are no longer applicable to vast masses of black people in the ghetto. These people have become alienated from those principles. For them, the system is no longer legitimate. By this we mean that the institutions of the society (the courts, the traditional political parties, the police, the educational institutions) are no longer seen as willing or able to meet the pressing needs of a majority of black people—*qua* black people—in this society. If an individual black person wishes to escape the oppression, he must renounce his black heritage, act as if he were white, conform to white standards and ideas of himself, and maybe then he will be permitted to climb out of the muck and mire. This is interpreted to him as conformity to the Anglo-Ethic of Work and Achievement; if he works hard, he will achieve, just like all other minority groups in the past. The fact has come home, however, that the Ethic (if ever it was applicable to white America) has no relevancy in the lives and history of masses of blacks. In addition, the explosions in the ghettos are not participated in by the handful of black middle class, but rather by the large lower class who correctly see themselves as perennial victims of public policy. They know that the system, as it is now constituted, has no intention of making room for them. Too much history to the contrary has shown otherwise.

Therefore, the *revolts* are the overt denials of legitimacy. True, they are threatening "law and order"—not to get a color television set, but to say to the larger society that a wholly new norm of "law and order" must be established. These are revolts against white America's conception of legitimacy vis-à-vis race in this country. This is a legitimacy which says that black people should accept their subordinated and suppressed status, that since they are only ten to twelve per cent of the total population, they must always accept the crumbs which the remaining majority (with all the economic, political and psychological power) is willing to drop down to them. This is a legitimacy which says that in a pluralistic society each group ultimately gets its grievances attended to, that changes do not come "overnight," but rather they come by stages. The accepted legitimacy says that we must pursue a politics of limited objectives, that the "democratic" mystique provides for ultimate alleviation of grievances.

The acts we have been witnessing for the last four consecutive summers are properly described as *revolts* against these anachronistic principles of legitimacy. They are *revolts* which say in no uncertain terms that the black people no longer believe in this system. They no longer believe that they will ever be able to improve their condition—even by stages—through the normal processes. This is *their* conception of socio-political reality; and *their* conception is the relevant one precisely because they are the ones doing the suffering.

Neither is this conception inaccurate. There is more than substantial evidence that while white America was lauding itself on the "progress" it had been making in race relations, the objective fact is that the day-to-day lives of the majority of black people were becoming progressively worse. Housing conditions were deteriorating, not improving; schools in the ghettos were getting worse and worse, not better and better; jobs were becoming harder to find, not easier. And yet we had more civil rights laws, more judicial decisions favoring black people, more white people marching side by side with blacks against segregation and discrimination. These were the surface impressions which covered up the fact that all those outward manifestations of systemic adaptation to black demands were sheer myths. The fact that a few black people received high public office or "made it" in the white world was set forth as living and breathing evidence of "progress," but this was blatantly irrelevant to the daily lives of the masses of blacks. And so when the revolts came, white America was shocked. It had actually believed its rhetoric, its concepts of what was legitimate. White arrogance is so imbedded that it could not allow for any notions contrary to its own.

Thus, the simmering summers of the sixties have been revolts, not just riots, and realization of that fact would be advisable for a society that must now give a response.

The revolts speak to the society in still another way. It has been assumed that oppressed, minority people in the country would ultimately not push their demands to the point of violence. After all, the assumption was that, given a majority in possession of the overwhelming predominance of power, the minority surely would capitulate. This assumption has completely overlooked the fact that the power equation is not *entirely* stacked in favor of the majority. The revolts have been saying: "You see, we too have some modicum of power, if it's only the power to destroy, to disrupt." Like all power, this minority weapon is as useful in the fact of its *potential* threat as in its actual use. Therefore, given clear evidence, now, that black people are willing to destroy their oppressors' property, to disrupt their normal business cycle, it may well be that the white decision-makers will be forced to view the relations between the races in different terms; the cards are *not* all stacked in their favor. The revolts have established the credibility of the blacks' willingness to use their power if they are forced to do so. *Now,* when the ground rules for bargaining are discussed, and when the agenda to be discussed is drawn up, it will not be a completely unilateral affair. The fact is—and apparently this was never quite clear to white America before— that black people have the power at their disposal to deny peace and stability to the larger society.

Relevant Response or Repressive Reaction.

At all times it has been clear that the ultimate decisions to change lie with the white community. That community can choose to listen to the demands of the black revolts and attempt seriously to deal with them, or it can diligently pursue a policy of extermination. If it chooses the first alternative, it must be clear what that involves.

Such an alternative clearly means that precisely because this society has lost its legitimacy vis-à-vis the black American, the solutions must take into account the imbedded distrust and suspicion blacks have of whites. Not only must programs be devised and funded to rebuild the black community, but black people must have a major share of the decision-making process. Black people need much more than benefits *from* the decision-making process; they must be viable participants *in* that process. It is not enough to develop and implement a crash educational program for the ghettos; blacks must control their local school systems, just as other ethnic and racial groups control theirs. It is not enough to implement employment programs; black people must have an initial voice in the planning of those programs. It becomes crucial to understand that this does not mean white hand-picked Negro leaders. The black participants must be products of the black community from which they come, and they must, first and foremost, be responsive to that community. I am suggesting that this is the only feasible way at this juncture to establish *legitimacy* in the minds of the black people. We need not talk at this point about the particular new forms or structures that will be devised to implement this. The fact is that those new forms will be devised to fit the particular indigenous situation. Relevant responses on the part of the larger society will recognize that only when black people feel a personal stake in the society will they move to protect that society. Only then will the society *deserve* protecting. Only then will the society be legitimate.

Thus far, most of the suggested remedies (short of military control) have overlooked this crucial factor of legitimate participation in decision-making. The "maximum feasible participation" formula in the Economic Opportunity Act is a farce and has been sacrificed to the priorities of irrelevant local political parties. Even the investigating committees have overlooked the possible contributions to be made by adding ghetto citizens to their deliberations, officially. All these decisions have been widening the legitimacy gap. And as these things happen, we should not be heard to register shock when the revolts occur time and again. We should not delude ourselves into thinking that incremental, half-hearted, non-participatory solutions will suffice.

The alternatives are clear, and the money used to rediscover this should be diverted to stimulating a relevant response. It is senseless and wasteful to continue mouthing the old clichés, advocating the anachronistic principles, issuing the same meaningless statements. This society is not faced with a traditional type of problem that lends itself to traditional approaches. If the revolts say anything, they speak to this with loud and unmistakable clarity.

FLOYD B. McKISSICK

Programs for Black Power

Hillel, the Jewish philosopher, once said,

> If I am not for myself, who will be for me?
> If I am only for myself, what am I?
> If not now, when?

This quotation summarizes in a real sense what Black Power is all about.

The time spent in definitions and in arguing the many ramifications of this concept has little significance if programmatic measures have not evolved to give life and breath, as it were, to the doctrine.

We should remember that the Black Power Movement attempts to secure power for Black Americans in six specific areas; in other words, it seeks to achieve power for Black people in six different ways. These are:

1. The growth of Black *political* power.
2. The building of Black *economic* power.
3. The improvement of the *self-image* of Black people.
4. The development of Black *leadership*.
5. The attainment of *Federal law enforcement*.
6. The mobilization of Black *consumer* power.

It is incontrovertible that these important ideals must pass beyond mere rhetoric. Programs must be initiated and relentlessly pursued in order to develop the wide organizational base necessary to achieve our ultimate goal of equality in American life. Some of these programs are herein described.

Among these efforts, none has been more difficult to implement than our political projects. In Louisiana, under the leadership of Ike Reynolds, CORE has developed a political movement that was instrumental in creating a series of Voter Registration organizations. This movement submitted nine candidates for election on November 8, 1966. Eight of them won seats; principally on the local school boards. For the first time in fifty years, Black people in several parishes in Louisiana now have officials that will serve their needs and make decisions to fulfill their aspirations. This is an example of Black Power in the political field.

In Opalousa, Louisiana, a sweet potato cooperative has been created. Farm laborers have bought land and are working it jointly and selling the produce for their own benefit. Organized by John Zippert, young CORE Task Force worker from New York, the cooperative now has 375 Black farmers. The success of this project has caused 15 small white farmers to join the combine. The special methods and marketing techniques learned there will be applied in other parts of the country. This is an illustration of Black economic power.

In Baltimore, Maryland, under the leadership of Antoine Perot, a CORE field secretary, a freedom school has been established with thirty teachers and two hundred students, ranging in ages from eight to eighty. Negro history, art, music and other aspects of Black culture are presented in order to make Black people aware of their contributions to the American heritage and to world civilization. More than anything else this showed Black people as important to the development of Western civilization. It is, therefore, an excellent example of the drive for the improvement of the Negro self-image.

Extensive conferences and leadership programs have taken place in Virginia, Maryland, New York and in California. These programs bring together the potential indigenous leadership of the Black community. Indoctrination in the new philosophy, training in leadership techniques and the development of verbal skills are aspects of this program. This is an example of the development of Black leadership.

Better and more extensive federal law enforcement is a constant objective of this phase of the Black Power doctrine. The Congress of Racial Equality maintains a legal department that seeks federal law enforcement in the numerous cases where local law enforcement officers have been guilty of discriminatory practices under cover of law or of failure to protect Black citizens and white Civil Rights workers from harm. Additionally, CORE chapters develop volunteer legal panels which appear in court to protect the rights of CORE workers who are arrested during demonstrations, detained without due process of law or involved in cases where constitutional considerations are present. Since all these instances press for improved federal enforcement, they show efforts in the search for the attainment of federal law enforcement.

The mobilization of Black consumer power is demonstrated by the urban chapters which developed consumer education and initiated protests and selective buying against economic exploitation by retailers in the poverty ghettos. The Brooklyn chapter recently made a survey of butcher shops and vegetable stands in the Bedford-Stuyvesant area and discovered that many of the merchants were offering inferior meat and inferior vegetables at higher prices than in the white neighborhoods. Unsanitary conditions prevailed in many of the facilities. The presence of an organized group protesting this disgraceful merchandising immediately improved conditions. Legal complaints were sought for the more intransigent merchants, who will now provide better merchandise or be forced to close shop. Here is an illustration of the mobilization of Black consumer power.

These programs and similar projects together constitute what has become known as the Black Power doctrine. Black Americans are aware that they live in a racist society that functions on the belief in white supremacy — sometimes open and sometimes secret. Black Power will serve to strengthen and encourage the Black American in his quest for equality; for united, he can fight against this evil. Thus, Black Power will become the key to the vast organization of Black people throughout the country so that they can, by the strength of numbers, effect meaningful change in the world in which they live.

The economic, political and cultural goals we have described, and the strength of people united for a cause that is just will be accomplished when sufficient power is developed by Black people to topple the bastion of discrimination and to end the long night of injustice.

NATHAN HARE

How White Power Whitewashes Black Power

Nobody much — let alone black people — had ever heard of the "Black Muslims" until the white press discovered them and the white liberals and their Negro cohorts began to speculate on how much they were "hurting the Negro's cause." This had the peculiar ring of an echo from those years when the same tune was sung about the National Association for the Advancement of Colored People — Communist front they called it, I remember. Now, whites wish they had the NAACP back and, soon it seems, the "Black Muslims" whom they were trying a few years ago to place on the subversive list. The lesson to be gained from this is that standards of militancy change with the times and the public definition of a social movement may affect it in unanticipated ways. The "Black Muslims" (nobody says "Black Baptists," though their liturgy may differ from white Baptists) might still be waddling in cultish oblivion had not white antagonism exposed them to angry and oppressed blacks elsewhere in the land. The same is true of the slogan "black power" and the farcical efforts to "define" it.

What is *white* power? That is what is most in need of defining. But "United States and European radicals accept white power as so natural that they do not even see its color," James Boggs wrote in *Liberator* magazine last Spring. It is not clear to me whether they really do not see its color or do not see that they are safely lying. What is white power?

White power is what causes black persons to earn a family income about half that of whites, now as half a century ago. White power produces the conditions (undernourishment, inadequate medical care, etc.) which cause black persons to die on the average ten years before their time; it is genocidal. White power sends black persons on the double to die in Vietnam, further depleting the ranks of black males and leading to further "family disorganization." Then it sends in missionary-minded white social scientists to make a report on the black family, study it and bemoan its high state of decay — which it, white power, produced!

The lexicographic confusion over the term "black power" is, then, but a whey-eyed conspiracy to defame it and its philosophy. Negro leaders and leading Negroes are trotted out one by one to give their particular connotation of it, or to denounce it for the same reasons they are placed before microphones to squash (or try to) any serious black rebellion which erupts.

And yet, what starts out as an effort to defame a concept quite frequently results in its promotion. People know what "power" means, even if they cannot quite put it into words. Power is the probability that the will of a person or group will be carried out by another, or the ability of a person to exercise influence over the behavior of another, even against his will when necessary. It may be institutionalized (authority) or charismatic (personal charm) or naked (force). Almost always it involves some assent on the part of the object of power. Nobody can make a person do anything but confine his body to a certain area or position, or make him die. Why is it, for example, that strong men such as Sonny Liston, Muhammad Ali, Bobo Brazil, and Nathan Hare will bow down to weak men such as Lyndon Baines Johnson and college deans? There is, somewhere, for whatever reason, some form of acquiescence. Both black and white children are taught in school to honor white Patrick Henry (yes, the color of his skin does and did matter) who stood and said "give me liberty or give me death." Should a Negro stand and say the self-same words, they would more than likely give him death. Still, the choice rests with the obedient.

People know, or eventually come to see, the meaning of power. They also know what black means — a word for the exotic, a word for mystery, the color of the clothes worn by men of the cloth and the color of the clothes generally worn to formal, dignified occasions. It is a word for something intriguing and terrifying. Such qualities can also, someday somehow, be those of men who are black. Presently they are not, not under white power.

Black Power means the exercise of influence over the behavior of white oppressors to the benefit of blacks — by any means available, by any methods which seem desirable. We take little stock in such lexicographers as Whitney Young who say they believe in polka-dot power: black and white together. Black power, they say, is the maroon of the textbook, the green of the dollar bill, the gray of the pay envelope. But my pay envelope is brown and what's inside, the paycheck, is blue and often leaves me feeling, if not looking, the same way.

We didn't believe James Meredith when he went hobbling down that Mississippi highway last summer, sporting piety, with a Bible tucked conspicuously in his palm. A white fellow took one blast of buckshot to correct the idea that a Bible has more power than a bullet. On Meredith's second march, he rightly left his Bible on the bookshelf, where it belongs. Many other shams from the fountain of white trickology are now being shelved by the proponents of black power.

Take the nonviolence hypocrisy. No doubt some white or white-minded readers were startled by the reference above to "any means available." Yes, that includes violence — repeat, yes — especially in retaliation. Allan Silver has pointed out in an essay in a book called *The Police* that rioting and pillaging, for example, comprise the only means black ghetto inmates have of addressing the white establishment and its black lackeys. But aggressive violence is one thing, retaliatory violence another. American mores and custom dictate that a man fights back when attacked, if only to preserve his honor. Legal norms decree that it is proper and pardonable to kill in self-defense. The American colonists who felt mistreated by the British tax collectors (though the matter is debatable) boarded a ship and chopped up the tea. (Not unexpectedly, the white men tried to place the blame on the Indians. The equivalent of this would be black men chopping up lunch counters which would not serve them in Florida and blaming it on the Cuban refugees. If black men were that ruthless, perhaps history would honor them too.)

"Ludicrous" accordingly is the only word I know that begins to describe the hypocritical way in which nonviolence is undemocratically infused into the black man's thinking by his enemies and "friends" alike. Yet, even Tom Paine, the white patriot, wrote in *The Age of Reason* that a turn-the-other-cheek philosophy is morbidly masochistic at best. Understand me, nonviolence under proper circumstances can be a good, if not the best, strategy; I am merely against the lopsided belief in nonviolence which Rev. King popularized to black folk. Unilateral tactics and absolute approaches are no more effective in collective contests than those of an amateur fighter who follows a set pattern re-

peatedly. When once the opponent catches on enough to anticipate your moves, it is necessary to vary them or prepare to meet
the canvas. Rev. King was named man of the year, flowered with honorary
degrees, and given the West's highest honor, the Nobel Peace
Prize, at a time when he hadn't even opened his mouth about
peace. Then he apparently got to thinking he *was* a peacemaker
and suggested going ten thousand miles to Vietnam to talk peace
at a Vietcong table instead of with their invaders cached here in
the Pentagon. Thinking no doubt that he was too close to espousing nonviolence for whites as well, his white supporters then said
he was no longer a responsible leader but was meddling in affairs
outside his realm. They said this despite the fact Rev. King was
a prizewinning peacemaker and black boys are disproportionately
killing and dying in a foreign land for a freedom they do not have
at home. I had thought it would be a good thing for Rev. King
to go to Vietnam. He would, I presumed, make the Vietcong
nonviolent. Then we could send a nonviolent army over there
and have some of all of that love and nonviolence he talks so much
about. Black power would not only be polka-dot; it would be
intertwined with yellow and red! The day was long overdue, then,
when black people came out of the nonviolence trick bag. (See
my "An Epitaph for Nonviolence," *Negro Digest,* January, 1966.)

In fact, one of our main problems in securing black unity —
aside from the facades of 'integration' and assimilation — always
just beyond reach — is the selection and promotion by the white
liberal establishment of acceptable black leaders. (This backfired
somewhat in the cases of the Honorable Elijah Muhammad,
Malcolm X, and Stokely Carmichael, where sustained condemna-
tion exposed them to potential black followers.) But only the
more dissident or astute can see through white evaluations of black
leaders. Most follow the white-praised, falling victim in a dual
way to the American addiction to hero-worship. They seek heroes
and open themselves to additional white manipulation insofar as
their heroes can be manipulated, either directly or indirectly.
Seldom are the heroes chosen truly heroic. Booker T. Washington, for example, was once regarded as a minor god because whites
honored him. Now many blacks regard him as an Uncle Tom.

The hero trap grows mainly out of the fact that we live in a
society where in order to reach our own people we must go through
white-controlled mass media. Many black power advocates who

reject the white press forget that white media made Malcolm a figure, otherwise he would probably be lost in obscurity. Most black radicals also forget or ignore the fact that the Negro press, serving and sustained by similar forces, is hardly better, if not in some cases worse, than the white press when it comes to reporting the black struggle.

Especially appalling in connection with the cult of nonviolence is the 'numbers' fallacy. The numbers fallacy pops up each time there is a riot or the threat of violence. White rulers immediately remind us that we are only one-tenth of the population, neglecting to mention the fact that it is by now probably closer to one-seventh, according to their own census tallies. Millions of black people surrender to the myth of dreadful numbers in spite of the fact that the white man rules, whether in a majority or a minority, all over this world. He is a numerical minority in the world taken as a whole, yet he rules it. When he is two percent of the population, say, in South Africa or Jamaica, he rules; forty percent in deep Southern counties or the District of Columbia; or ninety percent in remote Northern towns. His control represents a mental attitude supported by technology and social organization, not numbers. In Rhodesia, the blacks outnumbered the whites twenty-three to one yet whimpered in obedience.

The numbers terrorists advise the black man to seek salvation through voting. Voting is institutionalized and sacred, and it is virtually impossible to vote in a revolution; most certainly it is inconceivable, given the present methods of choosing candidates. Besides, I may be able, through superior fighting skills and stealth, to kill a number of men: slitting the throat of one, choking another, dropping a hand grenade among the rest. But I can vote only once. If my numbers are too few to fight back in self-defence, they are too few to vote out white supremacy.

The numbers fallacy also overlooks the obsolescence of numbers in certain kinds of civil disobedience or guerilla tactics. Many persons of a conservative hue would say such tactics are unreasonable, contending that emotion and reason cannot go together, that it is not proper to be bitter even in a bitter situation. On the contrary, if a man with a loaded pistol has just shot your companion after the count of five and is now pointing the gun your way, either you will get emotional, or you are unreasonable.

Similar examples of white deception could be discussed at length (see my "Brainwashing of Black Men's Minds," *Liberator,* September, 1966), but it is enough merely to indicate that the black man has suffered too long while permitting the white man to tell him when, how and how much to rebel. Victimized by a frantic desire to gain acceptance at all costs from the white world which rejects him, he trembles uneasily when his opponents, especially emissaries of the white liberal establishment, condemn black power or acts attributed to that source. This deepens white control over his rebellion, permitting his leaders and models to be selected in large part by the white establishment.

If black power is to survive and flourish it must create its own channels of communication. We have to develop an adequate grass roots network of communication since most of the information concerning ourselves and our struggle comes to us chiefly from white sources. Black power does show promise of helping to change this via a spirit of cynicism for white-produced ideas and the loss of contempt for black-produced ones. Black power advocates are turning away from white detours placed in the way of our togetherness. This is symbolized in part through "Afro" hairstyles (though not all militants need wear this badge), the brotherhood handshakes, and even the tendency to call each other "brother" and "sister." There is developing also a cultural bond shaped by the writings of nonwhite social thinkers: books which unify nonwhites under an anti-racist, anti-oppression banner. [*See Bibliography. — Ed.*]

All black power advocates, excepting the deceptive and dishonest few who occupy positions in all groups, appear to have lost faith in the old ways of righting the black man's wrongs. They have, to some degree, come to recognize, if only slightly, the failure of assimilation and the liberal moderate style of protest. They recognize the basic incompatibility of reform and revolutionary tactics. They see that integration, least of all equalization, does not mean the disintegration or absorption of the black race; they must also realize that unity involves a bringing together of diverse factions. There is need for a kind of interdependence between honest moderates and radical factions. Rather than fighting one another, diverting our agency from the attack on the true or foremost enemy, black activists might well establish a grass roots or underground system of functional interdependence. Moderates could then present one face to the white world and another privately to blacks.

Admittedly, this could open the movement to further subversion by moderates and enemies, but this is already occurring at too great a rate. Besides, cultish "more militant than thou" mysticisms handicap the movement. (I say "movement" because the black race is only in the early stage of a revolution, and there is a danger of jumping the gun, so to speak, injecting the tactics of a later stage prematurely into this one. Talk always precedes revolution, inasmuch as it is necessary first to create widespread discontent or sympathy before revolutionary bands can operate successfully. In this case, the blacks or nonwhites must first perceive that a revolution is necessary and feasible before they will be willing to make the necessary sacrifices. Timing is just as important to a successful revolution as it is to a knockout punch.)

No, intensity of feeling is not necessarily correlated with intensity of revolutionary knowledge, and there are roles for all to play. An apparent Uncle Thomas in the Pentagon or a Sapphire in a Governor's office might one day prove invaluable. White efforts to divide us might not then succeed so easily in cracking the cement binding black persons with similar goals.

This more inclusive concept of black power could utilize a general social movement as a blanket or launching pad for more specific revolutionary movements. Without the general movement, specific movements will find their tactics less prone to success. Nor would a broad-based black power movement need to fear the white-voiced deterrent that black power may simply replace white power. If that is the case, then turn-about is fair play. This will depend on the willingness of white power to cooperate in the just correction of grievances and inequities without delay. It is their decision, and this is not a plea. For I have no faith that — given the nature of its existing institutions, belief systems and practices — white America can fully rectify the situation.

But change it must, and if a civil war is necessary, then let it happen. We blacks who have come up against the obstinacy of white oppression understand what Brother Malcolm meant when he said that "we've been singing when we should be swinging." We have worried about the white backlash, about white reactions to us, when what we ought to have done is lashed the white backlash with a black lash! Black men must bring an irresistible black power force to clash with the immovable object of white oppression with such velocity that America will either solve her problems or suffer the destruction she deserves.

CHUCK STONE

The National Conference on Black Power

On May 29, 1966, Rep. Adam Clayton Powell, then Chairman of the Education and Labor Committee, declared in his baccalaureate address to Howard University:

Human rights are God-given. Civil rights are man-made. . . . Our life must be purposed to implement human rights. . . . To demand these God-given rights is to seek *black power*—the power to build black institutions of splendid achievement.

A week later, SNICK's chairman, Stokely Carmichael, marched through Greenville, Mississippi, leading the marchers in a new, militant chant, "We want black power, we want black power." It scared the hell out of white people and that fear, voiced in shocked editorials and public denunciations from both white and black leaders, nevertheless ushered in the era of black power.

Thirteen months later, on July 20, 1967, the black power movement was formally legitimatized by the National Conference on Black Power in Newark, New Jersey.

From 26 states, 126 cities, 286 different black or predominantly black organizations and institutions and two foreign countries (Nigeria and Bermuda), over 1,000 black people converged to write a glorious new chapter in black history.

What made this historic four-day Black Power Conference especially significant was the audacious decision of its conveners to hold the conference in Newark in the churning wake of the six-day black rebellion that had seared the city's racial complacency.

Newark's black rebellion which left 26 dead and 1,004 injured had finally spent itself by Sunday, July 17th, only four days before the Conference was scheduled to open. Still sensitive to the community's inflamed tensions and its atmosphere of undeclared war, both New Jersey State and Newark City Officials had pressured the Conference chairman, Dr. Nathan Wright, Jr., to postpone or shift the meeting to another city. He refused.

Instead, he arranged a telephone conference with the five-man Continuations Committee of the National Conference on Black Power. Members of the Committee included Dr. Wright, Omar A. Ahmed of the Bronx, N.Y., Ron Karenga of Los Angeles, Calif., Isaiah Robinson of New York and Chuck Stone of Washington, D.C.

This Continuations Committee had been appointed by Rep. Adam Clayton Powell on September 3, 1966, following the one-day Black Power Planning Conference which Powell had convened at the Rayburn House Office Building. The purpose of this Committee was to formulate plans for the first National Conference on Black Power in 1967.

Attending the 1966 Black Power Planning Conference in Washington, D.C. were 169 delegates from 37 cities, 18 states and 64 organizations. (The original Continuations Committee included Mrs. Jewel Mazique of Washington, D.C. who later resigned).

Dr. Wright and other members of the Continuations Committee unanimously agreed that the Conference should go on as scheduled. To postpone or shift the Conference at this late date, would, they felt, have been tantamount to a black knuckling under to the same white power structure whose oppressive policies had caused the black rebellions in the first place.

Furthermore, they concluded, such a conference held amidst yesterday's ashes of Newark's scorched black community would represent a phoenix of tomorrow's black power for all black communities.

Unexpectedly, the biggest vote of confidence came from black people themselves. No conference registrations were cancelled. "We're coming, baby!" exulted one elderly black lady who telephoned from New York City. It simply never occurred to black people that the Conference would not be held. And many began arriving on Wednesday, the day before the Conference was slated to begin.

From San Francisco, Calif.; St. Paul, Minn.; Shaker Heights, Ohio; Sturbridge, Mass.; South Ozone Park, N.Y. and Scotch Plains, N.J. to Monroe, N.C.; McComb, Miss.; Miami, Fla.; Marietta, Ga.; Memphis, Tenn. and Milwaukee, Wisc., black people came to Newark.

From the "little-old-ladies-in-tennis-shoes" of the civil rights movement—the Urban League—and its partner in conservatism, the NAACP, to the bearded militants of RAM (Revolutionary Action Movement) and the young firebrands of SNICK ("man, don't call us 'Non-Violent'—call us SNICK"), black people registered as delegates.

Wearing somber Ivy-leagued summer suits, flamboyant African robes, open-neck sport shirts, faded blue jeans, hippie beads and mini-skirts, black people sat together and swapped dreams.

It was to be the most splendidly diversified "in-gathering" of black peoplehood ever assembled.

This was no white-liberal-arranged civil rights conference where only certain selected, safe "Negro leaders" were invited. This was no Madison Avenue-showcased White House Conference on Civil Rights. Nor was it any "integrated" seminar on race relations to explore the therapeutic rhetoric of brotherly love.

Instead, it was a black peoples conference—conceived and organized by black people for black people to talk to black people on what black people must do to empower black communities. This was finally black power—searching, wondering, angry but supremely majestic in its expression.

The ideological eclecticism of black organizations and black people representing or affiliated with non-black organizations was astonishing. (One black delegate was listed as employed by the Christina Community Center of Old Swedes, Inc.!). But most of the delegates were employed by social work agencies, non-profit organizations, civil rights groups, businesses, the Federal government and various state and city agencies.

The following list is a *small cross-section* of the broad heterogeneity of some of the 286 organizations and institutions represented at the National Conference on Black Power:

Abyssinian Baptist Church of N.Y.C., Amsterdam News, Association of Black Social Workers, A. Philip Randolph Institute, Better Business Investors, Black Liberation Center, Black Muslims, Business and Industrial Co-ordinating Council, Catholic Inter-racial Council, Committee to Save Negro Lives on Foreign and Domestic Battlefields, Committee to Seat a Negro Congressman in Brooklyn, CORE, Delta Ministry, Detroit's Inner City Organizing Committee, Democratic Liberation Party of San Francisco, "Did You Know" Publication, Educational Marketing Associates, East Orange Housing Authority, Fisk University Poverty Research Group, Forum '66, Freedom Associates, Greater Hartford Council of Churches, Harlem Pastors Council of Civil Rights, Harvard University, Houston Mayor's Office, I.L.G.W.U., Indiana Herald, Jazz-Art Society for Social Research, Kappa Alpha Psi, Kansas City School System, Liberator Magazine, Lower East Side Community Reorganization, Mau Maus, Mississippi Freedom Democratic Party, Muhammad Speaks, NAACP, National Council of Negro Women, National Medical Association, New England Grass Roots Organization (N.E.G.R.O.), New York Police Dept., Northern Student Movement, Omega Psi Phi, Organization for Self-Improvement, Pepsi-Cola, Progressive Labor Party of Bermuda, People United Against Slum Housing, Princeton Co-operative School Program, Rochester's Dept. of Urban Renewal, Reformed Church of America, Self-Help Organization of America, St. Paul Urban Parish of Minn., Socialist Workers Party, Southern Christian Leadership Conference, Student Afro-American Society, Tanzania's Mission to the U.N., Training Resources for Youth of Brooklyn (TRY), TIME, UAW-CIO, "US", Urban League, The Worker, Washington Mobilization to End the War in Vietnam, West Side Conservation Association, Yale University Child Development Center, "Young, Black and Angry", ZOAR Baptist Ministry and Zimbabwe African People's Union.

Unified, *that's* black power! But their dissimilarity defined the problem. How could those organizations be organized, harnessed and made to work for black people in one efficient unit? The Conference delegates were convinced the effort was worth making.

As the delegates arrived, they were quickly and expeditiously registered at the Conference's headquarters, the Episcopal Diocese of Newark at 24 Rector Street where Dr. Wright, the Conference chairman, and an uncommonly brilliant minister and educator, was director of Urban Affairs. Directing the vast network of secretaries, volunteers and registration procedures was Dr. Wright's brother, Benjamin, a New York City business executive.

The registration fee was $25.00 which included meals for the Conference's four days.

Delegates were given their choice of 14 Workshops and were

asked to indicate second choices in the event some of the Workshops were filled. These Workshops and their co-ordinators were:

1. The City and Black People — Lee Montgomery
   Oswald Sykes
2. Black Power Through Black Politics — Chuck Stone
   Dan Watts
3. Black Power in World Perspective:
   Nationalism and Internationalism — Ron Karenga
4. Black Power Through Economic
   Development — Robert Browne
5. The Black Home — Nathan Hare
6. Black Power and American Religion — Rev. C.
   Lincoln McGhee
7. New Roles for Black Youth — Cleveland Sellers
8. Black Artists, Crafts & — Ossie Davis
   Communication Carol Green
9. Black Professionals and Black — Hoyt Fuller
   Power Gerald McWhorter
10. Developmental Implications of
    Black Power — Dr. James Comer
11. Black Power and Social Change — John Davis
    Lou Gothard
12. Fraternal, Civic and Social Groups — Fay Bellamy
13. Co-operation and Alliances — James Farmer
    Vivian Braxton
14. New Trends for Youth — William Strickland

These 14 Workshops were divided into six sessions. At each session, a different paper was delivered which dealt with a particular aspect of that Workshop's topic. For example, in the Workshop on Economic Development, papers were presented on: "Economics of Poverty: We Do Not Control Black Money"; "Which Businesses for Black People?"; "Black Co-operatives and the Capitalist System"; "Why Buy Black?"; "Research Marketing, Advertising and Production"; "Economic Control of Urban Rebuilding."

After presentation of the papers and discussions, the Workshops were to hammer out resolutions calling for specific programs of action in their respective areas. These resolutions were then to be presented to the Conference's final plenary session on Sunday, July 23rd and either accepted or rejected.

Depending upon which newspaper or magazine you read or television network you watched, the National Conference on Black Power somehow managed to be all things to all reporters. It was simultaneously hailed and condemned as a success, a failure, a separatist movement, a thoughtful effort for black power, an exercise in futility, a constructive undertaking, the bellow of angry voices, the beginning of a revolution, black racism and the glorious in-gathering of black people.

But the delegates were unconcerned about labels. They were a thoughtful, serious and single-purposed group. One fact alone bound them together—white oppression because of their black skins.

The question they had hoped to resolve was a simple one: how can the new wave of black militancy as expressed by the concept of "black power" be mobilized into an actionable unity involving the black masses and then translated into constructive programs of black empowerment?

When one realizes that the average black person has never joined a civil rights organization (less than 4% of all black people in America are paid members of the traditional civil rights organizations), has never walked a picket line and has failed to involve himself or herself in the black man's freedom struggle, then the task confronting the National Conference on Black Power was as monumentally complicated as the evasive answers which have eluded civil rights leaders in the past.

But there was an élan of hope and confidence—almost arrogance—among the black delegates in Newark. They knew the black power movement represented the future and they weren't taking a back seat for anybody. They felt a common obligation and a renewed mandate from black people to chisel out new black solutions on history's tablet of white progress.

When the smoke of misinterpretive press reports and the fall-out from dissensions and disagreements had subsided, a course for black people had been charted for the next 100 years.

If the National Conference on Black Power did nothing else, it buried once and for all the traditional civil rights movement, raised serious questions about the ultimate values of integration, shoved the myth of the so-called "Big Five" of "Negro Leadership" into the dungeon of obscurity and forged a new weapon of mass black leadership ready to take charge of the black man's destiny.

The National Conference on Black Power was not a leaders' conference, but a peoples' conference. Whitney Young, Roy Wilkins, Rev. Martin Luther King, Jr. and Bayard Rustin were not there and nobody missed them. Floyd McKissick's presence more than equaled their collective absence. The only other nationally prominent black leader the delegates wanted to hear and whose presence was sorely missed was Adam Clayton Powell. "If Adam had showed up here", mourned one delegate, "he would have been elected President of all black peoples for life." Powell was scheduled to speak at the Conference, but cancelled his appearance when he learned it would not be possible for him to enter New York City because of his legal difficulties.

It would be almost impossible to record here the more than eighty resolutions which came out of the fourteen Workshops and which were all read and considered by voice vote at the Conference's final plenary session. Only one resolution was officially passed by the Conference and that was the "Black Power Manifesto."

It read, in part:

"Black people who live under the racist governments of America, Asia, Africa and Latin America stand at the crossroads of either an expanding revolution or ruthless extermination. It is incumbent on us to get our own house in order, if we are to fully utilize the potentialities of the revolution, or to resist our own execution.

"Black people have consistently expended a large part of our energy and resources reacting to white definition. It is imperative that we begin to develop the organizational and technical competence to initiate and enact our own programs. . . .

"Control of African communities in America and other black communities and nations throughout the world still remains in the hands of white supremacist oppressors. . . .

"It is, therefore, resolved that the National Conference on Black Power sponsor the creation of an International Black Congress, to be organized out of the soulful roots of our peoples and to reflect the new sense of power and revolution now blossoming in black communities in America and black nations throughout the world.

"The implementation of this Manifesto shall come through the convening of regional Black Power Conferences in America and in black nations of the world."

The other resolutions were adopted by the following procedure: "It is the sense of this Conference that the spirit of the resolution be adopted, etc."

These were some of the more important resolutions whose spirit was adopted by the National Conference on Black Power:

ECONOMIC

1. Accelerate "buy black" policies within all black communities.
2. Establish neighborhood credit unions in black communities.
3. Initiate programs to facilitate upgrading of black workers at all levels of industries by mobilizing selective buying campaigns in all black communities.
4. Establish a guaranteed income for all people or else black people will move to disrupt the economy of the country.
5. Establish a Black Economic Power Fund to provide funds for non-profit and co-operative ventures within and by the black community.

POLITICAL

1. Assign a political task force to assist in the Newark recall election of Mayor Addonizio.
2. Establish a Black Power Lobby in Washington, D.C.
3. Reseat Adam Clayton Powell with all of his seniority and his Chairmanship. Mobilize efforts to defeat the three Congressional leaders in their fight to unseat Powell—Rep. Thompson of Trenton, N.J., Rep. Gibbons of Tampa, Fla. and Rep. Van Deerlin of San Diego, Calif.
4. Elect 12 more black Congressmen in 1968 to triple our present black Congressional representation. Target districts are Atlanta, Baltimore, Brooklyn's Bedford-Stuyvesant, Cleveland, Gary, Newark, Richmond, St. Louis, Chicago's West Side, two from Mississippi and one from South Carolina.
5. Hold a national black grass roots political convention following the conventions of the two major political parties in the same city.

EDUCATIONAL

1. Establish a National Black Education Board.
2. Require all black educational jurisdictions to be administered and controlled by black boards of education and black administrators.

INTERNATIONAL

1. Establish an international employment service to serve as a skills bank for exchanges by Africans and black Americans.
2. Confer with the appropriate representatives of the Organization of African Unity on their recommendations for needed services and skills from the black community.
3. Hold an International Black Congress within 15 months.
4. Support the freedom struggle of all non-white peoples throughout the world against their white oppressors.

MISCELLANEOUS

1. "Initiate a national *dialogue* on the *desirability* of partitioning the U.S. into separate and independent nations, one to be a homeland for white America and the other to be a homeland for black Americans."
2. Boycott all sponsors of televised boxing until Muhammad Ali's title is restored.
3. The right to self-defense is proclaimed.
4. Establish a permanent national organization of black college and non-college youth, concentrating on programs to develop these two groups.
5. Establish a National Black Clearing House for information, research and reports on all activities of all black people.
6. Encourage black homes to be centers of learning and growth by helping black adults to assume responsibility for learning more about our black heritage.
7. Establish a Black Protective Association for black communities.
8. Assign only black police captains to black neighborhoods.

Black pie-in-the-sky? The National Conference on Black Power never deluded itself into believing that the mere act of convening would achieve an overnight transformation of black communities from inter-racial powerlessness to black power.

But the more than 1,000 delegates were confident that the fact that they did meet, the fact that they did come to some agreement on a wide variety of resolutions, the fact that they represented the broadest spectrum of ideological thought ever to convene in the black community, the fact they laid plans for future national and international conferences of black people, and the fact that they held this conference without the co-operation or assistance of the traditional "Negro leaders" and without administration by the white power structure, were in themselves towering citadels of achievement.

History will ultimately enshrine this great event as one of the finest efforts of black people to emancipate themselves psychologically as well as politically and economically from the white man's enslavement. "Let's get our minds straight" and "We've got to be a 'together' race before we can achieve real power in this racist society" were two themes recurring constantly in discussions among the delegates.

Disagreements were expected and most of them were resolved. As would be expected, a few were left hanging in mid-air. Violence had already saturated several major black communities and it came as no surprise or shock when it spilled over into the National Conference on Black Power. The day before the Conference concluded, a group of young black militants from New York City invaded a press conference, denounced the "white racist press", broke up several television cameras, and drove the newsmen from the room. Order was quickly restored, a plenary session was immediately convened by the Conference chairman, Dr. Wright, and the Conference got back on the track of solving the problems of black people.

July 20, 1967, Newark, New Jersey must be remembered as the day when one of the most representative cross-sections of black people—the young, middle-aged, elderly, rich, poor, the Protestant, Catholic, Muslim, agnostic, militant, moderate, conservative, the laborer, businessman, college student, writer, social worker, teacher, secretary, janitor, doctor, lawyer, minister, government employee, politician, public official, policeman, fireman, journalist, actor, hustler, numbers banker, waiter, salesman, real estate broker and the unemployed—all came together at the National Conference on Black Power to write the boldest and most radical chapter in the black man's four-century old struggle to be a true equal among equals.

July 20, 1967 infused a new legitimacy into the revolutionary era of black power, giving it both definition and direction.

America doesn't know it yet, but she is going to feel for a long, long time the effects of what those 1,000 independently minded black folks did in Newark, New Jersey, for four fateful days.

JULIUS W. HOBSON

Black Power: Right or Left?

At the Black Power Conference in Newark, New Jersey, I visited a half dozen committee meetings on subjects ranging from political theory to education, but perhaps the most important, and the most revealing, was the discussion by the committee on economics. The general concensus of this gathering was that we needed to transfer the economic power wielded by white men in the Black ghettos of America to Black men. There were many proposals forthcoming on how this should be done. One minister proposed collecting a dollar from each Black man in the United States with which we would open up a bank. One self-styled revolutionary pointed out that the answer to the economic problems of Black people was the formation of cooperatives throughout the country, under Black control of course. There were lengthy papers prepared on the merits of Black ownership of ghetto housing, community control of service institutions and facilities, and even on the economic merits of a completely Black police force. Probably the most startling observation made in the economics committee meetings was the proposal that money be somehow kept in the Black community, and that that community become an economic entity or island on the larger American continent of capitalism.

The discussions within the political committee centered around the voting power of concentrated black enclaves within American cities. Somehow, it was pointed out, we could control our own destinies within the framework of the present political system, if we remained in the center cities and voted in blocks.

In still other committee meetings there were discussions and assurances on the subject of the beauty of blackness, and a reaffirmation of the obvious fact that men of color were handsome, and women of color were beautiful. So impressive were these discussions that one of the leading "revolutionaries" suggested in line with the disdain for all things white or light, that we change the English language to read "endarken" me instead of enlighten me.

The most obvious conclusions that could be drawn from all of this are (1) that the well-meaning proponants of these ideas were completely unaware of the degree to which they have already been "endarkened" by the good old American political and economic concepts of the status quo; and (2) that the agents of these ideas had little or no understanding of the nature of their political and economic surroundings; and (3) there was and still is a grave need to adopt a consistent philosophical base for the Black power movement.

The reality which the conference did not confront is this: that the history of social protest and change within the framework of capitalism everywhere, and at all times, has always been a history of the complete destruction or absorption of the agents of change.

The recent history of the American Labor Movement is an excellent case in point. In the middle 1930's the American Labor Movement came into its own, and reached its zenith with the passage of the National Labor Relations Act. The Federal, State and local governments throughout the Country officially recognized the right of workers to join unions, and to bargain collectively with the system in order to share in its many goodies. The leaders of these unions were predominantly men who made pronouncements about the possibility of doing business with the system. One labor leader gained fame with the statement that there really was, after all, no conflict of interests between the capitalistic owners of the means of production and the capitalistic workers.

A few dissenters publicly refuted this thesis in the name of real revolutionary change, but they were soon dislodged and by the mid 1950's had either recanted or were in jail as Communists. The "let's do business with the system" crowd ended up engaged in "business unionism," as opponents of even the mildest changes in the structure of capitalism. Labor Union membership declined, and leaders of the working man ended up advocating the murder of workers by workers in Korea, Africa, Vietnam, and every other place on earth where serious revolution threatened.

Another example of the futility of trying to make capitalism work, is the recent history of the late civil rights movement. From

1960 through 1964 the cry was integrate, Black and white together, and we shall overcome. The agents of these concepts (and I was taken too) spent immeasurable energy and time in freedom rides, sit-ins, live-ins, and marches, all designed to bring us into the promised land of the good old American economic system which we affectionately call capitalism.

Like the labor leaders of two decades earlier, civil rights leaders counseled their followers on the merits of gaining compatibility within the economic and political frameworks, and in a nonviolent fashion, no less. And in the mid 1960's as in the mid 1950's the skeptics either were dislodged from the "respectable" civil rights organizations and branded as militants, or recanted, and were invited to the White House as "responsible Negro leaders."

The Head of the Urban League, the "cleanest" civil rights organization, traveled to Vietnam and like the absorbed leaders of the past and present, endorsed the destruction of workers by workers, and all in the name of freedom, the free enterprise system, and Jesus Christ.

In my graduate student days my old and respected teacher of economic theory introduced his courses with the statement that "a capitalist is a capitalist regardless of race, creed or color." In his many enlightening lectures he proceeded to support this statement by pointing out that capitalism in all its history has been a system characterized by the unequal distribution of goods and services, by economic class structure, by exploitation, by profit motivation and by expansionism. The system has always found rationalizations for its behavior. My teacher defined racism as a rationalization for economic exploitation. It therefore followed, he said, that we cannot hope to eradicate racism from the United States and at the same time maintain capitalism. Private enterprisers have always and everywhere attempted to justify or rationalize their behavior, sometimes in the name of "progress," "civilization," Christianity, or as in Vietnam, in the name of world freedom and self-determination.

It was within the framework of the Socialist economics of Karl Marx that my teacher lectured. He pointed out what was indeed true, namely, that the Marxist doctrine was the most logical, most consistent and most obvious theoretical guide available to the oppressed who are seeking revolutionary change. The experiences in some Scandinavian countries give substance to the wisdom of my teacher's argument.

The logical conclusion drawn from all of this is that, given the same set of economic circumstances, a black slum lord will act exactly as the white slum lord acts. The black entrepreneur will be forced into perpetuating the system of exploitation if he operates as a capitalist. Black bankers will be dealing in the same money markets with their white counterparts and will thus be guided by the same rules of the banking game. In any system with primary property values, black policemen will protect black haves against the black have nots.

There is no evidence anywhere in the literature to support the idea that money can be kept within the geographical boundaries of any community. The characteristics of socialist as well as capitalist economic systems would not allow any such arrangement.

Any one familiar with the history of American cooperation, the farm cooperatives of the Mid-Western United States or the Rural electric cooperatives anywhere in the United States, is aware of the fact that cooperative efforts in this country have done little more than produce managerial classes with private enterprise mentalities.

Thus, we black power advocates face the decision either of duplicating the white man's mistakes by attempting to build an equally exploitative and racist black capitalism, or of internationalizing the struggle and moving with the tide of the oppressed peoples of the world toward an economic system based upon the socialist economics of Karl Marx.

If we adopt the latter, we will move in the direction of creating a world economy that produces for need rather than for profit. We will begin the creation of a system which has proven that it can eliminate starvation. We will foster the ownership of the world's natural resources by the people of the world, and we will create economic circumstances in which men will cease the exploitation of other men for personal gain. And most important, we will be able to hail the beginnings of a selfless society in which property values will no longer supplant human values.

Black beauty indeed! I was glad to be kicked out of CORE in 1964 for running the Washington Chapter in an "undemocratic fashion" which facilitated Black control. Not that I thought Black control would bring about immediate revolution, but because I was sure then, and I am sure now, that if we are to have a revolution in America, Black men by virtue of their positions in this society must be the ones to lead it. I believed then, and I believe now, that the struggle for world freedom must move to the left toward socialism, and not to the right in any attempt to live with capitalism.

Black people in the United States are in dire need of the psychological freedom which the emphasis of blackness affords, but lest we forget, the struggle is multi-racial and worldwide. There are resources outside of our color-camp which we need and should utilize. There is a thin line between the concept of virtuous blackness and the concept of racism—the rightist doctrine for which we have justifiably condemned the white man. Let us learn from his history.

And so to the youthful black power advocates I would say, go left young men, for it will be a great day indeed when the world socialist camp prepares to receive this black division of the army of the proletariat which has been wandering in the American economic wilderness since 1865.

IV

BLACK

POWER

AND

ME

JEAN SMITH

I Learned to Feel Black

I think that once you knew me. It was a time not long past, about four years ago. I was the bright, well-mannered girl who lived down the street from you. My grandmother was always stopping you on your way to the grocery store; she would call you to the door to show you, proudly, college-newspaper clippings about her granddaughter's winning a scholarship or achieving a place on the dean's list.

Or possibly you remember me from church. I was the girl who helped sustain the small, overambitious choir by appearing faithfully every Sunday to sing the praises of the Lord in songs that often were too difficult or out of my range. Sometimes you would stop and offer me a few words of encouragement because, you said, you liked my spirit.

Or you may remember me as the girl in the neighborhood who went off to join the civil rights movement or the Peace Corps. You might even have been among those who tried to persuade me not to waste my talents on those other people when there was so much work to be done at home. I could build a fine professional career, you told me; I could make a starting salary of $7,000.

I'm sure you knew me once. At least you knew a something in me, something that continued to grasp at the reality of the American image of the full person, blessed by our society with the resources and opportunities to be whatever he wants to be. I kept trying to be that full person, to use the talents I had toward widening opportunities for other people so that they also could make the most of their lives.

And so I tried to know everything and to be the best at everything I tried. I wanted to learn all about science, art, music, Greek mythology, Oriental philosophy. I wanted to learn the newest theories, study the most difficult courses and sing the hardest songs. It all would be useful in the refinement of this society where every man could be his best.

Thus I studied chemistry at college and planned to go to medical school, because I felt that I could be most useful in this way. And I had to join the civil rights movement because I saw in it a basic method of making our society stand completely behind its image of the full person and of every man's right to be a full person. I felt sure that once the country was made aware that some of its Negro citizens were being deprived of very basic rights and was brought face to face with the contradiction between its image and what was happening to the Negro people, then our society would necessarily correct the oppressed condition of the Negro people.

Yes, I'm certain that you knew, if only superficially, that *something* in me which reached toward the American image.

What was the source of my belief? It was based on my assurance that in this country there was room for everybody, that for every man there was, or soon would be, some place where he could be free to explore and employ the creative potential within him. So that my job was simply to develop the skills I possessed and then to fit my abilities into the massive machinery that, I trusted, was working day and night to create for every person a place of comfort and freedom. In short, I believed in guaranteeing everyone freedom, equality and democracy as the means of living full lives, and I thought that the rest of the country believed in these things too.

I had good reason to believe all this. My family was sort of upper lower class. There were just four of us, my mother, my two sisters and I. (My father, a pilot in the Army Air Force, was killed in World War II.) My mother worked as a practical nurse in Detroit, Michigan, when we were young, and she managed to get two of us through college. She herself graduated from college at the age of 40 and has just embarked on a new career, teaching deaf children. My youngest sister is in college now. All of us have or can get any *thing* we really want (a house, a car, a trip to Europe).

Thus my early personal experiences suggested that there was room for everybody. After all, I was nobody special and yet I was doing quite well. In fact, it was a long time before I became conscious that being a Negro made me different. I thought I was like everybody else.

It was in the context of my belief in our society's potential for making good on its promise of full men through freedom and democracy that I responded to the urgings of some of my classmates at Howard University. They were members of the Students' Nonviolent Coordinating Committee (or SNCC, pronounced "Snick") and I joined the Movement. I truly felt, and I think that many SNCC workers then felt similarily, that most Americans believed in these principles, and that when confronted with our documentation that they were being violated in the South, Americans would move to support the rights of Negro citizens.

When I left Washington, D.C., in 1963 to go South with SNCC, you knew me. Now, four years later, I am a different person.

Essentially the difference is that I became consciously black. I came to understand that there wasn't room enough in the society for the mass of black people, that the majority of Americans are acting either in unbearably bad faith or in tragic ignorance when they project to their children the image of an American society where all men are free and equal.

Since, in a way, I was once a friend of yours, perhaps you'll invest a little time and emotional energy in trying to understand what happened.

I went South after the sit-ins that were aimed at desegregating eating places. In the summer of '63 I went to Georgia and then to Mississippi as a SNCC field worker. The focus of SNCC's activity in the Deep South then was voter registration. The logic of it seemed very clear to me. Negroes had a right to vote, to participate in our democracy. In fact, our society wanted everyone's participation. Because of some curious isolation from the rest of the country, the white Southerners had managed to deprive Negroes of this right. But the South was still part of the United States. What we had to do was to show the rest of the United States that democratic participation was being denied our people. Then the rest of the country would insist that the South allow Negroes to vote.

I saw the relationship between political representation and economic and social development: If Negroes could get the vote, then we could use it to attack the poverty and misery which plagued the Negro community. If we could vote, we would be well on our way to full economic and social participation in the larger society. And so I worked with the other SNCC staff people to show the rest of the country that Negroes in the South wanted to vote and couldn't.

We got our people to go down to the courthouse to try to register to vote. After they were turned away from the courthouse or were not allowed to "pass" the test of eligibility for voting or were intimidated by threats of violence from whites, we appealed to the Justice Department, documenting carefully the instances of refusal and intimidation. Next we organized picket lines and marches to the courthouse to demonstrate to the rest of the country that Negroes *did* want to vote. The marches often ended in mass arrests and in violence, but they were reported in the newspapers and on television and the Movement's case was made clear to the public. After there had been much marching and many protests, Congress passed the 1965 Voting Rights Act, which assured Negroes the right to vote.

It would seem that this was a great victory. It was certainly a goal into whose attainment I had put my heart. I worked every available minute at reaching it. I used to walk through the whole town every day, canvassing neighborhoods to tell people about voting. I canvassed until evening; I took part in the mass meetings that were held every two or three nights. Then I went back to the office to work until one or two o'clock in the morning to establish files on potential voters and help organize our new library.

When finally I went home it was to a deep, satisfying sleep. I would be ready to go again at six the next morning, awakened by my eagerness to start a new day of efforts to secure the right of my people to vote and be represented. We all worked so hard. And Negroes did get the right to vote.

We found it was a shallow victory. After the earlier sit-ins, the civil rights movement had had to stop and ask: "What have we gained by winning the right to a cup of coffee downtown?" In the same way, we who had worked for voting rights now had to ask ourselves what we had gained. In both cases the answer was the same: Negroes were in fact not basically better off with this new right than they had been before; they were still poor and without the power to direct their own lives.

It is a subtle problem to acknowledge that there was some value in having achieved these rights and yet to understand that there was no basic gain. The value was in the way Negroes could feel like real men and women as they broke old traditions about "staying in their place" and went up to the courthouse to vote. The value was in the solidification of the Negro community, in our recognition of the possibility that we could work together to build decent lives. But you must see that there was no basic change. I personally resisted seeing this for a long time. I had invested so much of myself in the fight that I didn't want to admit that it came to so little.

The best way to understand is to look at what the Negro people who cast their lot with the Movement believed. They believed, I think, that their participation in the drive for voting rights would ultimately result in the relief of their poverty and hopelessness. They thought that with the right to vote they could end the exploitation of their labor by the plantation owners. They thought they could get better schools for their children; they could get sewers dug and sidewalks paved. They thought they could get adequate public-health facilities for their communities. And of course they got none of these.

The crux of the matter is that they believed there was a link between representation in government and making that government work for you. What they—and I—discovered was that for some people, this link does not exist. For most black people, voting has not much more benefit than the exercise of walking to the polls. Why is this the case? Because the link between voting and partaking of the benefits of society exists at the pleasure of society. The society must be willing to respond to the legitimate needs of the people; only then can the channels for the expression of these needs, such channels as voting, be meaningfully employed.

A dramatic example is glaringly visible today on the national scene. In January of 1967, when Adam Clayton Powell was barred from his seat in the House of Representatives, he was prevented from acting for his Harlem constituents, the people of the 18th Congressional District of the State of New York, who had elected him. When he was stripped of his chairmanship of the House Education and Labor Committee, which shaped and handled most of the antipoverty legislation, he was stripped of his power effectively to represent the Negro people, a power it had taken him 22 years to build. He was prevented from representing these people because the majority of Congress, which in this instance speaks for the larger society, does not want him to. It is as simple as that.

Our effort in the South to enter the society through the use of the vote came to an anticlimax because we had been lied to. We had worked feverishly to qualify under objective standards for our rights, only to learn that these rights are arbitrarily conferred by those in power. In the end we learned that there are a thousand ways for a people who are weaker than the rest to be "kept in their place," appeals to good conscience notwithstanding. There are simple mechanisms, like last-minute changes in election laws and altering the boundaries of election districts. And there are subtler means, such as making bank loans to the "leaders" of a poverty-stricken community so that they can never afford to disagree with you; such as busing newly eligible voters off to Florida to pick fruit.

It was through my efforts as a SNCC worker to bring my people into the larger society through the channel of voting that I first gained insight into the fact that there was not room in American society for most black people.

In August of 1964 the Mississippi Freedom Democratic Party (MFDP) went to the Democratic National Convention in Atlantic City. The MFDP went to challenge the right of the white Mississippi delegation to represent Mississippi at the convention where the Democratic candidate for President of the United States would be chosen. I helped to organize the challenge.

Our argument was that the regular white delegation had been chosen by a process from which Negroes had been excluded, and consequently that the delegation did not represent the total population. It certainly did not represent the 43 per cent of the state's population that was black. We knew it did not and we could prove it did not.

Negroes first tried to attend the series of meetings that were held by the Mississippi Democratic Party on the precinct, county and district levels to elect the delegation to the national convention. Most of these meetings were inaccessible to us. Only people who had registered to vote could participate in them, and it was not until a year later, under the 1965 Voting Rights Act, that our people were even *promised* the right to vote. In many cases, when our people arrived at the place and time appointed for a precinct meeting, there was no meeting. In many other instances, we were simply refused admission to the meetings.

After we had been refused participation in the precinct and county meetings from which the regular Democratic party delegates to the convention were ultimately chosen, we set out to hold our own meetings. The MFDP organized precinct, county, district and state meetings open to everybody, meetings from which the MFDP elected a sixty eight man delegation to the Democratic National Convention. The delegation, primarily black but including those few whites who were willing to stand with us, was to ask the national convention for seats as the Democratic delegation from Mississippi.

There was real fire in the civil rights workers as we organized the MFDP and held precinct, county and district meetings all over the state. We thought that this time we would surely make a breakthrough. As I helped to run educational workshops preparatory to the formal precinct meetings I thought, Yes, this is what democracy is all about.

But the delegation that could have represented us never got the chance to speak. Mississippi Negroes were never allowed to participate in the choice of the Presidential candidate. Although the rules of the convention provided that a delegation could be challenged as not representative of the constituency that it claimed to represent, our challenge was never heard by the convention. Our challenge was heard by the Credentials Committee preceding the convention.

We had worked for almost a year to substantiate our legal case that the only reason we were not represented in the regular Mississippi delegation was that the white Democrats in Mississippi had not allowed us to be: they hadn't allowed us to register to vote and they hadn't allowed us to participate in the process by which the delegation was selected.

After our case was heard by the Credentials Committee, the committee voted not to seat the MFDP delegation at the convention; it offered to seat two of our sixty eight man delegation, members whom it would specify, whom we would not even be permitted to choose. We rejected this offer. The only concrete gain we could show for all our work, for all our documentation and the eloquence of our members' testimony before the committee, was a promise that the delegation to the next convention would be integrated.

In retrospect, I think that in our hearts we knew our flawless arguments would fall on deaf ears. We were aware, at least subconsciously, that no group of white people was going to send some of its own packing in order to make room for us. No matter that that group had said to the world that it regarded all people as equals and no matter that we had a right to representation in that group. It took a few more turns at knocking our heads against stone walls (walls that, according to our society, did not exist) before we became fully conscious that this was the case.

In this experience can be seen one of the origins of the call for black power, which I consider the other side of the coin of black consciousness. One cannot exist without the other. Imagine the MFDP's 1964 experience repeated hundreds of times in hundreds of conventions and back-room meetings. Imagine that in every corner of the United States black people are coming face to face with the fact, never before so widely or so publicly acknowledged, that it is through the exercise of power that decisions are made, and that those decisions have little or nothing to do with morality. The next logical step is the call for black power.

I think for many Negroes it was our experience with the poverty program that finally crystallized our consciousness of how black we really were. It was through the poverty program that we were forced to admit that the society apparently had no use for us and that assurances to the contrary were, unfortunately, instances of white deception.

Along with several other civil rights people, I worked with the Child Development Group of Mississippi when it was first established in the summer of 1965. CDGM is a Head Start program in Mississippi, with funds from the Office of Economic Opportunity. We worked with CDGM because we thought this would be a chance to put thousands of poor people in command of one small sector of their lives, the preschool education of their children. It was a chance to have a several-million-dollar program actually run by poor Negroes. OEO's expression for this was "maximum feasible participation of the poor." The theory was that programs for helping the poor were best run when poor people, who best know their own problems, are given the power to solve them. For a while CDGM was actually allowed to be this sort of program. In each community poor people were running their own centers and hiring their own people to work in the centers.

All this lasted until white Mississippians began to realize that Negroes were benefiting from a program that white people did not control. The program was then attacked, primarily on the grounds that it was hiring civil rights workers and mismanaging funds. (Dispute still rages as this is written over how much money was "mismanaged" out of a total of $7,100,000. The amount ranges from the $1,100,000 charged by Mississippi Senator John Stennis down to the $65,653 that a national firm of accountants reported may have been spent in "technical violation" of regulations. Meanwhile, according to one estimate, investigations of CDGM have cost about $300,000.)

But think for a moment about the accusations. Why shouldn't the program hire civil rights workers, people who had proved their interest in and ability to work with the poor? Consider too that most of the Negro people involved in the program traditionally had been excluded from handling any money at all. How could they develop a perfect fiscal system in so short a time? Yet Negroes must have the experience of handling money if they are ever to participate in the economic life of the country.

It is impossible to trace here the complications of the CDGM fight. Through attacks and counterattacks, appeals and counter-appeals, through periods when the program was held together completely by volunteer labor and donated funds, CDGM managed to keep its Head Start program going. OEO was sufficiently satisfied with CDGM's responses to its accusers that it provided funds for the program several times. The current grant is for more than $5 million over a twelve-month period.

But the re-funding has been at great cost to the character of the program. Because of the jeopardy in which the charges of mismanagement placed CDGM, Negroes themselves, fearing to lose the program entirely along with the benefits it brought to their children, did not insist that they continue to have a large part in running it. Its working area in the state is being decreased continually, and an effort is now under way to replace CDGM with a group more politically acceptable. In another year it is very possible that there will be no more CDGM; the whole program will be run by the public-school system without even token participation by the poor.

It amounts to a paradox: The poverty program says it wants

"maximum feasible participation of the poor" but it *doesn't* want the poor to participate. For me it was a devastating paradox. It required me to abandon my last hope that American society would willingly make room for us. When I surrendered this last hope I had also to surrender my belief that American society was honestly trying to create conditions where, through promised freedom, equality and democracy, men could be their best. I felt the great loss of this belief on two levels.

On one level I was damaged as a member of a race of people who could no longer look to society for the means of relief from their poverty and from their condition of powerlessness over their own lives. The depth of this damage was crystallized for me one evening in Washington, D.C., in the park that faces the White House. I had come to Washington with a group of ninety people who sought funds from OEO to build houses with their own hands in Mississippi to replace the shacks and tents in which they lived. When after several days of meetings with OEO officials we had no positive response, we set up tents in Lafayette Square Park to demonstrate to the President and to the country that our people were in desperate need of decent places to live. This happened last year, at Eastertime.

On the second evening of sleeping in the tents there was a light rain, which continued for several hours. The rain curtained the trees of the park, reflecting the light of the street lamps and casting a wonderful warm glow over everything.

Because I felt too damp and cold to sleep, I got up and walked among the newly blooming tulips. I became aware that others who were awake were staring through the mist at the White House. They watched the beautiful, glowing White House from their tents. They watched and waited for some sign that they could abandon their hand-to-mouth existence and take up tools to build homes from which they could begin new, fruitful lives. And I was hurt for them because by then I knew their hopes were unfounded. There was nothing for them there. They would have to go back to their tents and shacks, back to hustling for $2 to pay a gas bill or 20 cents to buy a bag of pinto beans.

On another level, the loss of my belief was damaging to me as an individual. I had been stripped of a principle around which my life had been organized. No more could I seriously think that I was helping to build this country by making it stand behind its promises to all its people. I could no longer work at helping to build a society of full, free men. The image of that society was a joke. When considered in this light my work became meaningless. In existentialist terms, I was reduced to absurdity.

For me and many other black people the only allowable conclusion from these experiences has been that Negroes must turn away from the preachings, assertions and principles of the larger white society and must turn inward to find the means whereby black people can lead full, meaningful lives. We must become conscious that our blackness calls for another set of principles, principles on whose validity we can depend because they come from our own experiences.

We have to build a broad-based black consciousness so that we can begin to depend on one another for economic, political and social support. We have to build our own businesses to put money into the development of the Negro community, businesses to establish foundations to support our own new educational and social ventures. We have to make our politicians responsible to us so that either they improve our communities or they go. Living, growing communities must be built to replace our strife-ridden ghettos. The problems of illiteracy and the inability to communicate must be tackled.

Can we do all this by ourselves? Probably not. Obviously we need access to the capital and to the intellectual resources of the larger society. We need to know how to build lathes and how to market products. We need to learn the ins and outs of prevailing political forms and to have access to the body of scientific knowledge and cultural tradition. We need those few white people who are genuinely interested in helping.

It's not that we have to do it by ourselves. Rather it is that we have to reorient our efforts and to train ourselves, black people, to build for us. Our immediate objective must be the strengthening of the black community instead of the apparently unattainable goal of diffusion of all black people into the main stream of American life. We have to become strong so that we can depend on one another to meet our needs and so that we'll be able to deal with white people as we choose to, not as we are obliged to.

I realize that we are only ten per cent of the population and that in the end we may well need the large-scale assistance of the larger society. But I also realize that except on the level of tokenism, we can't win the fight for meaningful integration any time soon. (Soon, for me, means in my lifetime.)

I think the fight for integration must continue because we derive some benefits from it. It means better living conditions for a few of us, a few more low-cost housing units, a few more yearly incomes above the poverty level. It means that we can feel more like men and women because we've insisted on the rights that society says are ours. And we gain valuable knowledge and experience by being the only Negro architect in the firm or by being one of three Negro judges in the city or by being the agency's only black model.

Clearly there's much to be learned in the outside world. But basically I think we must have before us the objective of building strong black communities on which we and our children can depend and in which we can lead full, rich lives. I think that after the black community has become strong enough, the rules of the game may change; society may decide that it can live with us on equal terms. It may even decide to join hands with us to build a country where all of us, white and black, can live.

The call for black consciousness is at first painfully hard to answer. It's hard to start all over again and establish new principles and modes of operation. For we have struggled vainly for so long, trying to approximate white culture! Our artists, our scientists, our leaders, have been respected by us only after they have been "legitimatized" by the white world. For so long, events have not occurred unless they were recorded in the white press; world issues have not existed unless the President made a speech about them. The extent of our reality has been the width of our TV screens. We face a prodigious task. We've danced to the tune so long; and now it becomes necessary to stop and gather our senses, to stop and listen to the tune and decide which of its elements warrant our response.

Sometimes I am nostalgic for the days when you knew me. Sometimes I miss the clarity of those days, the assurance that what I was doing was right because it was helping to make a better country and, in turn, a better world. The black self that I am now has a difficult time, having to start all over again and discover the best ways to work in this new, black world. And yet, after a searching and painful evaluation of the last years' experiences, it is the only self that I can honestly allow.

BARBARA ANN TEER

Needed: A New Image

While the questions of the black woman and the exposure of her one dimensional roles portrayed in the theatre are important, they are relatively minor in the larger scheme of things. There are issues in the theatre far more basic and fundamental. The black woman's existence in the theatre or the lack of her existence is associated and related to issues of much greater magnitude. Yes, it is necessary to correct and clarify her image! Yes, she is more than a domestic, matriarch and/or sex symbol! However, it is far more important to establish a positive relationship between black men and black women in the theatre and all other mass media. It is vital that black artists project an image of love, respect, and solidarity for one another. It seems almost ludicrous to think that without this unity and understanding there can be fed into or sustained in any of the communicative arts anything of lasting and significant value for the race. Black people are spiritually very loving, and it is imperative that we begin to have stable romantic interests projected. America has never seen a Negro couple make love in any mass media. Does this not seem strange? The black artist must begin to recognize the necessity for and the many social ramifications involved in portraying this kind of unity.

The black writers and playwrights have a great responsibility here. They must become the spokesmen, the forerunners. They must pave the way with new thought patterns. They must set the pace and feed society a new image. This is a basic problem the black artist must contend with. However, before he can yet deal with this problem, he must first solve one even more fundamental—that of his individual racial consciousness.

The problem of racial equality which confronts the Negro performer in Show Business is no different from that which he faces in any other field of endeavor. What he is doing to alleviate this problem, however, is quite different. He is desperately lagging behind in social consciousness in this new struggle for black identity and racial solidarity. He is at the end of the totem pole mainly because he is struggling to be a part of or integrated into Show Business. The name itself is self-explanatory. It is a trade, owned, operated, and formulated by white people for the purpose of making money. In order for a black performer to become successful and/or accepted in this business, it is mandatory that he adapt to the values of that white system physically, spiritually, and morally. The compromises and sacrifices involved in making these adjustments are extremely dangerous. In order for the black performer to become successful in the dominant society which in this case is white, puritanically Anglo-Saxon, he must think in accordance with these values which necessarily dictate that he become the same as his white counterpart. Consequently, he begins to act out of their set of values and to pattern his life and personality after their way of life. The fact that he has allowed this to happen to him is indeed a misfortune. The American public, both black and white, can see the results of this compromise daily on television, in the theatre and on the screen.

Providing more jobs for black performers was one of the major solutions to this problem less than three years ago. A program of action was designed. As in most cases, we headed for the streets carrying picket signs, passing out pamphlets and chanting slogans such as "Last to be hired, first to be fired," "Don't exclude us," "We exist," "The image of the American Negro must be changed," "Employ us in roles that more realistically depict us as we really exist in America today," "We want to see more Negroes on television."

So now in 1967, the American viewer sees several handsome, virile Negro men fighting international spies, outwitting German prison camp commanders, capturing white hoods and facing down fast-drawing western sheriffs in dusty little western towns, and even telecasting the news.

While the problem of depicting the Negro male in roles natural to any actor has not been fully solved, it has been attacked with several dramatic and highly noticeable thrusts. He has dropped the broom, taken off the butler and porter uniforms and now clenches a Colt .45, a cocktail glass, a detective's badge, a computer, or a Geiger counter in his strong black hands.

Well, now we have accomplished the first phase of our program of action. We have been given a few more jobs by the white man. This was to be the beginning of an overall reform.

Television and movies, being mass media which influence millions of minds daily, are now establishing for the black man new patterns of behavior. The black performer should stop and appraise this situation. Is this the image that he wants portrayed? Is this the image that will further his racial identity or is it in fact simply reproducing more whiteness? Look around you. The proof is in the pudding. The few directors, choreographers, television and movie actors we have are doing in fact the same thing as the white man and not even as effectively.

Therefore, the answer to the problem of racial equality is far more complex certainly than simply "Employing more Negroes in roles that more realistically depict them as they really exist in America today." If this means that in order to "make it" we must deny our blackness—the very thing that makes us uniquely individualistic; if it means that we must blend into and become the same as whites, we should in fact refuse to perpetuate this image any longer. No one should or can dictate to us what our true cultural roots are.

It is true that the black performer has a dual cultural heritage. He is American with an African ancestry. (What an exciting theatrical combination!) However, he is often completely confused as to which of these images he should project.

It should be his duty as a public figure to reflect an image which his people cannot only identify with, but can emulate. More often than not he sacrifices his African heritage in order to become more commercial. If he is more commercial, which means more white, it therefore follows that he will become more successful financially. And if those performers who are at present more commercially successful could begin to change this image, it would certainly help those young performers, who are trying to make it now, have a much easier road to climb.

There is nothing wrong with being financially successful, or with being accepted by or in the white world. There is nothing wrong with living in comfort but there is something wrong with the attitudes which produce this success and the way in which one sets out to achieve acceptance. For instance, the height of accomplishment for a Negro performer is reached when he is bestowed with the signal honor of such catchy phrases as: "The fact that Joe Blow happens to be Negro is literally unimportant" or "Joe Blow is not Negro, he is universal, a first rate performer." Very few Negro performers have reached the level of achievement where this catchy phrase can be applied to them, but thousands are striving for it. You never see "The fact that Joe Blow happens to be white is literally unimportant", or "Joe Blow is not white, he is universal, a first rate performer." Why the double standard? This is a clear and open admission that the Negro must lose his unique identity and become molded in the image of the white man before he can be recognized as a human being in this country.

The black masses, i.e., the man in the street, do not have this problem of racial identity. The man in the street just by his very nature *Is*. With the exception of Rhythm and Blues singers, jazz musicians and performers of the magnitude of Nina Simone, very few black entertainers are clear as to what cultural image they should reflect. Culture is a way of life or the sum total of a way of living built up by a group of human beings which is transmitted from one generation to another, and this culture for theatrical purposes should be enhanced and enlightened. That means, the way we talk (the rhythms of our speech which naturally fit our impulses), the way we walk, sing, dance, pray, laugh, eat, make love, and finally, most important, the way we look, make up our cultural heritage. There is nothing like it or equal to it, it stands alone in comparison to other cultures. It is uniquely, beautifully and personally ours and no one can emulate it. It is the cultural responsibility of those before the public eye to wear our heritage like a badge of honor and project it whenever and wherever the opportunity arises. It is our responsibility as black artists not to assimilate another set of cultural values but to create and establish more realistic ones. This must be done before the black performer can truly progress. This double consciousness must be removed and replaced by a stronger black one. We must begin thinking and using more energy toward developing and sustaining our own cultural identity. Too much time, energy, pain and frustration is being utilized trying to maintain a dual personality. It is impossible for us to merge and identify at the same time.

An ideal situation would be to have black television stations, film companies and theatres. But, at this time, we do not have this kind of economic power. However, at this point in our growth, if we did have economic solidarity, we might just as easily fall into the same traps and pitfalls as whites. Essentially, there is no difference between the psyche of a white businessman and a black one. In this country, their sole concern is to make money. They stick to what has been tried and proven: the safe way; the easy follow-the-leader way. These narrow concepts have apparently, until now, been the code of ethics of the American businessman.

So in planning his own businesses, the black performer must be very careful to analyse his thought patterns so that he will not make the same errors. The seeds that the Negro performer plants in the mind of America and eventually of the world must reflect more positive attitudes concerning his blackness. The white businessman does not have the time, knowledge, nor inclination to do our research for us. Furthermore, it is not his responsibility. The black artist must solve this problem by himself and for his own salvation. The time has come to break down and destroy these antiquated stereotypes and concepts. The black youth of America needs a new image, and it should be the responsibility of the black artist to provide it for them.

JOHN E. JOHNSON, Jr.

Super Black Man

The Black Man has survived in this country in the face of what seemed insurmountable odds. Overwhelming odds! We have been black power since we set foot on these shores in the chains forged for us . . . Forced servitude! With our journey here, destiny placed a fate on us few modern peoples have had to face: the fight for our lives, our limbs, our liberty! The odds, then as now, were against us. This strong and fertile people . . . the mystique began!

The white man needed us. He raped, humiliated our women. He kept us in his cotton-fields, his house. We raised his children, scrubbed his kitchen. While he fulfilled his most sadistic fantasies, Miss Ann looked the other way—but had her black buck too!

In this foreign jungle, the Black Man began his struggle for freedom. The white man was not about to let us have it. Not until it became economically feasible did White Power free us. Or maybe loose us to decay. After all, we were not human beings, we were a means. A Thing.

This is a strange country. A country based on grandiose humane precepts to which it has no desire to adhere. Our heroes are gangsters, cowboys, unbelievable virgins, Mickey Mouse, and Rugged White Individuals. The white structure loves its mother and god, but at night or in the isolation of its guilt rejects both. Where is soul, U.S.A.-style? What is it? It is a non-descript gestalt which produces things on an assembly line. AMERICA! Corrupt, morally backward, cruel . . . and this is what they want black people to keep from aspiring to.

The white man is lucky. He can only gain. The Black American can lead this land into a new awareness . . . a new

Eden. A world of men psychologically secure in their socks. Generalities, however, are easy. Let's deal with facts. With recent uprisings in Black districts: "Criminals, vandals, looters, snipers, paupers . . . un-American, that's what you are. You have to choose! Either go back to your hole in the ghettos—roost with illiteracy, roaches, confinement, squalor, and early death—or we will help you out by killing you here and now!" They mean, there is no place here for black anger. They make us wonder whether there is really any place here for us.

White Power rejects and despises black boy for wanting out of the ghetto: How dare you? What's all this smoke about? You've got it good. You don't work, you're on welfare, and there're jobs for those who want them.

The dichotomies rise to the surface. We (all of us Americans) listen to our leaders. They rally us, they teach us: "Vietnam is good. We must stop the aggressor." Thirty-five million dollars a day to save a people from oppression. Pacification programs; build, rebuild new villages. Americans die to preserve the democratic way of life. We join up to defend our birthright, but must beg to have a rat extermination bill passed by our Congress to protect our children. Join up. But wait, if I fight and die in Vietnam, will this guarantee the black man's rights here?—"Hell, no, chump! You're doing what you oughta do, what you've always done!"

How many know that the death rate of the black child in this country is higher than that of the poor Vietnamese child we read about? . . . A weak smile crosses the faces of our American leaders when they talk about gross national product. Gross national product, that's right! The gross national product of this country is greater than all of the NATO nations and Japan combined. Not only can we afford a war overseas, we can afford some pacification work right here!

Black leaders tell me . . . "turn the other cheek—passive resistance." Others say . . . "Burn, baby, burn: Active insistence." White liberals tell me I have to prove I'm a man. I tell me I AM a man! That's right, I am a man, in fact, I am SUPERMAN! I'm no ordinary human. I am different. I'm capable of the worst crimes and laziness. I'm capable of true wisdom and folly. Everybody talks for me. I'm under a microscope from dawn to dusk. Well, I'm tired now. Tired of all the rationales. Rundown with putdowns. And I'm angry. But I've got something to hold onto. Black Power? Don't know. Slogans can't define my manhood . . . I am new man. I want to live for what I believe. I want to live. When the slaughter is over, I will survive. The world will be mine to corrupt anew. That's beautiful, but who believes it? . . . I am new man. I believe in me. I've proven myself too many times not to. I'm secure . . . I got soul. I can love and make love. I can hate and destroy hate. I don't need to die anymore.

The one thing I know is how to survive and this I will do. This we will do . . . HERE IN AMERICA!

BYRON RUSHING

I Was Born

I was born July 29, 1942.

On July 29, 1962, I pedaled my bicycle across the Massachusetts Avenue bridge from Cambridge to Boston and Roxbury to hear Elijah Muhammad speak at a Muslim rally in the Boston Arena. Mr. Muhammad was sick; Malcolm X was the main speaker.

For two quick hours Malcolm told the truth. He raised only one contradiction—discussion of the response of the Nation to the murder of one of its members by a white cop outside the Mosque in Los Angeles. A murder with no retaliation. The freedom of cops to murder like that and get away with it haunts me still, and still raises the question of the Nation's seriousness. Yet, I was born on July 29th.

Leo. I realize that birth now as I did not then. I pedaled my bike back to Harvard where I was making up a physics course I had flunked during the year. I majored in linguistics. Planned to go to med school. Later that summer I attended the Ninth International Congress of Linguistics.

The argument against infant baptism is that the infant doesn't know what's going on. I was baptized by the Rev. Edler Hawkins, June 13, 1943, at St. Augustine Presbyterian Church in the Bronx. I didn't know what was going on. *June, 1963:* After a completely useless year at school, I returned home to work as a surgical technician in Syracuse Memorial Hospital before going to work for SNCC in the South for the next academic year.

WE CAN STOP URBAN RENEWAL (NEGRO REMOVAL) if the city continues to relocate Negroes into:

—segregated areas of the city

—areas that will be doomed by urban renewal in the next 5 years

—houses that are worse than those Negroes are being forced to move from

Negroes must refuse to be forced into unsatisfactory housing CORE DIRECT ACTION has stopped Urban Renewal at Madison and Townsend. CORE sit-ins drove the wreckers off the lot!

The issue is
Housing Discrimination
We want a better deal for Negroes who have to relocate! We plan to hold this lot and take other action until positive steps are taken to *desegregate* housing!

MEET WITH CORE
THURSDAY, 8 P.M.
PEOPLE'S A.M.E.
Zion Church
711 E. Fayette St.
Help us plan further action.

I never went South. I began doing volunteer work in Syracuse CORE. Instead of going on the March on Washington, a few of us sat in on an urban renewal site and blocked the demolition of a gas station—Pelnick's Construction firm wasn't tearing down any houses that day—in what was quickly becoming the ex-black community. No one came out to persuade us to get off the site—almost the entire local urban renewal staff had gone on the March.

I stayed in Syracuse working for CORE at $25 a week.

While I was at Harvard, I went to Muhammad's Mosque on Interval St. in Roxbury one Sunday afternoon. Minister Louis X gave the address. More truth. But still that contradiction: notwithstanding his persuasive arguments against the white devil and his innate brutality, the only people he encouraged his listeners to take into back alleys and whip were Negro pimps. One of the brothers gave me a ride back to Cambridge. He told me I was lucky to be at Harvard and "if you'd combine that Harvard thing with Mr. Muhammad's program, brother, nothing could beat you." It is very tempting.

I don't know how to deal with a prophet or a saint; I didn't know how to deal with Malcolm. It was a struggle to understand that I had to struggle—with the truth, with the prophets and the saints, with the devil. And then there was Jesus. And the truth was my slavery, my death, my escape, my ambivalence, my cowardice. My brother. My enemy.

In the winter of 1963 I came closest to committing suicide. In that immense, frozen, *white* despair, I discovered that if God was real, he was *black* and I sought a nappy-haired, thick-lipped Jesus.

FIGHT INJUSTICE
IN SYRACUSE

1. All of CORE's charges in the Presley case have been substantiated by the report of the Mayor's Commission on Human Rights. The Mayor said that CORE was lying. Now the Mayor's Commission has said that the charges by CORE were true. Will Mayor Walsh apologize to CORE and the Negro community?

2. CORE pressure has improved the city jail. People are no longer kept in Willow Street Jail for more than one night. Last fall Negroes were kept in that jail for two, three, and four weeks. Negroes will only get equal treatment if they KEEP THE PRESSURE ON.

3. The case of Marine Private Joseph Brooks is still in the courts. As you remember, Brooks claimed that

We are all baptized as infants. We must grow to understand the significance and implications of that sign and seal. I now know that what seemed to be the temptation to commit suicide was the beginning of the tortuous, rupturing experience of dying/borning. And it didn't last for only one night, or one week, but on and on. The slow destruction of the old, the sinful, the white self. I was lying and I had to admit the truth. I thought I was safe; I had to be insulted; I had to Tom for some dumb, white cop. And watch myself again and again and not be able to help myself. It was the cops who taught me that we black folk are a formidable community, they knew our potential better than I did. Although I usually saw the police as the guardians of the city's enforcement of seghe was beaten by a policeman. Brooks took his complaint to the police chief. For the next week he was harassed by the police and city officials. (Eleven CORE members were arrested helping Brooks obtain justice.) After Brooks was beaten, he was charged and convicted of public intoxication. *He was not drunk.* But there is NO JUSTICE FOR NEGROES IN SYRACUSE CITY COURTS. These cases are being appealed. JOIN CORE AND FIGHT INJUSTICE IN SYRACUSE.

regation, I soon experienced them as the occupation troops in the black colony, free to beat, insult, shoot black natives with the total, defensive, calculated, paranoiac support of the white administrators. The administrator was the power, and he enforced that power through his alter ego, the cop. Want to know what the mayor, governor, president, bishop, think of black people? Look in the face of some dumb cop.

Paul wasn't struck blind on the road to Damascus; he was struck with the realization that he was already blind. At Harvard I had the fantasy that somewhere, deep in the stacks of Widener, there was the book, ignored, unnoticed, that, upon my reading it, would make my life right. Would give me the shocking bright light of discerning truth from irrelevance. *Get your ass up off the ground and go to the city. Get out of the stacks, there ain't nothing there for you.* I was blind and blind I rode my bike across the Charles and Ananias spoke to me and the scales dropped from my eyes.

Malcolm was smooth. Outside the arena, NAACP members were passing out leaflets: Go in and listen, but here's a program that *can* get you into the mainstream. . . . I was talking to the two brothers in front of me: about Jack Johnson (and how they wouldn't let him sail on the Titanic) and about some talented local boys out of some gym on Washington Street.

I have heard Malcolm so much since that day; I can't remember what he said. Just his description of Ronald Stokes' murder and the humiliation of the Muslims in L.A. Stokes' widow was on the platform and told that when she had heard, several months later, that two of the white cops involved in the murder had been killed in an auto crash, she cried, "All praise is due to Allah!"

I went up and shook Malcolm's hand; I didn't ask him anything. A black father introduced his daughter to him. The father had sent her to Moscow to get a decent education. Malcolm replied, "When I talk about the white man I mean the white devil in America." A white woman walked up to him and began talking—quickly, asking rhetorical questions. She held in her hand a white plastic crucifix on an opened Bible. Strange satanic talisman.

RUSHING OUTLINES CORE TACTICS "To change the status quo, you have to be willing to do the unpopular," Byron Rushing, Executive Secretary of the Syracuse chapter of the Congress of Racial Equality (CORE), told a heavily attended session of the Catholic Neighbor Training Council last night.

Rushing, speaking to more than 700 persons at Bishop Ludden High School, explained the aims and operations of Syracuse CORE as part of a survey of interracial and civil rights groups. Last night's fifth meeting of the eight-part series drew the largest audience to date.

"Negotiation is always first," Rushing declared as he outlined CORE tactics, "but when it fails there are other means." He described these as picketing or sitting-in or its variations.

The object of such actions is "direct confrontation of the public with the problem", Rushing noted, but he stressed

I grew up in Syracuse. When I returned to work for CORE, white people would always ask me "What do you know about our city? Where are you from?"

I believed in the integration goal and the nonviolence method. I wanted to love white people, openly, brotherly, sexually. I sat on that urban renewal site, scared in my gut, as a white crane operator dropped a demolition ball closer and closer toward me. I led mass meetings of blacks and whites singing, "Black and white together."

I cannot pinpoint the day when the idea of integration, of confronting this white society's conscience and nonviolently forcing it to respond with humane acts, all became irrelevant. Birth. Baptism. The old life lingers, lingers. Malcolm sank into me slowly; yet he had already laid his hands on me. There was the response of the white dominions and principalities to two that CORE advocates only nonviolent action.

"Action outside the usual channels of redress is necessary," he added, "because our society is so structured as to keep the Negro in a subordinate position."

He said the Negro's difficulty is different from other minority groups in the past, because the Negro's "inferiority" was written directly into the Constitution in three places.

"You can win court battles but lose the war," Rushing asserted, "because the majority of the people are not in the court room, don't hear the case, and thus do not learn about the crimes of racial injustice."

Results are realized "when you leave the courtroom and go downtown and confront the people when and where they are not used to it," he said.

Rushing reviewed the housing demonstrations downtown last fall, and remarked, "The whole community was aroused by these demonstrations—not necessarily in favor of us, but at least they were aroused, which in itself is good."

He said the tangible results of the demonstrations were non-existent, however, and promised demonstrations of a

police harassment cases we were handling. There was the frustrating CORE demonstration at the World's Fair and ACT's stall-in which never materialized. And after each draining act, all we could say as we analyzed our loss was: "Next time bigger and better demonstrations."

Inside I knew that there were two movements and I had been sucked into the wrong one. That one was the movement to free white folks' consciences, to make white folks human. And so you invent demonstration-dramas to confront them, and they organize fair housing groups or Equality Projects and get homes for thirty-five Negro families in the suburbs or stop their church from buying from a firm that discriminates, and, by their standards, they have put their bodies on the line, they have suffered courageously. Yet their acts do not affect the other movement one bit. Black people continue to be murdered in increasing numbers, housed in increasing squalor, supported by increasing unemployment, made more powerless, and the gap between white and black grows greater and greater. In my haste to express my birth, I had not listened, I was new type in the future here, in which "more than 100 persons will be arrested," but he did not elaborate.

Dear Neighbor,

Plans are being made to move the Greyhound Bus Station into the Loblows store building on East Adams Street.

If this happens it will mean: YOUR CHILDREN WILL BE IN DANGER OF BEING HIT BY BUSES entering and leaving the station;

NOISE from the buses entering and leaving the station DAY AND NIGHT;

FUMES from the buses in your backyards and in your houses.

We know of no other city that has a LARGE BUS STATION IN A RESIDENTIAL AREA. There are about 700 residential units in this area. Most of the families that live here are Negro. Is that why City Hall doesn't think they have to ask us before they put a bus station in our neighborhood?

City Hall and Urban Renewal say that this bus station is only "temporary"— BUT THAT COULD MEAN YEARS OF THESE DANGERS!

Plans to place the bus station next to Pioneer Homes only show how City Hall feels about us. The city has again

duped by the white conspiracy in myself, I had forsaken the movement for black freedom and power.

I met Malcolm five years ago. I left Syracuse three years ago. I never returned to Harvard.

I am scared. And even with my lucky, easy life I am sick and tired. I want to join a monastery in Ethiopia and tend Abyssinian cats and the mummies of long gone emperors. But he has turned me around. Sell your coats and buy swords.

Like most black people I have spent my life being both an obedient child and a responsible parent to white people. That self is dead. And although I have spent too much time in preparing that carcass for burning, it is being consumed. And at my young/ old age I must learn to love my true parents, learn to be obedient; I must learn to love my true children, learn to be responsible. I must learn my brother, learn my enemy. I must learn my God. Learn my devil.

I do not hate this enemy. I know him too well. He has been too close, inside me. It is not his money or his power that makes him evil, it is his godlessness, his idolatry. It is not that he is politically or and again demolished areas of the Negro community for projects that no other community would stand for. The city has repeatedly placed things in the Negro community because they know that Negroes "never complain." Well, all that has got to end. WE MUST SERVE NOTICE ON THE CITY THAT OUR COMMUNITY WILL NO LONGER BE THE AREAS OF LEAST RESISTANCE WHERE THE CITY CAN EXECUTE PROJECTS THAT IN NO WAY ADD TO THE WELFARE OF OUR COMMUNITY. This is a petition to show the city and tell the mayor that you are protesting the use of the Loblows building as a bus station. Please sign this petition: this is the *first* step in keeping our neighborhood *safe*.

Yours truly,

Inez Heard,
Citizens of Pioneer
Byron Rushing,
Syracuse CORE

economically unable to stop being racist, it is that he is psychologically and spiritually unable.

I know how I am blind. I know the devil. I am baptized. It does not make it any easier.

Once you have been baptized you are born again. No matter what you do from then on, you *are* different. And that difference will save you or destroy you.

GWENNA CUMMINGS

Black Women—
Often Discussed but Never Understood

This is not an article in defense of Black Womanhood, but rather
an article to suggest the inner complexities of being a Black
Woman in America. Let us begin.

As you read this, I want you to imagine you are not only black
but a woman as well. I want you to take a trip with me from
infancy to adulthood, and hopefully you will be able to see and
feel what it is like to be an Afro-American Woman in the United
States of America. I hope I am not asking too much of you, but
a great deal has been asked of *my people* in this country for many
years.

. . . We have just been born and we are part of a community
which, except for a spot of black here and a spot of black there, is
predominantly white (ghetto in reverse). Our families try hard
to instill racial pride at tremendous odds—what are they? They
are many—but to name a few: Segregation, American-style,
through the communications media re: newspapers, television,
movies etc. Employment: finding out through your environment
that only certain types of jobs will be open to you when you become an adult. Education: absolutely swamped by either too
many whites confronting too few blacks; or all blacks fighting
within themselves or with each other because the learning process
in the school teaches us to negate our own history (or the possibility that we might have had a history to be proud of). The
negation is a subtle process which does not rear its ugly head
until later in life when one has to confront his or her own self-
image, or lack of self-image. Then people have the nerve to
wonder *why* we fight with each other when we need each other
so much. We've never had the chance to develop this type of

sophistication. I am stating here that no matter what the environmental circumstances are in a given situation—when it concerns
Blacks—the cards are stacked to prevent any self-identification
process from occurring. Erik Erikson, in his *Eight Stages of Man,*
provides the evidence which shows that when a child is not given
the type of environmental and social learning situation which can
develop him as a whole person, he tends to be distrustful of himself and others he comes into contact with. . . . I ask you as
joiners in a distrustful group—how does it feel? Come along
with me a little further—*things get better—for you.*

The pendulum swings back and forth in perfect rhythm—
making equal responses to an equal stimulus—the stimulus is
the regulated manner in which self-denial is heaped upon the
unwary Black individual—and when we wake up we find that we
have been *tricked—but good!* Do you blame us for getting
angry? If so— why? . . . We are now blossoming into womanhood. We are many women—the high school girl, the potential
college student, the secretary, the factory worker, the domestic,
the prostitute, the wife and the mother. Why in that order, you
ask? Because we are the strongest quantity at the *END,* not the
beginning where it matters the most. Man caters to us—WHITE
MAN—he has made the rules of the game—we are the puppets
and he is the puppeteer. I mentioned the development of strength
as a criterion for survival. White man has made his mark long
ago. We have learned our responses well.

Now let us do some role-playing. . . . You are a participant in
the following drama. You have a choice of characters that you
may wish to play—if you dare.

We are a house of BLACK WOMEN—our aspirations vary
according to the way the decks have been stacked against us at
a given time in our history. One of you is a grandmother—
employed as a domestic in a house in the suburbs. One of you
is a mother—housewife on WELFARE—husband done gone—
White Man, Listen. Do you know what it means to be brought
up without a father—wife without a husband, because your husband has given up on everything that could have mattered because he had never developed self-respect nor dignity in his
surroundings? Don't blame the Black Woman—she has had to
build strength, but in so doing the Black Man has become weak
in every position affecting the family organization—WHITE
MAN, LISTEN!

Daughters are important to a household—how would you react if you were part of a family which included a prostitute with her pimp; a high school girl with a baby; a potential college student with nowhere to go; a factory worker endlessly searching for something better, and a clerical assistant who is *always* available? Where would *you* get the motivational spurt necessary for a more enticing existence? I've asked all of you to choose one role for yourselves—if you dare. Each one of us in this drama sees his world differently. Would you believe that you as a Black Woman, in order to fulfill any real objectives in this country, will have to combine at least three of these worlds before you find yourself, the self that can feel comfortable, confident and unafraid. *Unbelievable?—not at all.*

In this society the Black man has been depicted as a drunkard or addict (depending on the source of the information), a pimp, an abandoner of his children; lazy, unwilling to work, weak, stupid—therefore a thief, a sex fiend, and a lover of white women. Quite a few adjectives on the negative side of the ledger, isn't it? Think about how you could expect a great deal from people who are respected so little, who are daily subjected to mental, moral and physical anguish from the status quo. *Any twinges of conscience? None? Too Bad!*

In these roles you can't make any changes alone. Everyone has to assist each other. One of the many things that Black Women have had to do throughout history is tackle a course almost single-handedly to make change occur. Community leadership has therefore developed because of the tremendous need for such a leadership. I as a Black Woman have made a commitment to myself and my community to do something for the community children by giving them, hopefully, a sense of dignity through an educational experience.

My commitment has deepened with several activities I have participated in, namely: 1) the two school boycotts engineered by the NAACP when 20,000 children went to Freedom Schools in Boston. Historically, these boycotts were to stress the whole issue of racial imbalance in the schools. And 2) the March on Washington and the March on Roxbury which highlighted the educational plight of the Black Children in the inner city schools. Absolutely no changes occurred after these events, even though many conferences were held with the school committee. In discouragement, a group of Black parents met and decided to bus their children out of the area to schools still in Boston. In September, 1965, one bus-load of children left an office on Blue Hill Avenue. This mushroomed into the program now known as Operation Exodus which buses almost 1,000 children. The enormity of the situation is such that the program originally conceived to alleviate a temporary situation has now gone into its third year with no end in sight.

It has become quite obvious to our community that if we want any changes we have to pressure for them ourselves, as tax-payers, in the city of Boston. The Exodus program has enlarged itself to include tutorial and cultural enrichment services for both bused and non-bused alike. Our program involves testing and counseling along with home visits to parents so that they can keep abreast of their children's progress; a research component has been designed by the Harvard School of Education; a recreational program for the children is directed by the Black men of Exodus (the office staff is all Black women except for the transportation department); and a building-fund exists to make renovations on our present structure for expansion into an educational complex. A fund-raising committee raises money to support our program which costs approximately $2,000 a week. We are almost entirely funded by private donations and have been able to survive against tremendous odds.

It is obvious the whole idea of "self-help" as propounded by the Government does not imply any financial commitment on the part of the Government to grass roots programs. Therefore, we have not been able to get Federal funds to help run this program. It is also becoming more and more difficult to assume we shall receive such assistance. But, with or without Federal aid, we shall continue to run our program, and, because of this, we are grateful the Friends of Exodus are so many.

The problem that exists is that people still refuse to face the responsibility for the state of affairs as they stand today. We are not going to get a drastic change until this *is* realized. I do, as a community Black Woman, hold on, for I feel that day is a-coming when the scene will shift for the better.

I have asked you to imagine you were both Black and a woman; I have taken you to my office at Exodus; I would like you to remember this, that Black is strength in itself. That in the face of white America's refusal to recognize this, our strength has maintained its medium of power from a perpetual need for defense against injustice or misunderstanding. A hungry man only understands satisfaction and it is only through cooperation and competence that the power incapable of realization at present will blossom into a concrete absolute gain for all.

MALCOLM X

Because Malcolm was continually changing while seeking a deeper under-standing of himself and our people, it is difficult to single out any one given moment from his career. Even so, we turn to his extended trip abroad in 1964. Before returning on May 21, he travelled in Egypt, Lebanon, Saudi Arabia, Nigeria, Ghana, Morocco, and Algeria. He pilgrimaged to Mecca, and became known in the 'Muslim world as El Hajj Malik El Shabazz. Besides expanding his comprehension of orthodox Islam, he spoke with students, journalists, members of parliament, ambassadors and govern-ment leaders. The African press greeted him warmly, finding it an ex-tremely important fact that Malcolm was the first Afro-American leader of national standing to make an independent trip to Africa since Dr. Du Bois went to Ghana.

Malcolm's first trip was to prove important in his later efforts to "inter-nationalize" the black man's struggle. His trip was also to prove regenera-tive to him. When he returned to Chicago he said:

"In the past, I have permitted myself to be used to make sweeping indictments of all white people, and these generalizations have caused injuries to some white people who did not deserve them. Because of the spiritual rebirth which I was blessed to undergo as a result of my pilgrimage to the Holy City of Mecca, I no longer subscribe to sweeping indictments of one race. My pilgrimage to Mecca . . . served to convince me that perhaps American whites can be cured of the rampant racism which is consuming them and about to destroy this country. In the future, I intend to be careful not to sentence anyone who has not been proven guilty. I am not a racist and do not subscribe to any of the tenets of racism. In all honesty and sincerity it can be stated that I wish nothing but freedom, justice and equality: life, liberty and the pursuit of happiness—for all people. My first concern is with the group of people to which I belong, the Afro-Americans, for we, more than any other people, are deprived of these inalienable rights."

The following excerpts, reprinted from Malcolm X Speaks, *describe his reactions as he relayed them in letters from abroad:*

LETTERS FROM MECCA

Jedda, Saudi Arabia
April 20, 1964

Never have I witnessed such sincere hospitality and the over-whelming spirit of true brotherhood as is practiced by people *of all colors and races* here in this ancient holy land, the home of

Abraham, Muhammad and all the other prophets of the Holy Scriptures. For the past week I have been utterly speechless and spellbound by the graciousness I see displayed all around me by people *of all colors.*

Last night, April 19, I was blessed to visit the Holy City of Mecca, and complete the "Omra" part of my pilgrimage. Allah willing, I shall leave for Mina tomorrow, April 21, and be back in Mecca to say my prayers from Mt. Arafat on Tuesday, April 22. Mina is about twenty miles from Mecca.

Last night I made my seven circuits around the Kaaba, led by a young Mutawif named Muhammad. I drank water from the well of Zem Zem, and then ran back and forth seven times between the hills of Mt. Al-Safa and Al-Marwah.

There were tens of thousands of pilgrims from all over the world. They were *of all colors,* from blue-eyed blonds to black-skinned Africans, but were all participating in the same ritual, displaying a spirit of unity and brotherhood that my experiences in America had led me to believe could never exist between the white and non-white.

America needs to understand Islam, because this is the one religion that erases the race problem from its society. Throughout my travels in the Muslim world, I have met, talked to, and even eaten with, people who would have been considered "white" in America, but the religion of Islam in their hearts has removed the "white" from their minds. They practice sincere and true brotherhood with other people irrespective of their color.

Before America allows herself to be destroyed by the "cancer of racism" she should become better acquainted with the religious philosophy of Islam, a religion that has already molded people of all colors into one vast family, a nation or brotherhood of Islam that leaps over all "obstacles" and stretches itself into almost all the Eastern countries of this earth.

The whites as well as the non-whites who accept true Islam become a changed people. I have eaten from the same plate with people whose eyes were the bluest of blue, whose hair was the blondest of blond, and whose skin was the whitest of white—all the way from Cairo to Jedda and even in the Holy City of Mecca itself—and I felt the same sincerity in the words and deeds of these "white" Muslims that I felt among the African Muslims of Nigeria, Sudan and Ghana.

True Islam removes racism, because people of all colors and races who accept its religious principles and bow down to the one God, Allah, also automatically accept each other as brothers and sisters, regardless of differences in complexion.

You may be shocked by these words coming from me, but I have always been a ,man who tries to face facts, and to accept the reality of life as new experiences and knowledge unfold it. The experiences of this pilgrimage have taught me much, and each hour here in the Holy Land opens my eyes even more. If Islam can place the spirit of true brotherhood in the hearts of the "whites" whom I have met here in the Land of the Prophets, then surely it can also remove the "cancer of racism" from the heart of the white American, and perhaps in time to save America from imminent racial disaster; the same destruction brought upon Hitler by his racism that eventually destroyed the Germans themselves. . . .

Lagos, Nigeria
May 10, 1964

Each place I have visited, they have insisted that I don't leave. Thus I have been forced to stay longer than I originally intended in each country. In the Muslim world they loved me once they learned I was an American Muslim, and here in Africa they love me as soon as they learn that I am Malcolm X of the militant American Muslims. Africans in general and Muslims in particular love militancy.

I hope that my Hajj to the Holy City of Mecca will officially establish the religious affiliation of the Muslim Mosque, Inc., with the 750 million Muslims of the world of Islam once and for all—and that my warm reception here in Africa will forever repudiate the American white man's propaganda that the black man in Africa is not interested in the plight of the black man in America.

The Muslim world is forced to concern itself, from the moral point of view in its own religious concepts, with the fact that our plight clearly involves the violation of our *human rights.*

The Koran compels the Muslim world to take a stand on the side of those whose human rights are being violated, no matter what the religious persuasion of the victims is. Islam is a religion which concerns itself with the human rights of all mankind, despite race, color, or creed. It recognizes all (everyone) as part of one human family.

Here in Africa, the 22 million American blacks are looked upon as the long-lost brothers of Africa. Our people here are interested in every aspect of our plight, and they study our struggle for freedom from every angle. Despite Western propaganda to the contrary, our African brothers and sisters love us, and are happy to learn that we also are awakening from our long "sleep" and are developing strong love for them.

Accra, Ghana
May 11, 1964

I arrived in Accra yesterday from Lagos, Nigeria. The natural beauty and wealth of Nigeria and its people are indescribable. It is full of Americans and other whites who are well aware of its untapped natural resources. The same whites, who spit in the faces of blacks in America and sic their police dogs upon us to keep us from "integrating" with them, are seen throughout Africa, bowing, grinning and smiling in an effort to "integrate" with the Africans—they want to "integrate" into Africa's wealth and beauty. This is ironical.

This continent has such great fertility and the soil is so profusely vegetated that with modern agricultural methods it could easily become the "breadbasket" of the world.

I spoke at Ibadan University in Nigeria, Friday night, and gave the *true* picture of our plight in America, and of the necessity of the independent African nations helping us bring our case before the United Nations. The reception of the students was tremendous. They made me an honorary member of the "Muslim Students Society of Nigeria," and renamed me "Omowale," which means "the child has come home" in the Yoruba language.

The people of Nigeria are strongly concerned with the problems of their African brothers in America, but the U.S. information agencies in Africa create the impression that progress is being made and the problem is being solved. Upon close study, one can easily see a gigantic design to keep Africans here and the African-Americans from getting together. An African official told me, "When one combines the number of peoples of *African descent* in South, Central and North America, they total well over

80 million. One can easily understand the attempts to keep the Africans from ever uniting with the African-Americans." Unity between the Africans of the West and the Africans of the fatherland will well change the course of history.

Being in Ghana now, the fountainhead of Pan-Africanism, the last days of my tour should be intensely interesting and enlightening.

Just as the American Jew is in harmony (politically, economically and culturally) with world Jewry, it is time for all African-Americans to become an integral part of the world's Pan-Africanists, and even though we might remain in America physically while fighting for the benefits the Constitution guarantees us, we must "return" to Africa philosophically and culturally and develop a working unity in the framework of Pan-Africanism.

Today

the tone of my life takes
the future as a growl mingled
with the groan of the past
however, the growl must be
hidden, because the jungles of
the past have gone. . .
deflowered by napalm
shot down carrying white refrigerators
murdered bringing the liberators charisma, in a
hall full of my black people. . . . . .

So you see, the warrior, must look
like the old woman.
the warrior must stand straight in
the dark
we must whisper to each other, and
dare to tell. . . .
we must get our own together
with the revelation of the truth or
the pain of death
then the outer circles of strange alliances
the slow tedious math of power will begin
to creep into our shoulders. . . .
the child of years from me
the eyes of a grandfather days from me
will know this strange word
freedom. . . . .

—Gaston Neal, 1967

CONTRIBUTORS

STOKELY CARMICHAEL was born in Trinidad and grew up there, in New York City, and in Washington, D. C. He attended the Bronx High School of Science and received a bachelor's degree from Howard University in 1964. While at Howard he was active in student government, as well as in the local civil rights organization, the Nonviolent Action Group. Carmichael has worked with the Student Nonviolent Coordinating Committee almost since its beginning in 1960. He has been arrested more than fifteen times while participating in demonstrations in Mississippi, Louisiana, Tennessee, Maryland, Virginia, and New York. Before his election as chairman of SNCC in May 1966, he helped organize the Lowndes County Freedom Organization in Alabama, and played a major role in the 1964 Mississippi Summer Project as director of civil rights activities in the Second Congressional District. Since the expiration of his term as SNCC chairman, he has been active in Black Power liberation activities in both North and South, with primary emphasis on ghetto organizing in Washington, D. C. He is co-author with Charles V. Hamilton of the recent book, *Black Power: The Politics of Liberation in America.*

JAMES P. COMER is a fellow in psychiatry at the Yale School of Medicine. He received his B.A. from Indiana University in 1956 and was graduated from the Howard University College of Medicine in 1960. Following two years as a fellow in public health at Howard, he took a master's degree in public health at the University of Michigan in 1964. He joined the psychiatric residency program at Yale the same year.

GWENNA CUMMINGS was born in Brockton, Mass., and attended Howard University and Harvard University. She worked for the Federal Government for ten years, and returned to school to major in secondary education in the area of social studies. She has been employed by Educational Services, Inc., and the International Marketing Institute attached to the Harvard Business School. She taught social studies for Upward Bound at the University of Massachusetts for two years, and was on the advisory boards of the Upward Bound programs of Brandeis University and Bridge, Inc. Formerly Tutorial Director for the Boys' Club of America (Roxbury Branch), she is now employed by Operation Exodus as the Educational Director, and currently teaches a course in tutoring techniques for "disadvantaged" children at the Cambridge Center for Adult Education. Mrs. Cummings is the mother of two children.

CHARLES V. HAMILTON is chairman of the Department of Political Science at Roosevelt University in Chicago, from which he also received his B.A. In addition, he holds a law degree from Loyola University, and an M.A. and Doctorate from the University of Chicago. Professor Hamilton has taught at Tuskegee Institute, Albany State College (Georgia), Rutgers University (Newark), and Lincoln University. The author of a monograph titled "Minority Politics in Black Belt Alabama" and co-author with Stokely Carmichael of *Black Power: The Politics of Liberation in America,* he has also published articles on constitutional law and civil rights in the *Wisconsin Law Review, Phylon,* and the *Journal of Negro Education.* He has been both a participant in and advisor to civil rights organizations in Alabama, Georgia, Illinois, and Pennsylvania.

VINCENT HARDING grew up in Harlem and attended public school there. He received a master's degree in journalism from Columbia University, and a master's degree and doctorate in history from the University of Chicago. He is presently head of the Department of History and Social Science at Spelman College in Atlanta, Georgia, where he has been teaching since 1965. Dr. Harding has done extensive work in the area of race relations in the

South, and has published widely in the field of Afro-American History.

NATHAN HARE is at present Chairman of the Washington Committee for Black Power. His enthusiasm for academic freedom and freedom of speech brought him dismissal without warning or benefit of hearing from Howard University, along with five other professors and twenty students. In his early years of study he distinguished himself both academically and as a boxer at Langston University. His master's degree and doctorate were conferred by the University of Chicago; he began teaching at Howard in 1961, but was compelled to desert his sport in order to do so. Dr. Hare has published in many journals, magazines, and newspapers, including: *Phylon Review,* the *Saturday Evening Post, Ebony,* and the *American Sociological Review.* In 1965, his first book, *The Black Anglo-Saxons,* was published, and he has an essay in a forthcoming book edited by LeRoi Jones. He is included in *Who's Who in American Education, Who's Who in the South and Southwest,* and *Outstanding Personalities of the South.*

ADELAIDE CROMWELL HILL was born in Washington, D. C., where she attended Dunbar High School. She continued her education at Smith College and holds a doctorate in sociology from Radcliffe College. Dr. Hill has been a lecturer at Hunter College (New York); an instructor at Smith College; and a teaching fellow at Radcliffe. In 1953, she acted as United States Cultural Exchange Specialist in Africa and Israel, and in 1959 as Visiting Lecturer in Sociology at the University College in Ghana. At present she is Assistant Professor in Sociology and Research Associate for the African Studies Program at Boston University. Dr. Hill has published widely and is co-author with Martin Kilson of the forthcoming anthology, *Apropos of Africa: Sentiments of American Negro Leaders on Africa from the 1800's to the 1950's.*

JULIUS W. HOBSON is chairman of the local chapter of ACT in Washington, D. C. Formerly he was a member of the National

Council of CORE. He held this position for four years until 1964, when, he states, he had the singular experience of being the only member of CORE to be expelled because of his views on Black Power. Recently, he figured prominently in the Washington landmark school case which resulted in the resignation of former school superintendent, Carl F. Hansen. Hobson has been and continues to be a long-distance runner for human rights.

JOHN E. JOHNSON writes: "My background has been one which has involved me with the arts since my high school days. I have a Master's in Fine Arts from the City University of New York. My experience includes directing the Adult Acting Program at the Dorothy Maynor School of the Arts, and acting in such plays as *The Little Foxes* by Lillian Hellman, and *Call Me By My Rightful Name.* I was Chairman of the Art Department and Asst. Principal in charge of students and arts for the New York City Board of Education. At present, I am Asst. Prof. of Fine Arts at Lincoln University."

LEROI JONES comes from Newark, N. J. He studied at Rutgers University, Howard University, Columbia University, and The New School in New York. His writings include *The Dead Lecturer* (poems), *The System of Dante's Hell* (a novel), *The Blues People* (an analysis of black music) and several plays. His *Dutchman* won the Obie Award for the Best American Play of the 1963-64 off-Broadway season, and was made recently into a motion picture. The foundation and direction of the Black Arts Repertory Theater and School in Harlem is one of his enterprises towards the growth of conscious Black culture. He has just published *Tales,* a collection of short stories.

MAULANA RON KARENGA is founder-chairman of US, the Black Nationalist Cultural Organization. He holds a master's degree in political science and African studies from the University of California in Los Angeles, and is a doctoral candidate. He was co-ordinator of the Watts Grass Roots Community Seminar at University of Southern California in 1966. He has been an instructor of Swahili for the Los Angeles Board of Education, and was formerly a social worker for Los Angeles County. As a consultant and advisor, Karenga has done much for community youth groups. He has lectured on urban problems, Afro-American and African history, politics and leadership at the grass roots level. Until recently, he was lecturer for the Social Action Training Center in Los Angeles.

MALCOLM X. At his birth in Omaha, Nebraska, in 1925, he was named Malcolm Little. His father, the Rev. Earl Little, was a staunch Garveyite who died a violent death. Malcolm always believed his father had been left across tracks for a streetcar to run over him. Later, he was to remember his father's telling him: "No one knows when the hour of Africa's redemption cometh. It is in the wind. It is coming. One day, like a storm, it will be here."

Malcolm's early life was one of dissent. He dropped out of school at the age of fifteen, and by the age of twenty-one was serving a prison term for burglary. In prison he heard about the Messenger of Allah from his brother, and subsequently joined the Nation of Islam. After prison, he devoted his energies to serving the Black Muslim movement. He took the name *Malcolm X*. In March, 1964, having left the movement, he organized the first Muslim Mosque Inc., and later founded the non-religious Organization of Afro-American Unity. During this year he visited Europe and the Middle East twice; the following year, three months after his last trip, he was assassinated in New York on February 21, 1965.

FLOYD BIXLER McKISSICK was appointed National Director of CORE in March, 1966, by its Board of Directors, succeeding James Farmer. Prior to this, he was admitted to the North Carolina bar in 1952, having received his degree from North Carolina Law School. He was admitted to the United States Supreme Court in 1955. He opened his law office in Durham, N. C., where he handled a record number of civil rights cases. His clients included businessmen, labor unions, Muslims and whites. During this time, he was directing the affairs of the Durham CORE, and acting as State Advisor of the NAACP Youth Groups. He has spoken at many colleges and universities across the nation; gave expert testimony to the Senate Committee on Urban Problems (Ribicoff Committee) in December, 1966; and has written many articles and essays. McKissick has won recognition for his work in reorganizing CORE from a business as well as a philosophical point of view.

GASTON NEAL writes: "Dead born—1934, reborn 61 with the knowledge of the beauty of my blackness, the unfailing destiny of my people and me. . . .
Born and raised in Pittsburgh, Penn. Black Hill district.

My philosophy after I destroyed the whiteness or most of it, for I believe somewhere in me there is still some hiding, however I will not rest until I am purged and linked completely with my brothers in the struggle to destroy the enemy and rebuild a Black Nation, right now my philosophy is simple:
    Discipline for Unity —
                    Unity for a Nation
    Discipline for Unity —

Have read all over the east coast, New York, New Jersey, Penna., Boston etc., wrote, directed, acted in, read a narrative play *Notes for a Suicide* with black music (Mickey Bass, bass, Kenny Fisher, tenor, Al Blairman, drums, Beaver Harris, drums) in Pittsburgh Art festival—published in *Soulbook, Liberator, Change, Wildfire* LeRoi Jones. . . .

Right now my life is involved in the New School of Afro-American Thought (Washington, D.C.)
I am the Cultural Director and am editing a volume of poetry of my time spent in St. Elizabeth's Hospital."

LAWRENCE P. NEAL was formerly arts and cultural editor of *Liberator* magazine. He is also co-editor along with LeRoi Jones of a forthcoming anthology of Black writing called *Black Fire*. His work has appeared in *Soulbook, Negro Digest, Black Dialogue, Journal of Black Poetry,* and *Freedomways*.

ALVIN F. POUSSAINT is a native New Yorker who received his doctorate in medicine from Cornell University Medical College in 1960. He did his undergraduate work at Columbia College and holds a master's degree from the University of California. While in Los Angeles, he moved into the field of psychiatry, which he was later to teach at Tufts University Medical School in Boston, Mass., 1965-66. During the same year the Medical Committee for Human Rights in Jackson, Miss., claimed his services as Southern Field Director. Since then he has taught at the University of Oklahoma Medical School as Visiting Lecturer, and at present holds an assistant professorship in psychiatry at Tufts. Dr. Poussaint has been published in numerous periodicals and is a member of the American Psychiatric Association and the National Medical Association.

BYRON RUSHING writes: "After I left Syracuse and CORE in 1964, I went to work for the Northern Student Movement in Boston, mostly doing what we called 'politicization' in Roxbury. Later I directed a project in Black Boston for the Massachusetts Council of Churches. I am presently serving a two-year 'sentence' at Rochester General Hospital, giving enemas to whiteys because I refuse to participate as a dumb mercenary in godless white democracy's war against our yellow brothers. I see the piece published here as chapter one in my, as LeRoi Jones put it, twenty-volume suicide note."

JEAN SMITH is a graduate of Howard University in Washington, D. C., which she attended on a four-year scholarship and where she was elected to Phi Beta Kappa. With her husband, whom she met in 1964 when both were working for SNCC, she helped set up a foundation through which several black families in the Delta area of the Mississippi built their own concrete-block houses to replace tents and shacks. The Smiths now operate a janitorial supplies and household goods store in Greenville, Miss., hoping to develop an economic basis for the Black community. They are also working to establish a vocational training and literacy program.

CHUCK STONE was Director of Public Information and Press Relations at the National Conference on Black Power held in

Newark, N. J., in 1967. His activities as an international journalist and editor, and as television commentator (WCIU-TV, Chicago, 1965), had suited him excellently for the job. From March 1965 to February 1967 he acted as Special Assistant to the Chairman (Rep. Adam C. Powell) of the House Committee on Education and Labor. He received his undergraduate training in political science and economics from Wesleyan University and his master's in sociology from Chicago University. He has taught journalism at Columbia College in Chicago and been editor of newspapers in New York, Chicago, and Washington, D. C. Stone has acted as Overseas Representative of CARE in Egypt, Gaza and India. Since 1960, he has been the recipient of awards for journalism, and in 1964, he was named Outstanding Citizen of the Year by the Chicago chapter of CORE. At present, he is at work on two books *Tell It Like It Is* and *Negro Political Power in America.*

BARBARA ANN TEER is a native of East St. Louis, Illinois. She holds a B.S. degree from the University of Illinois and has taken advanced study at the University of Wisconsin and Connecticut College for Women. She made her Broadway debut in *Kwamina* and has played leads and featured parts in eight off-Broadway shows including *Day of Absence, Raisin' Hell in the Sun, The Living Premise,* and *Home Movies* for which she was awarded the Vernon Rice Drama Desk Award for off-Broadway's best actress of the year. She has appeared on Broadway in William Inge's *Where's Daddy;* has been on numerous television programs; and recently received high praise for her leading role in *Who's Got His Own,* the first play produced by The American Place Theater for their 1966-67 season.

MARGARET WALKER received her undergraduate training at Northwestern University and received the degree of Master of Arts from the University of Iowa. She married, raised a family, taught, and in 1963 received a fellowship at Iowa where she was granted a Ph.D., and completed her novel *Jubilee,* which was to win the Houghton Mifflin Literary Fellowship in 1966. At present she lives with her family in Jackson, Mississippi, where she teaches at Jackson College. The poem included in this volume was taken from her first published book, *For My People.*

ROBERT F. WILLIAMS was born in Monroe, North Carolina, in 1925. His tour of duty in the U. S. Marine Corps reinforced his belief in a man's basic right to defend himself and his home against any would-be violator. He returned to Monroe and became interested in civil rights activities. Later he was to become president of the local chapter of NAACP, and his efforts on behalf of his community were to receive nationwide attention. His long struggle with racist forces in the South, documented in his book *Negroes with Guns,* culminated in a frame-up against Williams for kidnapping. He is presently in exile.

NATHAN WRIGHT, JR., is Adam Clayton Powell's successor as Plans Committee Chairman of the 1967 National Conference on Black Power. An education and urbanization consultant, he is currently Executive Director of the Department of Urban Work of the Episcopal Diocese of Newark, New Jersey. A onetime Freedom Rider and CORE Field Secretary, Dr. Wright holds five college degrees, including a doctorate in education from Harvard University. He lectures in Urban Sociology at New York City Community College, and has written several books on religious subjects, including the award-winning *One Bread, One Body.* He is author of the recent *Black Power and Urban Unrest.*

ABOUT THE EDITOR

Floyd Barrington Barbour grew up in Washington, D. C. He is a graduate of Dunbar High School in Washington, and of Bowdoin College in Brunswick, Maine. He studied and traveled in Europe, and served as a teaching fellow at Howard University. He has written a number of plays, including *Auto Sacramental, Oranges, The Bird Cage, Sweet Jesus,* and *Day Work,* which have been performed at Bowdoin College, Yale University, Brandeis University, Howard University, the Institute for Advanced Studies in the Theater Arts, New York, and by the Garrick Players of Catholic University. *The Black Power Revolt* is his first book; he lives in Boston, Massachusetts.

APPENDIX I

HON. ADAM C. POWELL

My Black Position Paper

Taken from the Congressional Record, *Proceedings and Debates of the 89th Congress, Second Session*

Mr. Speaker, this year I celebrate a quarter of a century in politics.

In those 25 years, a philosophy which has guided my thought and my every act has evolved out of my life experiences as minister, politician, Congressman, and man from Harlem.

This philosophy is summed up in what I call my "Black Position Paper."

But it is an open-end continuing document whose contents are always subject to the influence of new ideas and changing events.

The black position paper is an outline for living and call to action for America's black people.

It is, above all, that passionate re-affirmation in what black people are today and what we can be tomorrow.

The following 17 points comprise my black position paper:

1. We must give our children a sense of pride in being black. The glory of our past and the dignity of our present must lead the way to the power of our future.

2. Black organizations must be black led. Other ethnic groups lead their own organizations. We must do the same. Jews lead the American Jewish Congress, American Jewish Committee and B'nai B'rith. Irish control the St. Patrick's Day Parade Committee and the Irish-American Historical Society. Poles head the Polish-American Congress and the Polish National Alliance. Italians lead the Italian-American Democratic organizations and

the Italian-American Labor Council. This kind of honest pluralism is a happy fact of American life.

3. The black masses must be primarily responsible for their own organizations. Only with black financial control can black organizations retain their honesty, their independence and their full commitment to the urgency of immediate equality.

4. The black masses must demand and refuse to accept nothing less than that proportionate share of political jobs and appointments which are equal to their proportion in the electorate. Where we are 20% of the voters, we should command 20% of the jobs, judgeships, commissionerships, and all political appointments.

5. Black people must support and push black candidates for political office first. This mandate should apply particularly where black candidates are at least equally well-qualified as other candidates.

6. Black people must seek audacious power—the kind of power which cradles your head amongst the stars and gives you the security to stand up as proud men and women, eyeball to eyeball with the rest of the world.

As Chairman of the House Committee on Education and Labor, I control all labor and education legislation. This year, my Committee will raise the minimum wage for the second time in five years—both during my chairmanship. When I first became chairman, the Federal commitment to education was $450 million. It is now $360 billion—an eightfold increase. The $1.7 billion for the war on poverty which has given the poor of America their first opportunity to be heard as a national voice derives its mandate from my Committee.

This is legislative power. This is political power. Above all, this is audacious power.

7. Black leadership in the North and the South must shift its emphasis to the two-pronged thrust of the Black Revolution: economic self-sufficiency and political power. The Civil Rights Act of 1964 (with the exception of Title VII or the "FEPC Title") has absolutely no meaning for black people in New York, Los Angeles, Chicago, Philadelphia, Detroit, or any of the northern cities.

It has been difficult for black leadership to grasp these new dimensions of necessary economic and political power for the black masses. This is because black leadership has been saturated too long with too many hustling social workers and professional "Negro leaders" whose only contribution they can make to American society is that they are white handpicked "leaders."

8. Black masses must produce and contribute to the economy of this country in the proportionate strength of their population. Rather than a race primarily of consumers and stockboys, we must become a race of producers and stock brokers.

9. Black communities of this country—whether they are New York's Harlem, Los Angeles' Watts, Chicago's South and West Sides, Philadelphia's North Side or Detroit's East Side—must neither tolerate or accept outside leadership, black or white.

Too many black communities in America today suffer from absentee black leadership.

Black communities must insist on black leaders living amongst them, knowing and sharing the harsh truths of the ghetto. These black leaders—the ministers, the politicians, the businessmen, the doctors and the lawyers—must come back to the black communities from their suburban sanctuaries or be purged as leaders.

10. The black masses should follow only those leaders who have true power—what President Kennedy called clout—and who can sit at the bargaining table with the white power structure as equals in power and negotiate for a share of the loaf of bread, instead of begging for some of its crumbs. These leaders will be chosen by the black masses themselves.

11. Demonstrations and all continuing protest activity must be non-violent. Violence even when it erupts recklessly in anger among our teenagers must be curbed and discouraged.

12. Black people must continue to defy the laws of man when such laws conflict with the law of God. The law of God ordains that "there is neither Jew nor Greek, there is neither bond nor free, there is neither male nor female: for ye are all one in Christ Jesus.

13. Black people must discover a new and creative involvement with ourselves. We must turn our energies *inwardly* toward our homes, our churches, our families, our children, our colleges, our neighborhoods, our businesses and our communities. Our fraternal and social groups must become an integral part of this creative involvement by energizing their resources toward constructive fund raising and community activities.

Too much time is spent on cotillions and champagne sips and running around sipping martinis in the homes of suburban white families. Some of those energies should be directed to helping black families who are starving in the inner city.

14. The War on Poverty must become that more productive crusade for jobs. The only thing that keeps a man impoverished is his incapacity to earn a living. Put some green in his pocket and some bread in his soul and he'll be that better citizen, that more productive father, that finer American.

15. The battle against segregation in America's public school systems must become a national effort, instead of the present regional skirmish that now exists. Title VI of the 1964 Civil Rights Act outlaws *de jure* racial segregation. It has no meaning or application to the hard core pockets of *de facto* racial segregation in Northern schools which is just as malicious, just as destructive of the human spirit.

16. We must put pressures on our predominantly black colleges to shift their emphasis from teacher education to nuclear physics and aerodynamics. Black colleges are still grinding out teachers and sociologists while other major schools are graduating space engineers and nuclear physicists.

17. Every black man who considers himself an American must become a *registered voter*. Freedom in a democracy rests on a free electorate. A free electorate only survives when people vote. But do more than vote. Learn to vote for those who are your friends, against those who are your enemies. No black person over 21 must be permitted to walk a picket line or participate in any demonstration unless he or she is a registered voter.

APPENDIX II

LETTER FROM ELIJAH MUHAMMAD

Dear Mr. Barbour:

. . . . . I hope that you understand me, and the Message of Allah given to me for the salvation of my people and the Blackman of the world. Of course the leaders of the Black Nation, Brown Nation and Yellow Nation recognize the Message God gave to me as being the salvation for the so-called American Negro. But, the desire of self-leadership among our Black people keeps them divided and working in opposition to our own salvation, unity, and universal recognition of the Nations.

I have been given an answer to the true way in which we can get the respect of the Nations, i.e. by teaching them the true knowledge of self and self-respect and the doing of something for self, seeking self-independence under the guidance of the All Wise God, who is on the scene to deliver us from the cursed way of our enemies and from the power of the enemy to control us according to his wishes.

A clear knowledge of the enemy makes us to resist the enemy; but without a clear knowledge of the enemy, we cannot resist the enemy's power to rule over us. Think over the smartest politicians or intellectuals of our people that want to be respected. They will not get out of the name of the white man, which binds them to the white man as a slave or servant. They want recognition by their people in Asia, and Africa, and even by the white man, wherever he may be. But, they cannot give you honor by your being a servant or a follower and doer of the white man's way of civilization.

By no means can we ever become independent under the names Mr. Jones and Mr. Culpepper (names of the white race). This shows a slave, and a people which has no knowledge of the value of being called by its own names, and names especially with Divine meanings. The so-called Negro could learn the whole of knowledge written in books of the Nations of the earth, but if he still desires to be called by his slave masters' and his children's names, he will not be recognized by the independent civilizations of the earth. I am proving this to you.

I made Muhammad Ali an example—after taking away the slave name Cassius Clay—giving him the name Muhammad Ali, then Africa and Asia recognized him immediately. And, whenever there, he can visit among them receiving respect. Regardless of the white man's dislike of calling him Muhammad Ali, the white man knows that he is entitled to be called that name or any of the 99 attributes of Allah. But of course, he is not going to tell the so-called American Negro to go out after these kind of names, which he knows relieve you as a servant or slave from his service, because if he wanted to cast you out of his society you have the membership of African and Asian societies. And, that if he wanted to drive you out of the country, you have a home among the Muslims of Asia and Africa. This, he knows; and, if he declares war against you, he knows that war will be declared against him by the Asians and Africans for the sake and protection of all the Muslims in America. So, why should he (the white man) endorse you to become a Muslim, when he knows that Islam frees you of his power and that you have greater forces backing you than he can muster?

Even to the modestly dressed girls and women followers of mine. The white man knows that you will not get respect by letting the women wear his short dresses, cut off knee-length and above the knee, like the Christian women. He knows that this is not decent. Even the white priests know but to get the so-called Negro, they tempt him to follow them, to marry their girls or boys (by being sexually tempted)—such characters will not see the Hereafter. He (the Black man) will go down with the white men with the destruction of their filth and evil. This is all that they want to do in everything. They tempt the Black man by offering him higher office positions in the government. They are only doing this to make him think that he has a great future now with them. But, we know better. We know they are doomed to be destroyed in the immediate future. This they know. If he will only just read the Bible, which they have poisoned, the truth in it bears me witness that they will do all of this filthy temptation of our people to get us to go with them in a lake of fire.

Thank you for reading this.

Sincerely,

Elijah Muhammad,
Messenger of Allah

APPENDIX III

"BLACK POWER"

A Statement By The National
Committee of Negro Churchmen
July 31, 1966

We, an informal group of Negro churchmen in America, are deeply disturbed about the crisis brought upon our country by historic distortions of important human realities in the controversy about "black power." What we see shining through the variety of rhetoric is not anything new but the same old problem of power and race which has faced our beloved country since 1619.

We realize that neither the term "power" nor the term "Christian Conscience" is an easy matter to talk about, especially in the context of race relations in America. The fundamental distortion facing us in the controversy about "black power" is rooted in a gross imbalance of power and conscience between Negroes and white Americans. It is this distortion, mainly, which is responsible for the widespread, though often inarticulate, assumption that white people are justified in getting what they want through the use of power, but that Negro Americans must, either by nature or by circumstances, make their appeal only through conscience. As a result, the power of white men and the conscience of black men have both been corrupted. The power of white men is corrupted because it meets little meaningful resistance from Negroes to temper it and keep white men from aping God. The conscience of black men is corrupted because, having no power to implement the demands of conscience, the concern for justice is transmuted into a distorted form of love, which, in the absence of justice, becomes chaotic self-surrender. Powerlessness breeds a race of beggars. We are faced now with a situation where conscienceless power meets powerless conscience, threatening the very foundations of our nation.

Therefore, we are impelled by conscience to address at least four groups of people in areas where clarification of the controversy is of the most urgent necessity. We do not claim to present the final word. It is our hope, however, to communicate meanings from our experience regarding power and certain elements of conscience to help interpret more adequately the dilemma in which we are all involved.

I. To the Leaders of America: Power and Freedom

It is of critical importance that the leaders of this nation listen also to a voice which says that the principal source of the threat to our nation comes neither from the riots erupting in our big cities, nor from the disagreements among the leaders of the civil rights movement, nor even from mere raising of the cry for "black power." These events, we believe, are but the expression of the judgment of God upon our nation for its failure to use its abundant resources to serve the real well-being of people, at home and abroad.

We give our full support to all civil rights leaders as they seek for basically American goals, for we are not convinced that their mutual reinforcement of one another in the past is bound to end in the future. We would hope that the public power of our nation will be used to strengthen the civil rights movement and not to manipulate or further fracture it.

We deplore the overt violence of riots, but we believe it is more important to focus on the real sources of these eruptions. These sources may be abetted inside the ghetto, but their basic causes lie in the silent and covert violence which white middle-class America inflicts upon the victims of the inner city. The hidden, smooth and often smiling decisions of American leaders which tie a white noose of suburbia around the necks, and which pin the backs of the masses of Negroes against the steaming ghetto walls—without jobs in a booming economy; with dilapidated and segregated educational systems in the full view of unenforced laws against it; in short: the failure of American leaders to use American power to create equal opportunity *in life* as well as *in law*—this is the real problem and not the anguished cry for "black power."

From the point of view of the Christian faith, there is nothing necessarily wrong with concern for power. At the heart of the Protestant reformation is the belief that ultimate power belongs to God alone and that men become most inhuman when concentrations of power lead to the conviction—overt or covert—that any nation, race or organization can rival God in this regard. At issue in the relations between whites and Negroes in America is the problem of inequality of power. Out of this imbalance grows the disrespect of white men for the Negro personality and community, and the disrespect of Negroes for themselves. This is a fundamental root of human injustice in America. In one sense, the concept of "black power" reminds us of the need for the possibility of authentic democracy in America.

We do *not* agree with those who say that we must cease expressing concern for the acquisition of power lest we endanger the "gains" already made by the civil rights movement. The fact of the matter is, there have been few substantive gains since about 1950 in this area. The gap has constantly widened between the incomes of non-whites relative to the whites. Since the Supreme Court decision of 1954, de facto segregation in every major city in our land has increased rather than decreased. Since the middle of the 1950s unemployment among Negroes has gone up rather than down while unemployment has decreased in the white community.

While there has been some progress in some areas for equality for Negroes, this progress has been limited mainly to middle-class Negroes who represent only a small minority of the larger Negro community.

These are the hard facts that we must all face together. Therefore, we must not take the position that we can continue in the same old paths.

When American leaders decide to serve the real welfare of people instead of war and destruction; when American leaders are forced to make the rebuilding of our cities first priority on the nation's agenda; when American leaders are forced by the American people to quit misusing and abusing American power; then will the cry for "black power" become inaudible, for the framework in which all power in America operates would include the power and experience of black men as well as those of white men. In that way, the fear of the power of each group would be removed. America is our beloved homeland. But, America is not God. Only God can do everything. America and the other nations of the world must decide which among a number of alternatives they will choose.

II. To White Churchmen: Power and Love

As black men who were long ago forced out of the white church to create and to wield "black power," we fail to understand the emotional quality of the outcry of some clergy against the use of the term today. It is not enough to answer that "integration" is the solution. For it is precisely the nature of the operation of power under some forms of integration which is being challenged. The Negro Church was created as a result of the refusal to submit to the indignities of a false kind of "integration" in which all power was in the hands of white people. A more equal sharing of power is precisely what is required as the precondition of authentic human interaction. We understand the growing demand of Negro and white youth for a more honest kind of integration; one which increases rather than decreases the capacity of the disinherited to participate with power in all of the structures of our common life. Without this capacity to *participate with power*—i.e., to have some organized political and economic strength to really influence people with whom one interacts—integration is not meaningful. For the issue is not one of racial balance but of honest interracial interaction.

For this kind of interaction to take place, all people need power, whether black or white. We regard as sheer hypocrisy or as a blind and dangerous illusion the view that opposes love to power. Love should be a controlling element in power, but what love opposes is precisely the misuse and abuse of power, not power itself. So long as white churchmen continue to moralize and misinterpret Christian love, so long will justice continue to be subverted in this land.

III. To Negro Citizens: Power and Justice

Both the anguished cry for "black power" and the confused emotional response to it can be understood if the whole controversy is put in the context of American history. Especially must we understand the irony involved in the pride of Americans regarding their ability to act as individuals on the one hand, and their tendency to act as members of ethnic groups on the other hand. In the tensions of this part of our history is revealed both the tragedy and the hope of human redemption in America.

America has asked its Negro citizens to fight for opportunity *as individuals* whereas at certain points in our history what we have needed most has been opportunity for the whole group, not just for selected and approved Negroes. Thus in 1863, the slaves were made legally free, as individuals, but the real question regarding personal and group power to maintain that freedom was pushed aside. Power at that time for a mainly rural people meant land and tools to work the land. In the words of Thaddeus Stevens, power meant "40 acres and a mule". But this power was not made available to the slaves and we see the results today in the pushing of a landless peasantry off the farms into big cities where they come in search mainly of the power to be free. What they find are only the formalities of unenforced legal freedom. So we must ask, "what is the nature of the power which we seek and need today?" Power today is essentially organizational power. It is not a thing lying about in the streets to be fought over. It is a thing which, in some measure, already belongs to Negroes and which must be developed by Negroes in relationship with the great resources of this nation.

Getting power necessarily involves reconciliation. We must first be reconciled to ourselves lest we fail to recognize the resources we already have and upon which we can build. We must be reconciled to ourselves as persons and to ourselves as an historical group. This means we must find our way to a new self-image in which we can feel a normal sense of pride in self, including our variety of skin color and the manifold textures of our hair. As long as we are filled with hatred for ourselves we will be unable to respect others.

At the same time, if we are seriously concerned about power then we must build upon that which we already have. "Black power" is already present to some extent in the Negro church, in Negro fraternities and sororities, in our professional associations, and in the opportunities afforded to Negroes who make decisions in some of the integrated organizations of our society.

We understand the reasons by which these limited forms of "black power" have been rejected by some of our people. Too often the Negro church has stirred its members away from the reign of God in *this world* to a distorted and complacent view of *an otherworldly* conception of God's power. We commit ourselves as churchmen to make more meaningful in the life of our institution our conviction that Jesus Christ reigns in the "here" and "now" as well as in the future he brings in upon us. We shall, therefore, use more of the resources of our churches in working for human justice in the places of social change and upheaval where our Master is already at work.

At the same time, we would urge that Negro social and

professional organizations develop new roles for engaging the problem of equal opportunity and put less time into the frivolity of idle chatter and social waste.

We must not apologize for the existence of this form of group power, for we have been oppressed as a group, not as individuals. We will not find our way out of that oppression until both we and America accept the need for Negro Americans as well as for Jews, Italians, Poles and white Anglo-Saxon Protestants, among others, to have and to wield group power.

However, if power is sought merely as an end in itself, it tends to turn upon those who seek it. Negroes need power in order to participate more effectively at all levels of the life of our nation. We are glad that none of those civil rights leaders who have asked for "black power" have suggested that it means a new form of isolationism or a foolish effort at domination. But we must be clear about why we need to be reconciled with the white majority. It is *not* because we are only one-tenth of the population in America; for we do not need to be reminded of the awesome power wielded by the 90% majority. We see and feel that power every day in the destructions heaped upon our families and upon the nation's cities. We do not need to be threatened by such cold and heartless statements. For we are men, not children, and we are growing out of our fear of that power, which can hardly hurt us any more in the future than it does in the present or has in the past. Moreover, those bare figures conceal the potential political strength which is ours if we organize properly in the big cities and establish effective alliances.

Neither must we rest our concern for reconciliation with our white brothers on the fear that failure to do so would damage gains already made by the civil rights movement. If those gains are in fact real, they will withstand the claims of our people for power and justice, not just for a few select Negroes here and there, but for the masses of our citizens. We must rather rest our concern for reconciliation on the firm ground that we and all other Americans *are* one. Our history and destiny are indissolubly linked. If the future is to belong to any of us, it must be prepared for all of us whatever our racial or religious background. For in the final analysis, we are *persons* and the power of all groups must be wielded to make visible our common humanity.

The future of America will belong to neither white nor black unless all Americans work together at the task of rebuilding our cities. We must organize not only among ourselves but with other groups in order that we can, together, gain power sufficient to change this nation's sense of what is *now* important and what must be done *now*. We must work with the remainder of the nation to organize whole cities for the task of making the rebuilding of our cities first priority in the use of our resources. This is more important than who gets to the moon first or the war in Vietnam.

To accomplish this task we cannot expend our energies in spastic or ill-tempered explosions without meaningful goals. We must move from the politics of philanthropy to the politics of metropolitan development for equal opportunity. We must relate all groups of the city together in new ways in order that the truth of our cities might be laid bare and in order that, together, we can lay claim to the great resources of our nation to make truth more human.

IV. To the Mass Media: Power and Truth

The ability or inability of all people in America to understand the upheavals of our day depends greatly on the way power and truth operate in the mass media. During the Southern demonstrations for civil rights, you men of the communications industry performed an invaluable service for the entire country by revealing plainly to our ears and eyes, the ugly truth of a brutalizing system of overt discrimination and segregation. Many of you were mauled and injured, and it took courage for you to stick with the task. You were instruments of change and not merely purveyors of unrelated facts. You were able to do this by dint of personal courage and by reason of the power of national news agencies which supported you.

Today, however, your task and ours is more difficult. The truth that needs revealing today is not so clear-cut in its outlines, nor is there a national consensus to help you form relevant points of view. Therefore, nothing is now more important than that you look for a variety of sources of truth in order that the limited perspectives of all of us might be corrected. Just as you related to a broad spectrum of people in Mississippi instead of relying only on police records and establishment figures, so must you operate in New York City, Chicago and Cleveland.

The power to support you in this endeavor *is present* in our country. It must be searched out. We desire to use our limited influence to help relate you to the variety of experience in the Negro community so that limited controversies are not blown up into the final truth about us. The fate of this country is, to no small extent, dependent upon how you interpret the crises upon us, so that human truth is disclosed and human needs are met.

SIGNATORIES:

Bishop John D. Bright, Sr., AME Church, First Episcopal District, Philadelphia, Pennsylvania

The Rev. John Bryan, Connecticut Council of Churches, Hartford, Connecticut

Suffragan Bishop John M. Burgess, The Episcopal Church, Boston, Massachusetts

The Rev. W. Sterling Cary, Grace Congregational Church, New York, N.Y.

The Rev. Charles E. Cobb, St. John Church (UCC), Springfield, Mass.

The Rev. Caesar D. Coleman, Christian Methodist Episcopal Church, Memphis, Tennessee

The Rev. Joseph C. Coles, Williams Institutional C.M.E. Church, New York, New York

The Rev. George A. Crawley, Jr., St. Paul Baptist Church, Baltimore, Maryland

The Rev. O. Herbert Edwards, Trinity Baptist Church, Baltimore, Md.

The Rev. Bryant George, United Presbyterian Church in the U.S.A., New York, New York

Bishop Charles F. Golden, The Methodist Church, Nashville, Tenn.

The Rev. Quinland R. Gordon, The Episcopal Church, New York, N.Y.

The Rev. James Hargett, Church of Christian Fellowship, U.C.C., Los Angeles, Calif.

The Rev. Edler Hawkins, St. Augustine Presbyterian Church, New York, New York

The Rev. Reginald Hawkins, United Presbyterian Church, Charlotte, North Carolina

Dr. Anna Arnold Hedgeman, Commission on Religion and Race, National Council of Churches, New York, New York

The Rev. R. E. Hood, Gary, Indiana

The Rev. H. R. Hughes, Bethel A.M.E. Church, New York, N.Y.

The Rev. Kenneth Hughes, St. Bartholomew's Episcopal Church, Cambridge, Massachusetts

The Rev. Donald G. Jacobs, St. James A.M.E. Church, Cleveland, Ohio

The Rev. J. L. Joiner, Emanuel A.M.E. Church, New York, New York

The Rev. Arthur A. Jones, Metropolitan A.M.E. Church, Philadelphia, Pennsylvania

The Rev. Stanley King, Sabathini Baptist Church, Minneapolis, Minn.

The Rev. Earl Wesley Lawson, Emanuel Baptist Church, Malden, Mass.

The Rev. David Licorish, Abyssinian Baptist Church, New York, N.Y.

The Rev. Arthur B. Mack, St. Thomas A.M.E.Z. Church, Haverstraw, N.Y.

The Rev. James W. Mack, South United Church of Christ, Chicago, Ill.

The Rev. O. Clay Maxwell, Jr., Baptist Ministers Conference of New York City and Vicinity, New York, New York

The Rev. Leon Modeste, The Episcopal Church, New York, N.Y.

Bishop Noah W. Moore, Jr., The Methodist Church, Southwestern Area, Houston, Texas

The Rev. David Nickerson, Episcopal Society for Cultural and Racial Unity, Atlanta, Georgia

The Rev. LeRoy Patrick, Bethesda United Presbyterian Church, Pittsburgh, Pennsylvania

The Rev. Benjamin F. Payton, Commission on Religion and Race, National Council of Churches, New York, New York

The Rev. Isaiah P. Pogue, St. Mark's Presbyterian Church, Cleveland, Ohio

The Rev. Sandy F. Ray, Empire Baptist State Convention, Brooklyn, N.Y.

Bishop Herbert B. Shaw, Presiding Bishop, Third Episcopal District, A.M.E.Z. Church, Wilmington, N.C.

The Rev. Stephen P. Spottswood, Commission on Race and Cultural Relations, Detroit Council of Churches, Detroit, Michigan

The Rev. Henri A. Stines, Church of the Atonement, Washington, D.C.

Bishop James S. Thomas, Resident Bishop, Iowa Area, The Methodist Church, Des Moines, Iowa

The Rev. V. Simpson Turner, Mt. Carmel Baptist Church, Brooklyn, N.Y.

The Rev. Edgar Ward, Grace Presbyterian Church, Chicago, Ill.

The Rev. Paul M. Washington, Church of the Advocate, Philadelphia, Pa.

The Rev. Frank L. Williams, Methodist Church, Baltimore, Maryland

The Rev. John W. Williams, St. Stephen's Baptist C h u r c h, Kansas City, Mo.

The Rev. Gayraud Wilmore, United Presbyterian Church U.S.A., New York, N.Y.

The Rev. M. L. Wilson, Covenant Baptist Church, New York, New York

The Rev. Robert H. Wilson, Corresponding Secretary, National Baptist Convention of America, Dallas, Texas

The Rev. Nathan Wright, Episcopal Diocese of Newark, Newark, N.J.

(Organizational affiliation given for identification purposes only.)

BIBLIOGRAPHY

PERIODICAL READINGS
COMPILED BY RICHARD NEWMAN
DEPARTMENT OF HUMAN RELATIONS, BOSTON UNIVERSITY

Allen, Gary, "Black Power," *American Opinion,* January 1967.
Analavage, Robert, "A Victory in Defeat in Lowndes," *National Guardian,* November 19, 1966.
_____. "Lowndes Party Girds for Future," *The Southern Patriot,* December 1966.
Bailey, Gordon, "Big Rally in Watts Hears Carmichael," *The Militant,* December 5, 1966.
Baldwin, James and Schulberg, Budd, "Dialog in Black and White," *Playboy,* December 1966.
Barnes, Elizabeth, "Black Power," *Young Socialist,* August-September 1966.
_____. "Independent Politics: The Significance of the Black Panther Party," *Young Socialist,* October - November 1966.
Bennett, Lerone, Jr., "Stokely Carmichael: Architect of Black Power," *Ebony,* September 1966.
Benson, John, "Interview with Stokely Carmichael," *The Militant,* May 23, 1966.
"Black Power and the White Radical," *19: A Radical Newspaper of the Committee for Independent Political Action,* October 21, 1966.
Boggs, James, "Black Power: A Scientific Concept Whose Time Has Come," *Liberator,* May 1967.
_____. "Power! Black Power!" *Liberator,* January 1967.
Bone, Richard, "A Black Man's Quarrel With the Christian God," *New York Times Book Review,* September 11, 1966.
Boyd, Malcolm, "Freedom Means Black Power," *Renewal,* August 1966.

Braden, Anne, "The SNCC Trends: Challenge to White America." *The Southern Patriot,* May 1966.

Breeden, James, "Demythologizing Black Power," *Christianity and Crisis,* August 10, 1966.

Breitman, George, "In Defense of Black Power," *International Socialist Review,* January - February 1967.

Brooks, Robin, "Black Power and White Liberals," *new left notes,* September 2, 1966.

Brown, C., "Power of Blackness," *Look,* June 27, 1967.

Carmichael, Stokely and Blackwell, Randolph. "Black Power: The Widening Dialogue," *New South,* Summer 1966.

——————. "SNCC-1966," Published by SNCC, n.d.

——————. "Symposium," *Negro Digest,* October 1966.

——————. "Toward Black Liberation," *The Massachusetts Review,* Autumn 1966.

Cave, Clarence L., "A Creative Response to Racism," *Social Progress,* March - April 1967.

Clausen, Oliver, "A Global Vision for Black Cats," *The Globe Magazine,* April 15, 1967.

Cloward, Richard A., and Piven, Frances F. "Desegregated Housing," *The New Republic,* December 17, 1966.

Cobb, Charles E., "Now More Than Ever," *Social Action,* December 1966.

Coles, Robert, "Two Minds About Carmichael," *The New Republic,* November 12, 1966.

Cook, Samuel, "The Tragic Myth of Black Power," *New South,* Summer 1966.

Danzig, David, "In Defense of Black Power," *Commentary,* September 1966.

Detwiler, Bruce, "A Time to be Black," *The New Republic,* September 17, 1966.

"Excerpts From Paper on Which the 'Black Power' Philosophy Is Based," *The New York Times,* August 5, 1966.

Feldman, Paul, "How the Cry for Black Power Began," *Dissent,* September - October 1966.

——————. "The Pathos of Black Power," *Dissent,* January - February 1967.

Fiddick, Thomas C., "Black Power, Capitalism and Vietnam," *Liberation,* September 1966.

Good, Paul, "A White Look at Black Power," *The Nation,* August 8, 1966.

————. "The Meredith March," *New South,* Summer 1966.

————. "The Gift of Blackness," *Katallegete,* Summer 1967.

————. "When Stokely Met the Presidents: Black Power and Negro Education," *Motive,* January 1967.

Hare, Nathan, "Behind the Black College Student Revolt," *Ebony,* August 1967.

————. " 'Black Power'—Its Goals and Methods," Interview, *U.S. News and World Report,* May 22, 1967.

Hentoff, Nat, "Applying Black Power," *Evergreen,* December 1966.

Hurt, H., "Negro Politics," *Reporter,* August 13, 1966.

Jackson, James E., "National Pride—Not Nationalism," *Political Affairs,* May 1967.

————. "The Meaning of Black Power," *Political Affairs,* September 1966.

Jehlen, Alen, "Black Power and Political Strategy," *new left notes,* November 11, 1966.

King, Martin Luther, Jr., "Black Power," *The Progressive,* November 1966.

————. "Martin Luther King Defines Black Power," *The New York Times Magazine,* June 11, 1967.

Kopkind, Andrew, "Lair of the Black Panther," *The New Republic,* August 13, 1966.

————. "Soul Power," *New York Review of Books,* August 24, 1967.

————. "The Future of Black Power," *The New Republic,* January 7, 1967.

Landy, Sy, "Powell and Black Power," *Independent Socialist,* March - April 1967.

Lawson, James M., Jr., "Black Power and the Mississippi March," *Fellowship,* September 1966.

Lincoln, C. Eric, "Black Power," *Together,* January 1967.

Long, Margaret, "Black Power in the Black Belt," *The Progressive,* October 1966.

McKissick, Floyd, "Black Power," *Interracial Review,* July 1966.

McNeill, Robert B., "Black Revolution: How Should Whites Respond?" *Together,* May 1967.

McWilliams, Wilson, "On Black Power," *The Activist,* Fall 1966.

MANAS, "The Psychology of Social Morality," reprinted in *Liberation,* October 1966.

Marine, Gene and Adam Hochschild, "Color Black Gloomy," *Ramparts,* December 1966.

Marion, John H., "Is Black Power Being Oversold?" *Social Progress,* March - April 1967.

Meyer, F. S., "Negro Revolution: a New Phase," *National Review,* October 4, 1966.

Millspaugh, F., "Black Power," *Commonweal,* August 5, 1966.

Moody, Howard, "White Integrationists and the 'Black Power' Movement," *Christianity and Crisis,* October 17, 1966.

Morrison, Derrick, "The Rise of Black Power," *Young Socialist,* October - November 1966.

Moulds, George Henry, "Color It Black or White: It's Still Power," *Vital Speeches,* April 1, 1967.

Newman, Richard, "Black Power: A New Direction for the Movement," *Concern,* September 1, 1966.

——————. "Black Power and White Liberals," *Register - Leader,* November 1966.

——————. "The Black Power Revolution," *Boston University Graduate Journal,* Fall 1967.

Nordin, K., "Interview with Stokely Carmichael," *The Christian Science Monitor,* September 22, 1966.

Patterson, William, "Black Power, Blackmail, Backlash," *American Dialog,* November - December 1966.

Payton, Benjamin, "Civil Rights and the Future of American Cities," *Social Action,* December 1966.

Peck, James, "Black Racism," *Liberation,* October 1966.

Peets, Tom, "On Black Power," *Junction,* June 1967.

Poussaint, Alvin F., "A Negro Psychiatrist Explains the Negro Psyche," *The New York Times Magazine,* August 20, 1967.

——————. " 'White Problem' Spawned 'Black Power,' " *Ebony,* August 1967.

Price, William A., "SNCC Charts a Course — an Interview with Stokely Carmichael, Chairman, Student Nonviolent Coordinating Committee," *The National Guardian,* June 4, 1966.

Proctor, Roscoe, "Notes on 'Black Power' Concept," *Political Affairs,* March 1967.

Roberts, Gene, "Negro Nationalism, A Black Power Key," *The New York Times,* July 24, 1966.

——————. "The Story of SNCC — From 'Freedom High' to 'Black Power,' " *The New York Times Magazine,* September 25, 1966.

Roberts, George, "Cassius Clay Warns 'Black Power Will Destroy Negroes!' " *Police Gazette,* April 1967.

Rowan, Carl T., "Crisis in Civil Rights Leadership," *Ebony,* November 1966.

Rustin, Bayard, " 'Black Power' and Coalition Politics," *Commentary,* September 1966.

Schuyler, George, "Negroes Speak Out Against Militants," *Christian Economics,* January 10, 1967.

Sheppard, Barry, "Black Power Attacked by Old Guard Leaders," *The Militant,* October 24, 1966.

—————. "Interview With CORE Leader," *The Militant,* August 8, 1966.

Simon, Alvin, "Black Power and Cambodia," *American Dialog,* November - December 1966.

Sinclair, John, "Stokely in Detroit: Who's Afraid of Black Power?" *The Fifth Estate,* October 16-31, 1966.

Smith, Leonard, "Not Black Power but Human Power," *Look,* September 6, 1966.

Stone, I. F., "SNCC Does Not Wish to Become a New Version of the White Man's Burden," *I. F. Stone's Weekly,* June 6, 1966.

—————. "Why They Cry Black Power," *I. F. Stone's Weekly,* September 19, 1966.

Thomas, Jay, "Negro-White Unity and the Communists," *Political Affairs,* May 1967.

Towne, Anthony, "Revolution and the Marks of Baptism," *Katallegete,* Summer 1967.

Walters, M. George, "Black Power and the Church," *Skandalon,* Fall 1966.

Wechsler, James A., "Killers of the Dream," *The Progressive,* December 1966.

Weinraub, Bernard, "The Brilliancy of Black," *Esquire,* January 1967.

Wilkins, Roy, "Whither Black Power?" *Crisis,* August - September 1966.

Wilmore, Gayraud S., Jr., "The White Church and the Search for Black Power," *Social Progress,* March - April 1967.

Wilson, C. E., "Black Power and the Myth of Black Racism," *Liberation,* September 1966.

Zinn, Howard, "The Healthful Use of Power," *American Journal of Orthopsychiatry,* January 1966.

FURTHER READINGS

1. Background

Clark, Kenneth B., *Dark Ghetto.* New York: Harper & Row, 1965.

Cruse, Harold, *The Crisis of the Negro Intellectual.* New York: William Morrow, 1967.

Dollard, John, *Caste and Class in a Southern Town.* New Haven: Yale University Press, 1937.

Du Bois, W. E. B., *Black Reconstruction.* New York: Harcourt, Brace, 1935; reissued, New York: Russell & Russell, 1964.

Fanon, Frantz, *Black Skin, White Masks.* New York: Grove Press, 1967.

Frazier, E. Franklin, *Black Bourgeoisie.* Glencoe, Ill.: Free Press, 1957.

—————. *The Negro in the United States.* New York: Macmillan, 1949.

Guzman, Jessie P., ed., *Race Relations in the South—1963.* Tuskegee, Ala.: Tuskegee Institute, March 12, 1964.

Hare, Nathan, *The Black Anglo-Saxons.* New York: Marzani & Munsell, 1965.

Hernton, Calvin C., *Sex and Racism in America.* Garden City, N. Y.: Doubleday, 1965.

Herskovits, Melville J., *The Myth of the Negro Past.* New York: Harper, 1941; reissued by Beacon Press Paperbacks, 1958.

Holt, Len, *The Summer That Didn't End.* New York: William Morrow, 1965.

Kenyatta, Jomo, *Facing Mount Kenya.* New York: Random House.

Killens, John O., *Black Man's Burden.* New York: Trident Press, 1965.

Kilson, Martin, *Political Change in a West African State, A Study of the Modernization Process in Sierra Leone.* Cambridge, Mass.: Harvard University Press, 1966.

Kozol, Jonathan, *Death at an Early Age.* Boston, Mass.: Houghton Mifflin Co., 1967.

Mphahlele, Ezekiel, *The African Image.* New York: Praeger, 1962.

Myrdal, Gunnar, *An American Dilemma.* 2 vols., New York: Harper, 1944.

Negro in America, The: A Bibliography, (compiled by Elizabeth W. Miller). Cambridge, Mass.: Harvard University Press, 1966.

Negro Reference Book (ed. by John P. Davis). Englewood Cliffs, N. J.: Prentice-Hall, 1966.

Nelson, Truman, *The Torture of Mothers.* New York: The Garrison Press, 1965.

Nkrumah, Kwame, *Africa Must Unite.* London: Heinemann Educational Books, Ltd., 1963.

Silberman, Charles, *Crisis in Black and White.* New York: Random House, 1964.

Thompson, Daniel C., *The Negro Leadership Class.* Englewood Cliffs, N. J.: Prentice-Hall, 1963.

Woodward, C. Vann, *Tom Watson: Agrarian Rebel.* New York: Oxford University Press, 1963.

2. History

Aptheker, Herbert, ed., *A Documentary History of the Negro People in the United States.* 2 vols., New York: Citadel, 1951; reissued 1962, 1964.

Bennett, Lerone, Jr., *Before the Mayflower: A History of the Negro in America, 1619-1962.* Chicago: Johnson, 1962.

Franklin, John Hope, *From Slavery to Freedom: A History of American Negroes.* New York: Knopf, 1947: 2nd ed., 1956.

Mannix, Daniel P., *Black Cargoes: The Story of the Atlantic Slave Trade: 1518-1865.* New York: Viking, 1962.

Quarles, Benjamin, *The Negro in the American Revolution.* Chapel Hill: University of North Carolina Press, 1961.

Woodward, C. Vann, *The Strange Career of Jim Crow.* New York: Oxford University Press, 1955; 2nd rev. ed. and Galaxy paperback, 1966.

3. Biography

The Autobiography of Malcolm X. New York: Grove, 1965.

Brown, Claude, *Manchild in the Promised Land.* New York: Macmillan, 1965.

Cronon, E. D., *Black Moses.* Madison, Wis.: University of Wisconsin Press, 1955.

Douglass, Frederick, *Narrative of the Life of Frederick Douglass, an American Slave, Written by Himself.* Boston: Anti-Slavery Office, 1845; Cambridge, Mass.: Harvard University Press, 1960.

Gregory, Dick, with Robert Lipsyte, *Nigger: An Autobiography.* New York: Dutton, 1964.

Hickey, Neil, and Ed Edwin, *Adam Clayton Powell and the Politics of Race.* New York: Fleet, 1965.

Williams, John A., *This Is My Country Too.* New York: New American Library, 1965.

Wright, Richard, *Black Boy.* New York: Harper, 1937; New York: New American Library paperback, 1950.

4. Literature

Baldwin, James, *Nobody Knows My Name.* New York: Dial, 1961; New York: Dell, Delta paperbacks.

_____. *Go Tell It On the Mountain.* New York: Dial, 1963; New York: Dell, Grossett, New American Library paperbacks.

Butcher, Margaret Just, *The Negro in American Culture, Based on Materials Left by Alain Locke.* New York: Knopf, 1956; New York; New American Library paperback, 1965.

Ellison, Ralph, *The Invisible Man.* New York: Random House, 1952.

_____. *Shadow and Act.* New York: Random House, 1964.

Himes, Chester B., *Third Generation.* Cleveland: World, 1954.

Hughes, Langston, *The Best of Simple.* New York: Hill & Wang, 1961.

Jones, LeRoi, *The System of Dante's Hell.* New York: Grove, 1965.

Kelley, William Melvin, *A Different Drummer.* Garden City, N. Y.: Doubleday, 1962.

Killens, John O., *Youngblood.* New York: Dial, 1954.

Pool, Rosey, ed., *Beyond the Blues: New Poems by American Negroes.* London: Headley, 1962.

Rollins, Bryant, *Danger Song.* New York: Doubleday, 1967.

Williams, John A., *The Man Who Cried I Am.* Boston: Little, Brown & Co., 1967.

5. Black Power

Brotz, Howard, *The Black Jews of Harlem: Negro Nationalism and the Dilemmas of Negro Leadership.* New York: Free Press, 1964.

Carmichael, Stokely, and Charles V. Hamilton, *Black Power: The Politics of Liberation in America.* New York: Vintage Books, 1967.

Essien-Udom, E. U., *Black Nationalism: A Search for an Identity in America.* Chicago: University of Chicago Press, 1962.

Fager, Charles E., *White Reflections on Black Power.* Grand Rapids, Mich.: Eerdmans, 1967.

Lomax, Louis E., *When the Word Is Given: A Report on Elijah Muhammad, Malcolm X, and the Black Muslim World.* Cleveland: World, 1963.

Malcolm X Speaks, ed. George Breitman, New York: Merit Publishers, 1965.

Muhammad, Elijah, *Message to the Black Man in America.* Chicago: Muhammad's Mosque No. 2, 1965.

Powledge, Fred, *Black Power, White Resistance: Notes on the New Civil War,* Cleveland, 1967.

Williams, Robert F., *Negroes with Guns.* New York: Marzani & Munsell, 1962.

Wright, Nathan, Jr., *Black Power and Urban Unrest.* New York: Hawthorn, 1967.

For further bibliography, see pages 102 and 146.

INDEX